PHILOSOPHY and JOURNALISM

LONGMAN SERIES
IN PUBLIC
COMMUNICATION

Series Editor: **Ray Eldon Hiebert**

PHILOSOPHY and JOURNALISM.

John C. Merrill
Louisiana State University

S. Jack Odell
University of Maryland

Longman
New York & London

Philosophy and Journalism

Longman Inc., 1560 Broadway, New York, N.Y. 10036
Associated companies, branches, and representatives throughout the world.

Developmental Editor: Gordon T.R. Anderson
Editorial and Design Supervisor: Joan Matthews
Production Supervisor: Ferne Kawahara
Manufacturing Supervisor: Marion Hess

Library of Congress Cataloging in Publication Data
Merrill, John Calhoun, 1924–
   Philosophy and journalism.

   (Longman series in public communication)
   Includes index.
   1. Journalism — Philosophy. I. Odell, S. Jack,
1933–   . II. Title.   III. Title: Philosophy and
journalism.   IV. Series
PN4731.M444   070'.01   82–7770
ISBN 0–582–28157–1   AACR2
ISBN 0–582–28383–3 (pbk.)

MANUFACTURED IN THE UNITED STATES OF AMERICA

Professor Merrill dedicates his part of the book to the youngest of his five children, Debbie, and to his two grandchildren in Missouri — Erin and Brett McBee.

Professor Odell dedicates his part of the book to his two daughters, Erin and Lynn, both of whom were seriously injured during the time it was being written.

Contents

Preface

In recent years the whole area of journalism and mass communication has increasingly opened itself to philosophical concerns. More and more articles, speeches, and books — by journalists and about journalism — have concerned themselves with topics mainly philosophical.

Journalists, at least on the level of language, seem to be interested in such subjects as objectivity, truth, credibility, ethical behavior, journalistic quality, meaning, logical discourse, propaganda and the news, persuasion, journalistic ideology, journalistic rights and responsibilities, censorship, social purpose, and the impact of journalism.

It is not difficult to ascertain the spiraling interest in such philosophical aspects of journalism, and it is interesting that, at long last, philosophical dimensions of journalism are beginning to compete in public discourse and academic circles with psychological and sociological perspectives which have dominated such discourse since the 1930s.

So far as we know, this is the first book which has attempted to deal systematically with journalistic philosophy in its main dimensions, to try to provide a philosophical context for the consideration of journalistic matters. Many readers may well question the value of such a book, for still philosophy is widely viewed as impractical and irrelevant in the hard-nosed and "real" world of professional journalism.

We feel that such a view is not only shortsighted, but is especially harmful to any intellectual and conceptual progress which journalism might make in our complex world. Philosophy should, in our view, be the foundation of modern journalism — an enterprise which, according to most of its practitioners, attempts to get at the truth and provide a reliable and interesting map of the territory of reality, or at least that part of reality that most impinges on our daily lives and needs.

Philosophizing in journalism helps us design meaningful definitions for ourselves which can help us in our work. A few concepts needing defining — common ones like "news," "fairness," "pluralism," "interpretation," "freedom," and even "journalism" itself — will show us very quickly how difficult, albeit stimulating, it is to traverse the byways of philosophy.

The journalist today is faced with a multitude of problems, questions, and issues. These are extremely complex and most of them cannot be resolved by recourse to common sense, personal biases, or even to insights and information gleaned from such fields as economics, political science, sociology, and psychology. It is not certain, of course, that even philosophy can give all the answers desired, but sooner or later the questioning and concerned journalist must put his mind to philosophizing.

Some of the criticisms often hurled at journalists (and journalism students) is that they are too mechanistic in their work and general outlook; that they are too insensitive to the complexities of the world; that they have put aside their humanistic concerns for a dedication to neutralism and objectivity; that they are invaders of privacy and conveyers of sensationalism and prurience; that they lack integrity and a basic moral sense; that they are superficial and biased in their news coverage; that they themselves are capitalistic materialists and are overimpressed with money and power; and on and on.

Regardless of the truth or falsity of these accusations, it is true that seldom, even in today's climate of greater philosophical concern, does one hear serious and knowledgeable conversations among journalists, journalism students, or journalism professors dealing with such questions. This does not mean that journalists are more oblivious to the philosophical dimensions of their vocation than anyone else; but it does mean that these dimensions do not yet seem very important to people who, because of the nature of their work, should be in the forefront of those who confront the world of philosophy with vigor and anticipation.

It seems to us that, too often, a kind of Machiavellianism dominates any philosophical thinking that might be done by journalists. A kind of hardheaded pragmatism that leads often to questionable tactics tends to be the guiding light for the seasoned journalist. Youthful optimism and idealism in journalism turn sour with the passing years, and a tough journalistic realism — often a camouflage for cynicism — takes root and often turns a person with a healthy ideology into an ideologue. The journalistic ideologue is quite common today in journalism even in the ranks of the self-styled liberals and progressives who claim to have open minds.

Philosophy — or a concern for philosophizing — will not automatically eliminate cynicism or a pessimistic *Weltanschauung*, but it will push the journalist's thinking into more systematic and logical channels and provide a more coherent foundation for his journalistic belief and value system. We hope that this book will serve as a catalyst for such a push.

There are, at least, two rather different ways to realize this goal. One approach is to explicate the fundamental concepts, distinctions, theories, methodologies, techniques, and procedures of philosophy, illustrating them with journalistic examples. This approach is motivated by the hope that journalism students introduced to philosophy in this way will become good applied philosophers. It is hoped that such an introduction to philosophy will cause students to appreciate and engage in keen and precise thinking and writing. They will learn to analyze and organize their thoughts, to express those thoughts clearly and unambiguously, to approach such topics as journalistic ethics, objectivity, truth, confirmation, and evidence with intelligence and critical acumen. Another approach to our task is to utilize philosophical concepts, themes, and theories to comment on the current state of journalism. More specifically, this approach applies philosophical thinking to such areas as journalism education, journalistic codes, social responsibility, and objectivity.

The first approach focuses on philosophy, the second one on journalism. We believe that both approaches are important and valuable. In Part I, S. Jack Odell, a philosophy professor, will cover the fundamentals of deductive and inductive reasoning, conceptual analysis, ethics, and the theory of knowledge, illustrating these fundamentals in journalistic contexts. In Part II, John Merrill, a journalism professor, will utilize philosophical themes to discuss the nature and the state of the art of journalism.

These approaches are not, as our text reveals, mutually exclusive. The reader will find that many applications are attempted in Part I and that various concepts are explicated in Part II. The emphasis is, however, quite different in the two parts.

Some readers will notice a certain unevenness in the pages which follow — especially between Part I (the first four chapters) and Part II (the last four). The style and content, admittedly, differ between the two sections — one mainly concerned with philosophical basics (Odell's) and the other mainly concerned with journalistic issues impinging on philosophy (Merrill's).

These differences perhaps reflect more than anything else differences in basic mannerisms with language and thought between philosophers and journalists. After considerable deliberation, we concluded that the unevenness was a natural result of our interests and backgrounds and does not harm the book. So we decided to segregate our ideas and styles in the two parts of the book as we approached the overall subject from two perspectives.

Also, we felt that the philosopher should set the stage, providing a basic philosophical foundation, and should orient the nonphilosophy student to the essentials of philosophical thinking. Odell has tried to do this in Part I. In contrast to a mainly philosophical perspective, Merrill, in Part II, has emphasized journalistic concerns. Thus the eight dimensions covered in the book have been dealt with from both angles: the first mainly philosophical and the second mainly journalistic. Although the two parts show some discrepancy in treatment and writing style, we feel both approaches are necessary for the journalism student interested in philosophy, the philosophy student interested in journalism, or the general reader interested in both philosophy and journalism.

Whether the reader begins at the beginning of Part I or at the beginning of Part II, or whether particular chapters are taken at random or because of special interests, we feel that philosophy and journalism will coalesce sufficiently to permit the reader to be drawn into areas of concern which undergird, or even overshadow, the more technical or pragmatic endeavors of the journalist or journalism student.

John C. Merrill
Louisiana State University

S. Jack Odell
University of Maryland

Acknowledgments

John Merrill thanks his many friends and colleagues in journalism education and the mass media who, through the years, have helped him refine many of his ideas and concepts about journalism. They have been serious and patient in their criticism and suggestions, even when they thought he was far off base in many of his presentations. Especially helpful have been colleagues at the University of Missouri and the University of Maryland who have contributed substantially through suggestions and discussions to Part II.

Jack Odell wishes to acknowledge a great debt to Professor Michael Petrick with whom he taught a course on philosophy and journalism, and from whom he received, during many discussions, many suggestions, some of which are incorporated into Part I. He also wishes to acknowledge a considerable debt to Judith Hammond Odell who made innumerable editorial suggestions for Part I, all of which were accepted. Professor Odell also wishes to thank the IBM Systems Research Institute for their support during the time the first draft of Part I was written, and Anita Barnes for her assistance in preparing the manuscript.

PHILOSOPHY and JOURNALISM

FOUNDATIONS

No other branches of philosophy can be said to have so fundamental an impact on society as a whole and on journalism in particular as do logic, semantics, epistemology, and ethics.

Logic and semantics, or conceptual analysis, are the most fundamental disciplines within philosophy. Together they constitute the methodology of philosophy. Logic determines for us what is to count as valid or acceptable reasoning. Conceptual analysis enables us to clarify what we mean. Those who are firmly entrenched in these areas of philosophy have a distinct advantage over those who are not.

Many important philosophers, for example, Aristotle, Leibniz, and Bertrand Russell devoted much time and effort to the refinement of logic. They all appreciated its role in the advancement of civilization and culture. By refining logic they were at the same time refining philosophical methodology. They isolated, and thereby helped to prevent, various kinds of fallacious reasoning.

Many contemporary philosophers, including Bertrand Russell, Ludwig Wittgenstein, G.E. Moore, and J.L. Austin, have contributed to the refinement of conceptual analysis. And even though not all professional philosophers agree regarding the importance of it, most professional schools in philosophy instruct their graduate students in its use. It is our belief that such training is invaluable.

One who masters logic, both formal and informal, and combines this knowledge with a mastery of analytic technique cannot help but be a better journalist for having done so. Such training leads one to think more carefully, and to express thoughts precisely and unambiguously. Who can deny that these are important characteristics for journalists to possess?

While by no means as fundamental as logic and conceptual analysis, epistemology, or the theory of knowledge, is of central importance to most other disciplines, and journalism is certainly no exception. All the great philosophers, including Socrates, Plato, Aristotle, Descartes, Spinoza, Leibniz, Locke, Berkeley, Hume, Kant, Russell, and Wittgenstein, were interested in epistemological questions. They were all concerned with questions having to do with the nature and limits of human knowledge. What we know and do not know affects everything we do.

Journalism is no exception. The great epistemologists were concerned with the nature of truth, evidence, objectivity, confirmation, and justified belief. No one, and especially no journalist, can elect to ignore these concepts or their implications. We depend on the journalist to keep us informed about the facts. We demand that the journalist seek the truth.

Unlike logic and conceptual analysis, both of which provide us with a methodology, epistemology consists primarily of a body of information. We say "primarily" because there are exceptions, as we shall see when we take up Mill's methods. Epistemology is less fundamental than logic and conceptual analysis, however, because the way one responds to the issues raised in it depends, in part, upon the way the issues are analyzed. Still, epistemology is of fundamental importance to journalists. The issues raised in epistemology are ones which journalists must take seriously.

Ethics is on par with epistemology in so far as it does not provide us with a methodology. But, also like epistemology, it is of considerable and fundamental importance; a society without ethics is a society doomed for extinction. The basic concepts and theories of ethics provide the framework necessary for working out one's own moral or ethical code. As is the case with the other three areas we shall investigate in Part I, ethics is of obvious significance to the journalist. Unethical journalists are of as little use to society as are stupid or poorly educated ones; perhaps of even less use. Whatever value they do have is negative. Stupid journalists simply misinform us; unethical ones also deceive us.

We will begin with logic and follow with conceptual analysis because they are the more fundamental of the four areas to be covered in this section. They will provide us with the methodological underpinnings necessary for subsequent sections. We will then pass on to epistemology because it provides some methodological techniques. We will finish with ethics. This procedure will show how methodology aids in understanding.

S. Jack Odell

CHAPTER 1

Logic: Journalism and Rationality

With the exception of having journalists who possess a fundamental grounding in ethics, nothing could be of greater importance to society than having journalists who are well grounded in logic. A journalist informs us. He alerts us. He cautions us. He instructs us. He does so through language. A journalist has the option of doing or not doing these things precisely and logically. Our journalists serve us well when they are careful to be both logical and precise. They serve us ill when they are not. When they are not careful, precise, painstaking, and unambiguous, they misinform us. They mislead us. This causes us to form mistaken judgments. It causes us to vote for the wrong people, sign the wrong petitions, harass the wrong persons, support the wrong causes, engage in meaningless debates, dislike and disregard people we would otherwise honor and respect.

No one doubts that many of our journalists reason imprecisely and fallaciously. Anyone familiar with introductory logic textbooks knows that many of their examples of fallacious reasoning are taken from journalistic contexts. If the reader needs to be convinced of this, let him look at Howard Kahane's *Logic and Contemporary Rhetoric*. This text abounds with examples of fallacious reasoning borrowed from media sources.

The examples in Kahane's text are primarily examples of *informal* fallacies. But just as great a need exists for instructing journalists in the art of avoiding *formal* fallacies. These arts are usually conjointly taught in courses in introductory logic. But they could just as well be taught in courses which integrate philosophy and journalism. The latter alternative has one major advantage over the former one, namely, the course can be tailored to the needs of journalism majors. Often, journalism majors find the traditional logic course too abstract, and, because of this, they fail to see the relevance of logic to the day-to-day practice of journalism.

We will begin our discussion of logic by discussing formal fallacies. But before we do so we will have to define some basic concepts of logic.

Basic Concepts of Logic

Logic is primarily concerned with the evaluation of arguments. But what is an *argument*? People say things all the time. They say them on the streets, in their houses, to their families, to their friends, to strangers, to enemies. People write articles, they write books, they write letters, they write editorials, and they write news reports. Humans give speeches, talks, courses, advice, lectures. In the course of doing all these things they make claims, and, if they are rational and responsible human beings, they are willing to provide reasons, in favor of their claims. The reasons provided in favor of what is claimed are called, by logicians, the *premises*. That which the premises support is called, by them, the *conclusion*. The conjunction of the conclusion with the premises is called an *argument* or, sometimes, an *inference*. So, logic is the evaluation of the relation between what people claim, i.e., their conclusions, and the reasons, i.e., the premises, which they provide in favor of their claims. This is not to say that every person is willing to back up his or her claims with reasons or evidence. Some people respond to "Why did you say that?" with "Just because," or "Are you getting smart with me?" or some equally bellicose and irrelevant expression. With people like this you can choose but one of two options. You can do as Aristotle suggested and take a stick to them, or you can, when possible, simply ignore them.

Here are some examples of arguments:

> Some reporters are illogical, because some reporters resort to name-calling when they can think of no better response, and anyone who does this is illogical.

> Reporters who favor advertisers are unethical, so, since this reporter always slants the news in favor of his newspaper's advertisers, he is culpable.

> Not all reporters are philosophically naive. One obvious example is George Will, whose father, a well known contemporary philosopher, trained him in philosophy.

Each of these passages makes a claim and offers grounds in favor of its particular claim. The *conclusion* of the first *argument* is the claim that some reporters are illogical. The *premises* are these: all who resort to name-calling when they are stuck for a response are illogical, and some reporters do this. When we make explicit what is the conclusion and what are the premises, we perform an *analysis* of the argument. Notice that the order of the premises and the conclusion, and the language used to *express* the first argument's premises on the previous page, differ from their order and the language used to express them in the *analysis* of the argument. In the original expression of the argument the premise which was expressed first was the one about some reporters acting in a certain manner. The second premise was the one about anyone who acts in certain ways. That order has been reversed in the first argument's analysis. In the original expression of the first argument the illogical behavior attributed to some reporters was spelled out, whereas it was simply referred to as a "this" in the premise about anyone. This is reversed in the analysis. Unquestionably, the first reversal is intimately connected to the second reversal. For the purposes of unambiguous communication, it is necessary for us first to describe what we are talking about before we refer to it in an elliptical manner. Still we should recognize that we can express the same thoughts in different language.

The second argument has as its conclusion the claim that some specific reporter is culpable. Its premises are these: reporters who slant the news in favor of advertisers are unethical, and some specific reporter has favored an advertiser in this way. Some interpretation is necessary. In order to interpret these premises to favor this conclusion we must assume that "culpable" means guilty of slanting the news so as to favor advertisers. Such interpretations are necessary in order to understand, and, ultimately, to evaluate, arguments. If we did not interpret in such cases as these, we would not see the relevance of the premises to the conclusion.

The need for interpretation is even greater in the case of the third example. The conclusion is, and here we state it differently, that some reporters are not philosophically naive. In favor of this conclusion we have a premise which states an exception to the rule that all reporters are naive philosophically. But this premise will not by itself yield the conclusion in question. In addition, we must *assume* that reporters who are trained as George Will was are not philosophically naive. We must supply a missing premise. That premise is the assumption about all reporters who have been trained by fathers who are philosophers. Arguments which have suppressed premises are called *enthymemes*. We also refer to arguments which have their conclusions suppressed, as enthymemes. Here is an example:

All humans are self interested; reporters are human beings, so, draw your own conclusion.

What all of this shows is that quite often we must interpret, even add a missing premise or conclusion, before we can evaluate an argument. But before we say anything further, we need to distinguish between *sentences* and *propositions*.

Underlying this distinction is the recognition that we can express the same thoughts in different languages. This recognition is very important to philosophy. The way philosophers express this recognition is by referring to our thoughts as *propositions* and to the various possible expressions of them as *sentences*. The following are all different sentences but they can be said to express the same proposition.

Most human beings like to eat.

Persons, most of them, like to eat.

The majority of people like to eat.

Most people enjoy eating.

Among those species whose members for the most part enjoy eating are to be found *homo sapiens*.

These sentences are all English sentences. But the same proposition can also be expressed equally in many ways in many other languages. So, for any proposition, there are many sentences which can be used to express it.

We need also to distinguish between sentence *types* and sentence *tokens*, and also to introduce yet another category, namely, *statements*. Many philosophers and logicians try to get along without all these categories, but this is a mistake. Each of the categories we have introduced should become part of the newsperson's basic vocabulary, and hence, part of his conceptual prowess.

Consider the group or set of things displayed below:

Jesse James liked to sack towns.

Jesse James liked to sack towns.

Jesse James liked to sack towns.

Consider the following group as well:

Bob Ford liked to shoot Jesse.

Bob Ford liked to shoot Jesse.

Suppose you were asked to count the number of sentences in each of these groups. How would you respond? Would you say that there are three sentences in the first group and only two in the second group? Or, would you say that there is just one sentence in each of these groups, though the sentence in each group is different? Either answer is correct. It depends upon whether you are counting *tokens* or *types*. The request to count the sentences is ambiguous. It can mean either count the tokens or count the types. The tokens are the actual physical entities displayed above. The type is what the mind must grasp in order to recognize that the first three things displayed above are different from the second two; it is what must be grasped in order for one to understand that the first three things are in some sense the same sentence.

Tokens are physical expressions of sentence types. They can be composed of ink as in the above instances, but they can also be composed of chalkmarks on a blackboard, impressions in the sand, vapor trails in the sky, sticks on a table, blocks in a game of Scrabble, and, in the case of spoken language, sounds in the air. They come in various sizes, shapes, and weights. They can even kill. One could carve the sentence about Jesse James out of heavy stone and drop it on Bob Ford's head.

Types, unlike tokens, and also unlike propositions or thoughts (which can be dangerous because of what they can cause or inspire), are never dangerous. They can, however, like propositions, be stolen or misappropriated. This is called *plagiarism* and it is most easily proved when the culprit steals another's "words," i.e., his sentence types, and not just another's thoughts or ideas, i.e., his propositions. Of course, one can also steal another's sentence tokens, and by doing so, even prevent a murder. One just as surely prevents a murder when he runs off with the weighty carving we spoke of a moment ago, as when one steals another's club intended for the head of that "dirty little coward who shot Mr. Howard." But this is not plagiarism.

Statements are the uses we make of sentences on particular occasions. They involve staters and a specific context of utterance. They are the proper subjects of the predicates "is true" and "is false." Consider the following example sentence from P.F. Strawson.*

The present king of France is wise.

This sentence can, as Strawson has pointed out, be used to make different statements, depending upon whether it is used in the reign of Louis XIV or Louis XV. To use it to say something about Louis XIV is to use it to make a true statement. To use it to say something about Louis XV is to use it to make a false statement. *What it means*, namely, is that whoever is at present king of France is wise, can be different from *what we use it to mean on some specific occasion.* In short, we must distinguish *what a sentence means* from *what we might mean by it.* One person will use the sentence to mean that Louis XIV is wise. Another will use it to mean that Louis XV is wise. Clearly, what they mean are

---

* "On Referring" in *Philosophy and Ordinary Language*, ed. by Charles E. Caton (Urbana, Illinois: University of Illinois Press, 1963), pp. 162–193.

two different things. Equally clearly, the dictionary meaning of the words has not changed. For this reason, as well as for others, we need to recognize the existence of what we will call *statements*, that is, a declarative use of a sentence by a speaker in a specific context. Statements are obviously not the same as sentence types or tokens. Less obviously, though nonetheless true, they are not the same as propositions, i.e., what the words mean.

If further evidence is required in favor of making this distinction it can be found in the fact that what we sometimes mean by a sentence is radically different from what it means. If one says "He is a real friend," while placing a certain sarcastic intonation on the word 'real', one can succeed in saying the very opposite of what the words mean. Besides, we sometimes wish to consider what a sentence means independent of what anyone might mean by it. One can ask another to consider a proposition which no one in his right mind has ever made a statement with. Just consider the proposition which the following sentence expresses, i.e., what it means:

> There is a purple polka-dotted chartreuse moose perched upon my left ear.

We understand perfectly well what this sentence means. It is, in fact, our perfect understanding of it which causes us to recognize that no one would ever make a statement with it. We could, of course, mark the distinction in question with the words 'statement' and 'possible statement' and abandon the word 'proposition'. But this would only complicate matters since 'proposition' is used throughout philosophy in the way explained here. Besides, it is shorter than 'possible statement'.

Just as we would do if we were contrasting statements with possible ones, we will consider statements, rather than propositions, to be the proper subjects of the predicates "is true" and "is false." It is only actual statements and not possible ones that are true or false. It is one thing to talk about the meaning of some sentence, e.g., 'He is tall'. It is another to talk about its being used to say something which is true or false. When we talk about the meaning or the proposition which the sentence expresses, we say things like: It can be used to make a true statement when its intended subject is a human six and one-half feet tall; it cannot be used to make a true statement when its subject is a six-and-one-half-foot tall giraffe. Such a giraffe would be a short one. We say things that are true and false when we use sentences, not when we discuss the ways they can be used. Still there are sentences whose meanings (propositions) are quite inextricably bound to the predicates "is true" and "is false." Examine the following sentences:

Triangles have three sides.

Nothing can both be and not be rhomboidal in exterior shape.

Colored objects are colorless.

If one were asked to examine the sentence 'He is tall' it would not make sense to ask, independent of any use of it, whether it is true or false. The sentences displayed above are different. The reason they are different is that it would make sense, not only to ask such a question of each of them, but to answer it as well. The answers are that the first two are true, the last one false.

Such sentences as these, i.e., ones the very examination or understanding of which involves the assignment of a truth value, were discussed early on in the history of philosophy. The great philosopher Immanuel Kant referred to them as *analytic apriori* sentences. He referred to ones like 'He is tall' as *synthetic aposteriori*. A controversy surrounds this distinction today. W.V.O. Quine and those who follow him deny the validity of the distinction, while many British philosophers, such as H.P. Grice and P.F. Strawson, defend it. We will simply specify that we believe that there are some sentences which, when used or interpreted in a standard way so as to preserve the meaning of their words, are either necessarily true or necessarily false. By "standard way" we mean just what we have asserted, namely, a way which preserves the ordinary meanings of the words which are used. A nonstandard use of a sentence can be illustrated by our previous example about a "real friend." Another example would be our using a sentence like 'He is tall' as the password of the week to gain entrance into the place where the floating crap game is being held. Here the sentence is used to mean something approximate to the utterer who is an approved member of this "club."

Previously we defined logic as being primarily concerned with the evaluation of argument. We can now explain what this means. Two sets of terms provide all the vocabulary we need for evaluating arguments. The first set contains these two terms: *valid* and *invalid*. The second set contains these two terms: *sound* and *unsound*. The first set is the more fundamental pair as far as logic itself is concerned.

To say of an argument that it is either invalid or unsound is to devalue it. To say either of these things about an argument is to make a negative judgment about it. Invalid or unsound arguments are unacceptable arguments. A sound argument is a good argument. It is an acceptable one. A valid argument is a partially acceptable one.

To say of an argument that it is valid is to say of it that it is *impossible* for its premise or premises to be true when its conclusion is false.

Another way to say this is to say that an argument is valid whenever the truth of the premise or premises *necessitates* the truth of the conclusion. To say then that an argument is invalid is to say that it is *possible* for its premise or premises to be true when its conclusion is false, and hence, that the truth of the premise or premises does not necessitate the truth of the conclusion. To be more precise, validity is a matter of *form*. To get across what we mean by this, consider the following argument:

> All outlaws admire Jesse James; Bob Dalton was an outlaw, therefore he must have admired Jesse.

The form of this argument can be expressed as follows:

> All things of sort x are things of sort y; a given thing is of sort x, therefore this given thing is of sort y.

The point is this: you could not have all things of one class be contained in a second class and not have any given member of the first class be a member of the second class. If all Jack's daughters are in Jack's house, then Erin, who is one of Jack's daughters, is in Jack's house. The conclusion could not possibly be false when these premises are true. Nor could any argument with this form have true premises and a false conclusion.

We are not saying, however, that you could not have an argument in this form which has premises that are false. The following argument will illustrate this possibility:

> All females are singers; Lynn Odell is a female, therefore Lynn Odell is a singer.

The first premise in this *instantiation* (example, instance, exemplification) of the argument form under scrutiny is false. For this reason we are not forced to accept the conclusion, even if, in fact, Lynn is a female. We are forced to accept the conclusion only if *both* of our premises are true. If one or the other or both of our premises are false, we say that the argument is unacceptable. It does not matter how many premises an argument has, if any one of them is false, the argument is unacceptable. Whenever this happens, we refer to the argument as *unsound*. A *sound* argument is an altogether acceptable argument. It is an argument with a valid form that has all of its premises true. The way we will use the term 'unsound argument' is to mean any argument, whether valid or invalid, which has one or more of its premises false. Such an argument is always unacceptable. It makes no difference whether or not the conclusion is true or false. The Lynn of the above example *is* a singer, but this fact does not follow from the premises because one of them is false. We can say that the conclusion is true, but not that the argument is acceptable. It would be acceptable only if all the premises were true. If the premises were both true, the argument would be sound.

With these concepts at our disposal we can now begin to discuss what philosophers classify as *formal* fallacies.

Formal Fallacies

The distinction between *formal* and *informal* fallacies is more a matter of emphasis than anything else. There are no hard and fast criteria for separating the one form of fallacy from the other. There is one thing which can, however, be said about all formal fallacies which can only be said about some informal ones: *all* formal fallacies are invalid arguments. And we already know what this means. It means that the form of the argument allows for the premise or premises to be true when the conclusion is false. There is, as we shall see, an exception to this rule in the case of informal fallacies.

Some formal fallacies have been isolated and named because of their prevalence. Consider the following argument:

> All reporters are concerned citizens; so, since they are all admirers of Lois Lane, all those who admire Lois Lane must be concerned citizens.

The form of this argument can be stated thus:

> All things of the first sort are things of a second sort; all things of a first sort are things of a third sort, thus whatever is a thing of the third sort must be a thing of the second sort.

The *subject term* of the conclusion is "Lois Lane admirer." Its *predicate term* is "concerned citizens." In logic we refer to the premise which contains the predicate term of the conclusion as the *major* premise of the argument. We refer to the premise which contains the subject term of the conclusion as the *minor* premise of the conclusion. When we put an argument into *standard form*, we state the major premise first. Even though it may be true that all admirers of Lois Lane are indeed good citizens, this by no means *follows from* the premises provided in the above example. If it did, it would have to follow that all animals are vegetarians because all horses are vegetarians and are also all animals. This fallacy is the fallacy of the *illicit minor*. It is called this because it illicitly goes beyond what the premises assert. The conclusion says something about all admirers of Lois Lane. The premise about Lois Lane admirers (the minor premise) does not. Another way of saying this is saying that although the term 'Lois Lane admirer' is *distributed* in the conclusion, it is not distributed in the premise in which it is found. To say that a term is distributed is to say that that term is found in a *sentence type* the meaning of which implies that the term in question is being used to refer to all the things to which it can refer.

Consider the following types:

All reporters are Lois Lane admirers.

Some reporters are Lois Lane admirers.

Independent of any speech actions — e.g., statements, inquiries, exhortations, or judgments — that we might use these sentences to accomplish, each one of them means something different, or expresses a different proposition. The first sentence has as its subject (means) *all* reporters. The second sentence has only *some* reporters as its subject. The term 'reporters' is *distributed* in the first sentence; it is *undistributed* in the second one.

If we were to conclude on the basis of the same premises we used when exemplifying the *illicit minor* fallacy that no citizens who admire Lois Lane are concerned citizens, we would be committing a different fallacy, the fallacy of *illicit major*. In this case the term 'concerned citizens', which, because of its position in the argument, is the *major term* of the argument, is distributed in the conclusion but not in the premise in which it occurs.

The following argument contains a different formal fallacy:

> All conservatives are Reagan supporters; all employees of this restaurant are Reagan supporters, therefore all employees of this restaurant are conservatives.

Again, while the conclusion might well be true, it does not follow logically from the premises. If it did, we would have to conclude that all cocker spaniels are beagles because both are dogs. This fallacy is the *fallacy of the undistributed middle*. The reason it is known under this description is because the middle term of the argument — the term which occurs in both of the premises — is undistributed. Although the argument refers to *all* conservatives and *all* employees of a given restaurant, it only refers to *some* supporters of Reagan. And for this reason, it is fallacious to conclude that all the employees of the restaurant under consideration are conservatives. For the same reason it would be fallacious to conclude the more obviously unwarranted contention that all conservatives are employees of the restaurant. The reason this conclusion is more obviously unwarranted is not a matter of logic. Each of these conclusions is equally invalidly inferable from the given premises. The only difference is that as a matter of empirical fact it is much more *likely* that all the employees of any given restaurant are conservatives than that all conservatives are the employees of a given restaurant. This fact is, however, irrelevant to whether or not the arguments are formally valid. The first one is more likely to mislead us, but it is no less *formally* valid than the latter. Formal validity is not a matter of degree or likelihood.

Another example of a formal fallacy is the *fallacy of denying the antecedent*. The following case is an example of this fallacy:

> Any reporter who constantly gets the facts wrong is a lousy reporter; Baston always gets the facts right, therefore Batson must not be a lousy reporter.

There are many ways of being a lousy reporter. The mere fact that someone gets the facts right does not show that he is not a lousy reporter. If this argument form were valid we would have to conclude that, since hardworking people succeed, anyone who does not work hard will not succeed. But clearly there are other ways of succeeding. One can inherit his mother's business.

The following passage contains the *fallacy of affirming the consequent:*

> Any reporter who constantly gets the facts wrong is a lousy reporter; Batson is a lousy reporter, therefore Batson must constantly get the facts wrong.

Obviously, Batson could be a lousy reporter for other reasons. He might, for example, be illiterate.

There are innumerable examples of formal fallacies which could be singled out and named. The reason some of them are singled out and named and others are not is because those selected for naming have been determined to be more seductive than the others. There are many examples which have been so honored but which we will not discuss. Four examples are quite sufficient for our purposes. What one needs to recognize is that any argument can be demonstrated to be invalid (to contain a formal fallacy) by a method which we have been using throughout this section: the *method of counterexample*. Armed with this technique one can usually determine when something is formally wrong with an argument.

The Method of Counterexample

All formally fallacious arguments can be shown to be invalid by this method. Formal or mathematical procedures exist for determining whether or not a given argument is valid. In a course in symbolic or mathematical logic one is taught various formal techniques for determining when an argument form is invalid. Most of these techniques are based on the method of counterexample. It is the only technique we really need.

To provide a counterexample to an argument is to show that its form is faulty. It is to provide an instantiation of that form such that the premises are undeniably true and the conclusion undeniably false. Remember that a valid argument is one which has a form such that it is *impossible* for the premises to be true when the conclusion is false. To provide a counterexample is to show that it is *possible* for the premises to be true when the conclusion is false. But the counterexample must be persuasive. That is why we have said that the premises of the counterexample must be undeniably true and its conclusion undeniably false. The method is best understood when one sees it applied to an example. Reconsider the example we used in the previous section to illustrate the *undistributed middle* fallacy. First we set out its form thus:

> All things of the first sort are things of a second sort, and all things of a third sort are things of the second sort; therefore all things of the third sort are things of the first sort.

Now think of the descriptions, things of the first, second, and third sort, as three separate *place holders* to be filled by three separate terms. We proceed by producing three separate terms which when substituted for the place holders will produce undeniably true premises and a false conclusion. This is what we were in effect doing when we previously asserted that accepting this argument form would force us to "conclude that all cocker spaniels are beagles because both are dogs." If you examine the following you will understand what it is to produce a counterexample to an argument.

> All beagles (things of the first sort) are dogs (second sort), and all cocker spaniels (third sort) are dogs (second sort); therefore all cocker spaniels (third sort) are beagles (first sort).

Having completed our explication of formal fallacies and provided a technique for refuting any invalid argument, we will now turn to what have been traditionally described as *informal* fallacies.

Informal Fallacies

We will begin with a caveat. Describing the unacceptable arguments which we are about to discuss as *informal fallacies* is not only a misnomer, but is apt to be misleading as well. We will use the term 'informal fallacy' to refer to certain kinds of unacceptable arguments only because there is a tradition of doing so. We will, however, make it clear, before we are through with this section, why it is a misnomer to refer to these things in this way. But we will start by further clarifying what we mean by the word 'fallacy'.

Many writers of introductory logic textbooks define informal fallacies as forms of reasoning which are altogether unacceptable, but which are, nevertheless, quite apt to mislead the conceptually unsophisticated. These writers often proceed to explain the concept of a fallacy in terms of the concept of a *counterfeit argument*. This is, in fact, an enlightening analogy, because some forms of fallacious argument, like counterfeit money, do fool us. Unfortunately, this analogy has only limited application. Many unacceptable arguments, traditionally classified under the label 'informal fallacies', do not exhibit the characteristic of being easily mistaken for the real thing. Consider the following dialogue:

> *Reporter:* "Mr. President, I understand that you intend to make future cuts in the funding of environmental agencies. Am I right about this?"
>
> *The President:* "There are all sorts of rumors in the air. Don't believe everything you hear."
>
> *Reporter:* "Mr. President, you are being evasive. I want a definite answer. Is the answer Yes or is it No?"
>
> *The President:* "Are you getting fresh with me? You are going to find it awfully difficult getting in here in the future. I don't want to see your face around here again."

The fallacy this dialogue exemplifies is well known as *argumentum ad baculum*. It is also known as the *appeal to force*. Instead of addressing the real issue, the President threatens the reporter with banishment. A threat never resolves an issue, but, under these circumstances, it may accomplish what is intended. It may very well silence the reporter. But the issue, which the reporter has raised, remains unresolved. The threat is *irrelevant* to whether or not the President intends to ask for further cuts in the funding of environmental protection agencies. For this reason this particular type of fallacy is often classified, along with certain others, as an informal fallacy of relevance. We have no objection to classifying it in this way. What we object to is explaining what is meant by a fallacy in terms of its ability, like counterfeit money, to mislead us, and then including *argumentum ad baculum* among those kinds of fallacies.

In this work we shall use the word 'fallacy' to mean simply any erroneous bit of reasoning. Aside from the fact that there is one informal fallacy that is not formally fallacious, there is no real difference between formal and informal fallacies. We separate them only because there is a long-standing tradition of doing so. The same tradition incorporates a distinction among informal fallacies that turn on the presence of an ambiguity and those that do not. This is a perfectly valid distinction and we will observe it. Unfortunately, this distinction is not as aptly marked as it ought to be. In fact, the terminology that is selected to mark the distinction is bound to mislead. The terms that are used are *fallacies of ambiguity* and *fallacies of relevance*. There is nothing whatever misleading in the traditional use of the former expression. The problem is with the traditional use of the latter expression. It is traditionally defined to cover those cases of fallacious reasoning where the premises are in some specifiable way irrelevant to the conclusion. It then gets used to refer to cases that do not exemplify this characteristic. The fallacy *petitio principii* is, as will be made clear when we discuss it, a case in point. So, while we will follow tradition and dichotomize between fallacies of relevance and fallacies of ambiguity, we will do so self-consciously, pointing out as we proceed just where the difficulties are.

Informal Fallacies of Relevance

There are many ways for the premises of an argument to be irrelevant to its conclusion. We will describe some of the ways and label them in accordance with tradition. We have already described one of these ways that reasoning can go astray, labeling it *argumentum ad baculum*. It looks like this:

> Premise: Threat of some sort, therefore conclusion (which could be anything).

In the case of *ad baculum* the premise is totally irrelevant to the conclusion. It makes no difference whether the conclusion is, for example, 'Reporters are ethical' or 'Reporters are unethical'. One could just as easily attempt to force acceptance of one member of this contradictory pair as the other. This observation actually provides us with a reliable test of whether or not an argument is a fallacy of relevance. We can, with few exceptions, claim that an argument is fallacious whenever its premise or premises can as readily be attached to its conclusion's contradictory.

The next fallacy we want to introduce is *argumentum ad hominem*. The following dialogue contains an example of this fallacy:

> *First reporter:* Boy, do I have a scoop! Mr. Grim, the secretary to the president of Optimal Motors, tells me that his company is planning to put a car on the road next year which will get over a hundred miles to the gallon of gas.
> *Second reporter:* Bull! That guy Grim is a jerk. He drinks tons and runs around on his wife. If I were you, I would forget whatever he told you.

The second reporter commits the fallacy. Instead of providing some kind of counter to the claim that a high mileage car will be forthcoming from the company in question, he (or she) attacks the man who leaked the information. Other names for this fallacy are *attack on the man and poisoning the well.* To show that what someone says is false it is necessary to produce evidence to the contrary. One can never establish that something is false by abusing the person who said it. If we could, all we would have to do in order to disprove anything is to wait until someone who was open to criticism said it. If you want to prove that someone is not smarter than you, just get some fool or villain to say that that someone is smarter than you.

Some care has to be exercised, however, when labeling something a fallacy *ad hominem.* Not every attack on someone's character is fallacious. If someone has promised to pay you fifty dollars an hour just to answer his phone, my informing you that he is a pathological liar is certainly relevant. The fact that he is a pathological liar does not *prove* that he will not keep his promise, but it certainly is worth knowing.

A variation on the *ad hominem* theme exists. It is illustrated by the following example:

> *First reporter:* You shouldn't drink and smoke so much.
> *Second reporter:* You are a fine one to talk. You drink all the time, and you smoke at least as much as I do.

The mere fact that the first reporter happens to smoke and drink himself does not bear at all on the question of whether or not such activities are harmful. The only thing which would show that the first reporter is mistaken is new scientific evidence sufficient to override the existing evidence that these activities are unhealthy. *Ad hominems* occur all the time. It is difficult to get through a day without encountering some instance of it. The explanation of its pervasiveness is to be found in the fact that the *principle of universalizability* which underlies our value judgments is easily, though mistakenly, carried over into nonnormative contexts. In his book *Ethics** William Frankena points out, "If one takes a maxim as a moral principle, one must be ready to universalize it.... if he is unwilling to share his basic normative premises, then he does not have a morality in the full sense." Although, as we shall see in Chapter 4, adherence to the universalizability principle is necessary in contexts of normative judgment, it is misplaced in nonnormative ones.

Another way of accounting for the pervasiveness of this fallacy is to recognize that sometimes when we use the word 'shouldn't' we mean to be saying that one *ought not* do something. In other words, we frequently use the word in question in a normative fashion. When we use it in this way we mean that *it would be ethically or morally wrong* to do something. So, when someone who smokes tells us we shouldn't smoke, this is apt to carry with it a normative tinge which discolors our perceptions and causes us to impose the principle of universalizability upon the speaker, when in fact the speaker is using the word 'shouldn't' in a nonnormative sense to mean something like *if you want to remain healthy, don't smoke*.

The fact that this commonly occurring fallacy has this explanation does not make it any less a fallacy. Our second reporter is guilty of committing an *ad hominem*. His objection is irrelevant to whether or not smoking is dangerous.

This way of viewing the matter in terms of recognizing that there are both normative and nonnormative senses of the word 'shouldn't' is interesting for another reason. This reason will be explained when we talk about the fallacy of *equivocation*.

It is common practice to refer separately to the two varieties of *ad hominem* which we have exemplified as the *abusive* and *circumstantial* varieties. Obviously, the first example exemplifies the abusive variety. The smoking case exemplifies the latter because the fallacy involved erroneously appeals to the relationship between a person's beliefs and the *circumstance* that he smokes.

Another form of fallacy that occurs far too often can be illustrated by the following dialogue:

> *Editor:* Did you see the article I'm running in our January issue regarding the government's stand on environmental issues?
> *Journalist:* I did, but I don't see why you persist in printing so many articles critical of the government's stand on that issue. Billy Graham has said he favors the President's environmental policies.

The fallacy is that of attempting to resolve some issue by appealing to the opinion of some figure in the public limelight. The fact that some

* *Ethics*, William Frankena (Englewood Cliffs, N.J. Prentice-Hall, 1973), p. 18.

celebrity? or famous person believes some proposition, call it p, does not make p true, or even plausible. If we were to accept this kind of approach, we would be stuck with many outrageous propositions. No matter how silly a view you imagine, there is some celebrity somewhere who accepts it. Were we to adopt such a procedure for argumentation, establishing a particular point of view would require nothing more than surveying the beliefs of the famous. The fancy name for this fallacy is *argumentum ad verecundiam*. Its less pretentious moniker is *appeal to authority*.

One has to proceed with care, however, because not every appeal to an authority figure is fallacious. Whether or not we reason fallaciously when we appeal to an authority is determined by whether or not the person cited is an authority in the field at issue. If the journalist in the above dialogue had cited some expert in the field of ecology instead of Billy Graham, he would not be guilty of arguing fallaciously, unless, of course, he claimed that the expert's favoring of the President's policies makes them true. What would follow from the expert's favoring the policies is that they are at least *reasonable* or *plausible* views to hold. No person's statement of any nonanalytic proposition makes it true. In order to establish any given nonanalytic proposition, one must produce factual evidence in its behalf.

Fallacious appeals to authority occur with deplorable frequency in journalistic contexts. Reporters commonly ask us to accept some point of view on the grounds that "A distinguished expert has said...." Advertising is practically based on it. If an advertiser's chrematistic endeavours contain a persona of sufficient charismatic caliber, you can even sell panty hose to football players. Such appeals are, nonetheless, fallacious. They must be avoided.

Another extremely common type of fallacy is what has been dubbed *argumentum ad ignorantium* or the *argument from ignorance*. It occurs, for example, when one reporter says to another, "The present administration must be quite honest because no evidence has emerged to prove otherwise." It occurs with unbelievable regularity whenever laymen discuss the question of whether or not God exists. For example, "How can you doubt that God exists since no one has ever proved that he doesn't?" The same argument is often used to show that ghosts, Martians, and so on, exist.

The form of the argument looks like this:

Premise: No one has ever proved that x does not exist.

Conclusion: Therefore, x exists.

Sometimes, in the context of the discussion regarding God's existence, the premise is strengthened on the grounds that not only has His existence not been disproven, it is *impossible* to do so. And, so, the argument becomes:

Premise: No one could ever prove that God does not exist.

Conclusion: Therefore, God exists.

But even this, the argument's strongest form, is demonstrably invalid. Suppose I claim that the second hand on my watch is turned by a wee bit of a leprechaun who inhabits the watch. You would quite likely take the watch, rip off the back and exclaim, "Look, you idiot! There is no leprechaun in this watch!" To which I could respond, "Wait a minute, don't get so worked up. I forgot to mention that he is also invisible." You have seen the old Claude Raines movies about the invisible man and you know that he leaves footprints in the snow, and his outline is visible in the fog. You grab the watch, which is an expensive Rolex, and much, to my chagrin, you put it in a vaporizer. You then, with exultation, vociferate, "Now I've got you! Do you see any leprechaun outline in there?" Your victory is short-lived, however, because I hasten to point out that my leprechaun is also intangible, and, hence, he does not leave an outline.

The leprechan is now characterized so as to make it impossible for anyone ever to prove that he does not exist, from which it would have to follow, if we were to accept the argument form in question, that the leprechaun exists. By parity of reason we could prove that all sorts of incredible, invisible, intangible things exist. One could, for example, prove that one's watch is inhabited by an invisible and intangible tyranosaurus rex.

Another equally serious objection to the weaker form of the argument is that by its means you can just as easily prove that x does not exist. If you start with an affirmative proposition p, its denial is not p. So if you start with not p, its denial is not not p. So, following the form of the argument in question, since no one has *proved* that God does exist, it follows that He does not. This also constitutes an objection to the stronger version of the argument, but only if its defenders concede that it is equally impossible to prove his existence. But this would be an inconsistency on their part since they think that His existence is proven by the fact that no one can prove that He does not exist. Inconsistency is not, however, unheard of in such contexts.

Let us now imagine a reporter who has just been pulled over by a policeman for exceeding the speed limit by driving eighty miles an hour in a thirty-mile zone. He says to the police officer:

Officer, please don't give me a ticket. If I get any more tickets the judge will suspend my driver's licence. I won't be able to drive, so I won't be able to do my job. I'll get fired. I'll lose my house. My wife and ten children will suffer.

The fallacy contained in this example is called *argumentum ad misericordiam*. It is also known as the *appeal to pity*. The real issue is whether the reporter did or did not break the law. If he (or she) did, he should be given the citation. Everything the reporter says in his own behalf is irrelevant. This is not to say that this kind of appeal is ineffective. Fallacious appeals of this sort are often quite efficacious. Trial lawyers would be practically powerless if they were not.

Appealing to pity is not the only fallacious emotional appeal. There is also *argumentum ad populum*. Frequently we are seduced by those who play upon our prejudices. Demogogues like Hitler or Napoleon manipulate the masses by appealing to their prejudices and biases. They play their tunes on the strings of *all* our emotions. They not only appeal to our sympathy or pity, but also utilize our fears, hopes, and apprehensions. So often when the appeal should be made to reason, it is instead made to our emotions. Editorial writers are guilty of this offense when they try to convince us that a certain stand is the appropriate one to take on some issue by tying the issue to some widespread prejudice or bias.

Another and closely related fallacious appeal is that usually referred to as the *bandwagon fallacy*. When this fallacy occurs, what happens is that someone attempts to convince us of the truth of some proposition on the grounds that a large number of others accept it. Such appeals are fallacious. The mere fact that a number of people think that something is right is a poor sort of reason for accepting it. One should never lose sight of the fact that one million times zero is still zero. In the history of mankind many outrageously wrongheaded propositions have been the coin of the realm. People have been persecuted, driven from their homes, starved, tormented, tortured, and killed because some group or culture was under the impression that some proposition, which we now know to be false, was sacrosanct. The bandwagon fallacy, like the appeal to authority, is at the very core of advertising, so much so that one wonders if there would be any advertising at all if we were to make the use of these two fallacies unlawful.

We can summarize what we have been doing in this section by saying that we have been looking at a variety of different ways for the premise or premises of an argument to be irrelevant to its conclusion, and thus for the relation that obtains between them to be a fallacious one. But are these the only ways for the premises to be irrelevant to the conclusion? No. There are an unspecifiable number of additional ways for an argument's premise or premises to be irrelevant. Consider the following example:

> *Advertising director:* We have just received word that Magnus Corporation is going to place a long term, full-page advertisement with us for its new shampoo, "Oodles-O-Suds." Isn't that great news?
>
> *Youthful employee:* I wouldn't get too excited about that news if I were you. I hear that it is a lousy product. It won't sell, and they won't advertise it for very long.

The fact that some product is lousy is irrelevant to whether or not it will be a commercial success. Many worthless products have had phenomenal sales.

Whenever, as in this example, the premise or premises are irrelevant to the conclusion, but not in any of the ways previously explained, it is common practice to name the offender a *non sequitur* or *ignoratio elenchi*, or simply *irrelevant appeal*.

All of the fallacies we have presented so far in this section are aptly described as fallacies of relevance in as much as the truth of the premises of each example can be seen to be irrelevant to the truth of the conclusion. The examples we are about to turn to are not properly so described.

The fallacy *petitio principii*, as we previously noted, tends to get classified as a fallacy of relevance. This fallacy, also known as *begging the question*, should not be so classified when, as so often happens, the claim is made that fallacies of relevance occur where the truth of the premise or premises is irrelevant to the conclusion's truth. Not only is the truth of the premise relevant to the truth of the conclusion, in the case of *petitio principii*, the one entails (which is to say, formally implies) the other. The following example is an example of this fallacy:

> God must exist. This follows from the fact that existence is a necessary attribute of God.

The premise has the same meaning as the conclusion. Or to put it differently, but in keeping with a distinction we drew earlier, although the sentence used to state the premise is different from the one used to state the conclusion, the proposition which they state is the same. So, since the truth of any proposition self-evidently insures its own truth, the truth of any given proposition is relevant to its truth. And so it will not do to classify this fallacy as one of relevance. Still it is a fallacy and should be avoided, even though the argument form in question (p, therefore p) is formally valid.

Petitio principii is the example which we had in mind when we previously said that not every informal fallacy is a formal one. It's a fallacy because simply repeating, in different words, what you want somebody to accept is not, ultimately, different from simply saying it again. No progress occurs.

There is a set of contrasting labels which are commonly introduced under the general heading 'fallacies of relevance' but which are, like *petitio principii*, mislabeled. The labels are *accident* and *converse accident*.

The following case exemplifies what is known as the fallacy of accident:

> *Excerpt from an editorial*: "I, for one, find it difficult to understand why it is that we should be expected to take a stand on the Afghanistan issue. Why should we be willing to commit our resources to help out a country we would not expect to come to our aid? I say this because I firmly believe that nations have to protect their own interests. They have to stand and shoulder the burden themselves. They cannot expect the rest of the world to do it for them."

The fallacy is that of attempting to apply a principle which has a certain validity to a context where the specific circumstances of the case render it inapplicable. In general, it is no doubt true that nations must stand up for themselves. But when the nation in question is as small as Afghanistan, and the agressor is as large as Russia, the rules of the game are radically altered. No one could expect Afghanistan to take on Russia. Of course exercise is healthy, but one does not expect a person suffering from severe asthma to run for health's sake. To commit this fallacy is to reveal a certain ignorance of the nature of generalization. Generalizations about the world as opposed to principles of mathematics and logic must be understood to be no more than what they are, namely, descriptions which are generally or for the most part true. We misunderstand their nature if we take them to be unqualifiedly true; to have no exceptions.

The other label in this set, 'converse accident', is used to refer to the opposite of accident. The fallacy involved here is that of taking some description, which is true of some specific set of circumstances, and wrongly assuming that it has general applicability. The following case is an example of this fallacy.

Newsperson: Hold on to your hat! A new phenomenon is about to emerge on the national scene. People aren't going to stand idly by and allow Reagan to cut welfare spending. They are going to take their cause to the streets and riot.

Editor: Why do you say that?

Newsperson: Because I just came back from the Bowery where I saw several people carrying signs saying "Rise up and fight against Reagan's budget cuts!"

The fallacy committed by the newsperson in the above example is that of putting too much stock in an isolated incident. From this one incident it by no means follows that a trend has been revealed. It may be that the events of subsequent days will provide further, even sufficient, evidence for such a generalization. But this one instance cannot by itself form the basis of generalization. It is easy to understand why we also refer to the fallacy of converse accident as *hasty generalization*. Evidential generalizations (inductions) must be based on an extensive factual base.

Another fallacy, which is also inductive in character, and which is usually classed a fallacy of relevance, is what is called *false cause*. An example of this fallacy exists whenever a reporter concludes that something is the cause of something else solely because the something which he (or she) takes to be the cause of the something else occurs more than once temporally prior to the something else. When a sports reporter says that he thinks he had better stop attending the Giant's games because they always lose when he attends, he commits this fallacy. Of course, he may only be kidding, in which case he is not guilty of asserting a false cause. When Lincoln responded to the charge of Grant's critics that Grant drank too much with "Have Grant send all my other generals some of his whiskey," Lincoln was not guilty, as some logic textbook writers would have it, of a fallacy of false cause. These authors do not seem to know the difference between a fallacy and witticism.

The next fallacy we want to explicate is the *slippery slope*, which is not classifiable as either a fallacy of relevance or a fallacy of ambiguity. It is, however, common. Whenever anyone argues that some step taken in some direction will inevitably lead to further steps being taken in that direction, one commits the fallacy of the slippery slope. It is sometimes referred to as the *snowball fallacy*. One commits this fallacy when one argues against allowing newspersons to protect their sources on the grounds that this will lead inevitably to a breakdown in our judicial system, because permitting this practice encourages other segments of the population to do likewise, and eventually no one will be willing to testify against anyone he has not got a grudge against. There is also the *false dilemma* or *it could always be worse* fallacy. One who argues that the present editor of a newspaper ought to be retained solely on the grounds that his replacement might be worse, is guilty of committing this fallacy.

A rather frequently occurring fallacy, not always included in logic textbooks, and rarely ever classified as a fallacy of relevance, is the fallacy usually referred to as *false analogy* or *faulty analogy*. This fallacy occurs when one considers one thing to be on an analogue with another on the basis of their having some characteristic or characteristics in common, but when the two things thought to be analogous are really quite different in other and more significant respects.

An interesting example of this fallacy occurred recently in the life of one of the authors of the present volume. While residing as an instructor and consultant at a research institute of a major corporation, he was notified that one of the managers was planning to allow a person without proper qualifications to teach a course in ethics in business and technology. Our author objected to this offering on the grounds that no one who is not certified in ethics should be allowed to teach such a course. He pointed out to this manager that certification in ethics can take years, that ethics forms a large part the works of the great thinkers Aristotle, Hume, Kant, Bentham, Mill, Sartre, and many others, and that one cannot be said to be qualified to teach these ideas until one has demonstrated mastery over such works. The manager's response, which was repeated by one of his underlings and his own manager, was that several other course offerings were being taught by men who had not had formal education in the area covered by the course. The author then pointed out that those courses were courses which involved material which was commonly learned through experience, and that the men who taught the courses were men who had had vast experience in the areas, and hence that this manager was guilty of drawing a *false analogy* between those courses and ethics. It was further pointed out to this manager that ethics was really analogous to subjects like medicine, law, and physics. The manager did not get it, which goes to prove that old adage about leading a horse to water. Fortunately for the institute the corporate executives of the company in question had a strong proclivity for water (reason).

Ambiguity Fallacies

As we pointed out previously, it is a common practice to classify all the fallacies we have discussed thus far under the general heading *fallacies of relevance* and to distinguish them from what are classified as *fallacies of ambiguity*. And, although we consider this way of proceeding misleading with respect to the so-called fallacies of relevance, we concur with referring to the ones we are about to discuss as fallacies of ambiguity.

They do, unquestionably, result from an inattention to language, and would not be possible were it not the case that language does contain the possibility of ambiguity.

One source of ambiguity is the fact that almost every word in a natural language has associated with it multiple senses or meanings. If someone says to you that a boy threw a rock into the bank, you may think that by 'bank' is meant a commercial institution, but you could just as easily think that by 'bank' is meant a certain arrangement of earth. It is possible for a person of sadistic inclination to take advantage of this ambiguity to mislead and thereby to torture another person. Suppose you have just discovered that you do not have enough money in your checking account to cover a check which you earlier today gave to the second meanest guy in town. Suppose you run into the meanest guy in town and you tell him your tale of woe. Smiling sadistically, he tells you he has just seen the second meanest man in town at the bank. After you faint and he has poured cold water over you, he chortles, "Yeah, I saw him fishing off the river bank." This kind of fallacious reasoning is referred to as *equivocation*.

In the mean guy case, the person who utilizes the ambiguity is perfectly aware of what he is doing. Quite often, the person who reasons fallaciously because of an ambiguity is not aware that he is doing so. The great English philosopher J.L. Austin was particularly adept at exposing equivocations in the writings of other philosophers. His discussion* of Ayer's confusions regarding the words 'looks', 'seems', and 'appears' is particularly enlightening and insightful. One of his points in this discussion is that because 'looks' can mean either 'visually looks' or 'seems' it is possible for one to confuse the fact that something has a certain look with its seeming to be that way. If something *seems* a certain way, say crooked, it follows that *there is some evidence, though not conclusive*, that it is crooked. But if it only *looks* a certain way, it may do so when it is perfectly certain that it is not. This ambiguity can lead one to conclude fallaciously that since every straight stick can be emersed in water and look bent, there is always some evidence that it is bent. And, since every straight stick will look straight when it is out of water, there is always evidence both that it is straight and that it is not. If, moreover, one believes, as many traditionally oriented epistemologists do, that we can never determine what properties a thing has, or even that it exists, when there is evidence both that it has and does not have certain properties, one will be apt to conclude that we can never have knowledge of physical objects. In other words, an equivocation on the word "looks" can lead to what is described as *epistemological scepticism*.

* *Sense and Sensibilia*, J.L. Austin (Oxford: Oxford University Press, 1962), pp. 33–43.

To establish that someone has committed an equivocation one need only demonstrate that some key expression is being used in one sense in the premise or premises and in another sense in the conclusion.

Previously, we explained accident and converse accident. There are a couple of fallacies which although difficult to distinguish from these, are nevertheless quite different because they are fallacies of ambiguity. They are *division* and *composition*. The following are examples of each. The first one is an example of division:

> *Editor:* Batson, I want you to get off your can and dig up something on Malone. The whole family is promiscuous. I don't care how much he's seen in the company of his wife, he's got a woman or two stashed somewhere.
>
> *Same editor, different day:* Batson, all those Malones are talented, devoted public servants. Just imagine what a terrific government we could have if we elected all of them to office at once.

Division and composition are really just subtypes of equivocation. They both involve an ambiguity on the word 'all'. 'All' can mean either a *collection* or *each member of a collection*. 'All' has both a *collective* and a *distributive* sense. If one is told that another's horses are for sale and that all of them are two thousand dollars, what one is told is subject to two interpretations and is hence ambiguous. It could mean that for two thousand dollars one could purchase the bunch of them, or it could mean that each horse costs two thousand dollars, in which case, if the seller has ten horses, a buyer will need twenty thousand for the bunch of them.

In the case of division the premise involves an 'all' in the collective sense, and the conclusion involves an 'all' in the distributive sense. While it may be true of the family or the bunch that they are promiscuous, it need not be true of each member that he or she is. The Malone in question could, for example, be altogether impotent. In the case of composition the opposite is true. The fallacy results because the 'all' involved in the premise or premises is the distributive one and the 'all' of the conclusion is the collective one. The fact that *each* member of the family is talented, hardworking, and devoted to public service is quite consistent with their being totally incapable of working together as a *group* or *collection*. They may, for example, suffer from intense sibling rivalry.

The difference, then, between this pair and the pair comprised of accident and converse accident, is that each member of this pair is just a more specific form of equivocation. Whether or not one is encountering a member of this pair depends upon whether or not there is in the argument a collective/distributive or distributive/collective equivocation on the word 'all' or some contextually equivalent expression like 'the group', 'the whole family', 'the members of a family', 'each of them', 'all of them'.

All the ambiguity fallacies discussed so far involve word or expression ambiguity. The ambiguities involved are ambiguities associated with, and, in fact, result because and only because of, multiple word meanings. Such ambiguities are said to be *semantic* ones. We have now to talk about ambiguities and fallacies that are a function of the whole sentence or its *syntax*. Consider the following sentence:

My son cares more for me than his mother.

This sentence could mean that the speaker's son cares more for the speaker than he does for his own mother. It could equally be said to mean that the speaker's son cares more for the speaker than the speaker's son's mother cares for the speaker. Badly constructed sentences of this sort can mislead us and cause us to infer what we are not really justified in inferring, and hence they can result in fallacious reasoning. Any fallacy which results from an ambiguity of this sort is called an *amphiboly*. The following quotation from *The Evening Press*, Binghamton, N.Y., provides an example of this fallacy:

> The wife of exiled physicist Andrei Sakharov says the government has turned down a request by a young family friend to leave the Soviet Union for the United States to marry her son by a previous marriage. (May 13, 1981)

Two interpretations are possible. We do not know whether to boo or applaud the Soviet Union. On one interpretation the Soviet Union is to be condemned for standing in the way of true love, but on the other interpretation the Soviet Union is to be congratulated for preventing incest. The rest of the article does make it clear to the reader that the former interpretation is the correct one.

Notice also that this passage contains an additional ambiguity. This passage does not make it clear which government is to be booed or applauded.

There are many other types of informal fallacies which have been recognized, described, and labeled. There are also other ways of slicing the pie. Various classifications are possible. We have chosen one. We have not even provided all the different kinds of informal fallacies that the classification system we have adopted is designed to accommodate. Still we have provided a fully representative set of examples. If one carefully studies these examples, he should be able to extrapolate to and recognize as fallacious examples of categories we have not covered.

Anyone who understands and is able to incorporate the contents of this chapter into his conceptual armory cannot help being a better equipped newsperson, able to spot errors of reasoning in the assertions of others and to avoid them. By doing so, the newsperson will better serve society by analyzing and clarifying issues, and forcing others to state their opinions, goals, intentions, and reasons unambiguously. Mankind will survive only by allowing kindness and understanding accompanied by reason to guide the future.

Suggested Reading

Allwood, Jens, Anderson, Lars-Gunnar, and Dahl, Osten. *Logic in Linguistics.* London: Cambridge University Press, 1977.

Barker, Stephen. *The Elements of Logic.* New York: McGraw-Hill, 1965.

Blumberg, Albert E. *Logic: A First Course.* New York: Knopf, 1976.

Carney, James D., and Scheer, Richard K. *Fundamentals of Logic.* New York: Macmillan, 1980.

Copi, Irving. *Introduction to Logic.* New York: Macmillan, 1978.

Fearnside, W. Ward, and Holter, William B. *Fallacy: The Counterfeit of Argument.* Englewood Cliffs, N.J.: Prentice-Hall, 1959.

Guttenplan, Samuel D., and Tamny, Martin. *Logic: A Comprehensive Introduction.* New York: Basic Books, 1971.

Kahane, Howard. *Logic and Contemporary Rhetoric: The Use of Reason in Everyday Life.* Belmont, Calif.: Wadsworth, 1980.

Manicus, Peter T., and Kruger, Arthur N. *Logic: The Essentials.* New York: McGraw-Hill, 1976.

Thomas, Stephen N. *Practical Reasoning in Natural Language.* Englewood Cliffs, N.J.: Prentice-Hall, 1977.

Toulmin, Stephen, Rieke, Richard, and Ianik, Allen. *An Introduction to Reasoning.* New York: Macmillan, 1979.

CHAPTER 2

Semantics: Journalism and Meaning

Since journalists are constantly dealing with the written word they are inescapably concerned with meaning. In the chapter on logic we distinguished between *sentences* and what they mean, i.e., *propositions*. In this chapter we will elaborate on that distinction, but, in addition, we will distinguish between *words* and what they mean. In order to talk unambiguously about word meaning we need to distinguish it from other uses of the word 'meaning'.

But before we turn to this topic it is necessary to explain more fully why it is important for journalists to study semantics and conceptual analysis. In the course description of their jointly taught course in philosophy and journalism at the University of Maryland, a journalism professor, Michael Petrick, and Jack Odell put the matter thus:

Conceptual analysis (and semantics) are not separable from logic. Logic involves sentences and sentences involve words which are the vehicles of our concepts. The distinction between logic and conceptual analysis on the one hand and semantics on the other is more a matter of emphasis than anything else. In logic the emphasis is placed upon whether or not arguments or inferences (which consist of sentences) are valid. In conceptual analysis and semantics the emphasis is placed upon what certain concepts or words *mean*.

Much of twentieth century philosophy has been concerned with linguistic or conceptual analysis. Philosophers like G.E. Moore, J.L. Austin, Wittgenstein, W.V.O. Quine, Nelson Goodman, and A.R. White have provided us with subtle and sophisticated analyses of such concepts as "memory," "perceiving," "thinking," "responsibility," "meaning," "referring," and "possibility." That the work of such philosophers has application to journalism can be illustrated by a couple of examples.

On the surface it might appear that J.L. Austin's analysis* of

---

* "A Plea for Excuses" in *Philosophical Papers*, J.L. Austin, ed. by J.O. Urmson and G.J. Warnock (Oxford: Oxford University Press, 1961), p. 133.

the difference between doing something "by mistake" as opposed to doing something "by accident" have little use to a journalist. Yet it is not too difficult to imagine a journalistic context in which this distinction would be relevant. As Austin points out, in order for someone to shoot another's donkey "by mistake," he must be intending to shoot a donkey and mistake the other's donkey to be the donkey he intends to shoot.

One can, however, shoot another's donkey "by accident" when he has no intention whatever to shoot any donkey. If intentionally shooting donkeys is against the law, then one who shoots another's donkey "by mistake" is guilty of breaking that law, whereas one who has shot another's donkey "by accident" is not. By parity of reasoning, if one country destroys "by mistake" a ship belonging to another country, this has ramifications that destroying the same ship "by accident" would not have. A reporter who is judicious in his observance of that distinction will not misrepresent to the public the ramifications of such an event.

The distinction between "possible for" and "possible that" (introduced into the philosophical literature by G.E. Moore and explicated by A.R. White) serves as a further example of the relevance of conceptual analysis to journalism. According to this analysis, someone who says that something "is possible" can mean either that it is possible *for* that something to be the case or that it is possible *that* that something is the case.

If, for example, the United States were to claim that its intervention into the internal affairs of another nation were possible, such a claim would be subject to two rather different interpretations. If all that is being claimed is that it is possible *for* the United States to do so, this needn't cause much alarm — since this is consistent with the United States having no real intention of intervening. (It is possible *for* a door to be open when it is in fact closed.) But, if what is meant is that it is possible *that* the United States will intervene in the other country's internal affairs, then there is reason for alarm. For the implication now is that the United States is actually considering such intervention. Again, the competent journalist who is aware of such a distinction, and who has for this reason developed the proper critical awareness as regards claims to the effect that something is possible will not be satisfied until he has determined what is meant by the claim under consideration.

Numerous other examples from the writings of contemporary analytical philosophers can be provided to illustrate the importance of conceptual analysis to journalism. The writings of these philosophers abound with relevant examples. The word 'meaning' has itself been the subject of much analysis during this century. In fact it has probably received more attention during the last fifty years than any other single concept. We will turn now to this concept.

Meaning

The word 'meaning', like all words in a natural language, is multivocal. It has many meanings. We are not, however, nor should we be, interested in all its meanings. In his very useful little book *The Philosophy of Language* (pp. 10–11), William Alston tries to prevent confusion by isolating nine meanings of 'meanings', all of which are distinct from the sense it has in 'word meaning', which is the sense with which we ultimately will be most interested. He asks us to consider all of the following:

1. That is no mean accomplishment. (insignificant)
2. He was so mean to me. (cruel)
3. I mean to help him if I can. (intend)
4. The passage of this bill will mean the end of second-class citizenship for vast areas of our population. (result in)
5. Once again life has meaning for me. (significance)
6. What is the meaning of this? (explanation)
7. He just lost his job. That means he will have to start writing letters of application all over again. (implies)
8. Keep off the grass. This means you. (refers to)
9. Lucky Strike means fine tobacco. (indicates)

Concerning the first seven of these, Alston claims, "In these cases we are talking about people, actions, events, or situations rather than about words, phrases, or sentences." For this reason we are less apt to confuse these with word meaning than we are the last two.

Eight seems to involve word meaning because the 'this' seems to refer to the meaning of the words 'Keep off the grass.' But it really does not. If it did, its meaning would be a person. Persons cannot be the meanings of sentences or expressions, otherwise it would make sense to look for persons in dictionaries.

If the 'means' of (9) was word meaning, we would expect, as Alston points out, to find 'Lucky Strikes' defined in the dictionary as, fine tobacco. Alston points out that the 'means' of (9) is synonymous with the 'means' of 'That look on his face means trouble.' He concludes his discussion with the observation that in such cases as these,

"We are saying that one thing or event is reliable indication of the existence of another."

Word meaning is the meaning which 'meaning' has in the following:

I just looked up the meaning of the word 'bachelor' in the dictionary, and it means *unmarried male*.

"What Our Words Mean" and "What We Mean By Them"

We want to keep the meaning of 'word meaning' distinct from the other nine Alston has isolated, but we also need to recognize that there is a use of the word in question which though not synonymous with word meaning, is nonetheless of considerable interest to us. It is the sense of 'meaning' tied to the sense of 'implication' which H.P. Grice illustrates in his paper "The Causal Theory of Perception"* with the sentence 'Jones has beautiful handwriting and his English is grammatical.' We will illustrate Grice's point with an example set in a journalistic context. Suppose several people are involved in the process of interviewing a would-be reporter. They meet after each of them has interviewed the candidate. One of them starts things off saying, "He stinks, he'd make a lousy reporter." Another is quick to agree. And a third observes, with a sarcastic intonation pattern, "He dresses well." What the third person *meant by* 'He dresses well' is precisely what the other interviewers meant, namely, his prospects are poor. It is one thing to talk about *what the words mean*, it is quite another thing to talk about what someone might *mean by them*.

When your local bartender asks if you want another drink, you can respond with, "Why not?" But when you do so, you are not requesting him to provide you with reasons why you should not drink. That is what your words mean. But it is not what you mean. What you mean is that he should serve you another drink.

If one is asked to describe another person, one might well respond with, "He dresses well." Here, in contrast to the above use of these words, you mean what your words mean. And if one person notifies another person that some third person is not coming to the movies with them, the person notified may request an explanation of the third person's change of plans by asking, "Why not?" He also means what his words mean. These uses of these expressions, in contrast to the uses made of them in the above examples, are what we shall refer to as *standard* uses. The use of the one to pass judgment on the would-be report-

* "The Causal Theory of Perception" in *Perceiving Sensing and Knowing*, ed. by Robert Swartz (Garden City, N.Y.: Doubleday & Company Inc., 1965), p. 448.

er, and the use of the other to order a drink, we will refer to as *non-standard uses* of these expressions.

When we simply talk about what a collection of words (sentences) mean, we are, to make use of a distinction we made in the previous chapter, talking about the *proposition* a sentence expresses. But when we talk about a declarative use of some sentence by a speaker in some specific context, we are talking about a *statement*. Some statements correspond to *standard* uses of a sentence, and some correspond to *nonstandard* uses of a sentence. What is *meant by* a standard use of a sentence is equivalent to what the words mean, and is, accordingly, equivalent to the proposition the sentence is said to express. It follows from this that there are times when there is no real difference between *what the words mean* and *what we mean by them*.

We can, however, use the same sentence to accomplish many things besides statement-making. The philosopher J.L. Austin developed a theory of meaning around this fact. This theory is known as the *speech-act theory of meaning*.

The Speech Act Theory of Meaning

This theory is presented in Austin's marvelously cogent and finely wrought little masterpiece, *How to Do Things with Words*. It has been explicated elsewhere* by Odell. We will quote from that exposition:

> One can take the view that the basic units of communication are, not *words*, but *strings of words*, usually *sentences*. J.L. Austin takes this line in . . . *How to Do Things with Words*. According to Austin the same string of words can be used in a variety of ways with a variety of meanings in order to accomplish a variety of tasks. The same sentence can be used to warn, state, request, acknowledge, promise, express one's emotions, etc. *Where, when,* and *how* a given sentence is used will determine what it means. Consider the following sentence from Austin (1962):
>
> There is a bull about to charge.
>
> If you and I are short-cutting our way across a pasture and I yell out the sentence displayed above, there is very little doubt in my mind concerning whether or not you would get the point of my outburst. If not, you are apt to get a rather different sort of point(s). No doubt, one can fail to hear or heed a warning, nevertheless, it is true that I have tried to *warn* you.
>
> If you and I are on our way to a bullfight at the *Plaza de Torros*

* "Are Natural Language Interfaces Possible?" IBM Systems Research Institute Technical Report # TR 73–024 (August 1981), pp. 10–12.

and hear on the car radio an announcer use the displayed sentence, we will take him to be *making a statement* either true or false. We will assume that it is true and hasten to make up for lost time.

Once we arrive at the bullring, you, who are at your first bullfight and don't understand very well what is going on, may use the displayed sentence, with the appropriate emphasis or speech pattern to *request* information regarding what the bull is about to do.

Following your request, I can use the same sentence to *acknowledge* that you are correct in the assumption underlying your request.

If, however, you have been disappointed several times already and are fast approaching utter boredom accompanied by exasperation, you may seek further assurance and ask me if I promise what I have just acknowledged. You have provided a setting that allows me to accomplish what you desire (a *promise*) by simply asserting the displayed sentence while nodding my head affirmatively.

After a rather long and tedious afternoon, you have become totally exasperated with the whole "bloody" business. You jump up out of your seat, shrug your shoulders and assert the displayed sentence as you hurriedly seek the exit. You have clearly and quite unambiguously succeeded in *expressing your feelings* about bull-fighting. You hate it!

These are just a few examples of the many speech actions one can accomplish with the displayed sentence. In each of these contexts the displayed sentence can be said to have a different meaning. What we shall say that the displayed sentence means is, as the examples demonstrate, a function of at least three variables. These variables are, *where, when*, and *how*. The meaning of the sentence in question changes depending on whether it is said in a pasture, in an automobile, or at the *Plaza de Torros*. It also depends on when it occurs. One cannot easily promise with it unless it has been *preceded by* a certain kind of event. Whether or not a given utterance of it is to be understood as a question, statement, etc., depends also on how it is said. When we wish to ask a question with it we must accent it a certain way. Accentuated a different way it will mean something else. I will use the term 'intonation contour' throughout the remainder of this paper when I want to talk about the way something is accentuated. The stater's *body language* (including such things as facial expression, eye contact, eye movement, body stance, etc.) also plays an important role regarding what the stater happens to mean by something he says. Austin referred to the various kinds of things which we can *do* with language as *speech actions*.

The Logical Positivist's Theory of Meaning

Certain positivistic philosophers, among them Rudolph Carnap, equated talk about word meaning and semantics with empirical verification. They claimed that asking for the meaning of some word, for example, 'arthropod', is synonymous with asking for a list of that thing's observable characteristics. To express fully the meaning of a given term is to list those characteristics which are essential to our understanding what it is to fall under the term. It is to provide a set of conditions which are both *necessary* and *sufficient*.

The difference between a sufficient and a necessary condition is explicable in terms of the fact that although being a dog is *sufficient* for being an animal, being an animal is *necessary* for being a dog. If it is true that something is a dog, then it must be an animal, but if it is not an animal, it is not a dog. As the example reveals, something can be sufficient but not necessary, and necessary, but not sufficient.

Carnap once attempted to define 'arthropod'. According to Carnap,* 'x is an arthropod' means:

1. x is an animal.
2. x has a segmented body.
3. x has jointed legs.

Carnap's point is that if (1), (2), and (3) are true of some thing, then it is true that the thing in question is an arthropod. But, if any one of (1), (2), or (3) is false of that thing, then it is not an arthropod.

Objections to Logical Positivism

The philosopher Wittgenstein provided an insurmountable obstacle to the logical positivist's conception of meaning and the notion of analysis it supports by demonstrating in *The Philosophical Investigations* that few, if any, of our general empirical terms are governed by necessary and sufficient conditions. He says regarding the word 'game':

> Consider for example the proceedings that we call "games". I mean board-games, card-games, ball-games, Olympic games, and so on. What is common to them all? — Don't say: "There *must* be something common, or they would not be called 'games'" — but *look and see* whether there is anything common to all. — For if you

* "The Elimination of Metaphysics through Logical Analysis of Language" in *Logical Positivism*, ed. by A.J. Ayer (New York: The Free Press of Glencoe Inc., 1959), pp. 60–81.

look at them you will not see something that is common to *all*, but similarities, relationships, and a whole series of them at that. To repeat: don't think, but look! — Look for example at board-games, with their multifarious relationships. Now pass to card-games; here you find many correspondences with the first group, but many common features drop out, and others appear. When we pass next to ball-games, much that is common is retained, but much is lost. — Are they all 'amusing'? Compare chess with noughts and crosses. Or is there always winning and losing, or competition between players? Think of patience. In ball-games there is winning and losing; but when a child throws his ball at the wall and catches it again, this feature has disappeared. Look at the parts played by skill and luck; and at the difference between skill in chess and skill in tennis. Think now of games like ring-a-ring-a-roses; here is the element of amusement, but how many other characteristic features have disappeared! And we can go through the many, many other groups of games in the same way; we can see how similarities crop up and disappear.

And the result of this examination is: we see a complicated network of similarities overlapping and criss-crossing: sometimes overall similarities, sometimes similarities of detail.*

In the article about natural language interfaces, Odell summarizes Wittgenstein's point thus:

Wittgenstein's point is that most, if not all, of the general empirical terms of our language are not, *as a plain matter of fact*, susceptible to analysis in terms of necessary and sufficient conditions. To search for some characteristic or set of characteristics which functions in this way for any given empirical term is to search for the non-existent. It is like looking for that secret ingredient which turns the base metals into gold. Philosophers and linguists who carry out such investigations are best compared to the medieval alchemists. [p. 21]

Waismann, following Wittgenstein to some extent, argues a different but closely related point. He argues that any attempt to provide an analysis of the meaning of an empirical concept in terms of conditions both necessary and sufficient is, *in principle*, impossible. According to Waismann, most of our empirical terms are what he calls *open textured*. In "Verifiability," he explains what he means as follows:

What I mean is this: Suppose I have to verify a statement such as

---

* Ludwig Wittgenstein, *The Philosophical Investigations* (New York: Macmillan, 1953), p. 31e, paragraph 66.

'There is a cat next door'; suppose I go over to the next room, open the door, look into it and actually see a cat. Is this enough to prove my statement? Or must I, in addition to it, touch the cat, pat him and induce him to purr? And supposing I had done all these things, can I then be absolutely certain that my statement was true? Instantly we come up against the well-known battery of sceptical arguments mustered since ancient times. What, for instance, should I say when that creature later on grew to a gigantic size? Or if it showed some queer behaviour usually not to be found with cats, say, if, under certain conditions, it could be revived from death where as normal cats could not? Shall I, in such a case, say that a new species has come into being? Or that it was a cat with extraordinary properties? [p. 119]

In the article on natural language interfaces, Odell explains Waismann's views on this matter as follows:

Waismann's point is this: if any of the things he imagines as possible did happen, we wouldn't know what to say. The rules which govern the expressions of ordinary language are not hard and fast. The rules we observe when communicating with each other cover only the kinds of cases we customarily encounter. The logic of an ordinary expression is not exhaustive. The boundaries of application of a given empirical term are not fixed. One way to come to appreciate Waismann's point is to contrast an ordinary everyday term like 'cat' with a term from mathematics which does have fixed boundaries of application. A term like 'triangle', unlike 'cat', is governed by fixed rules. One cannot even *imagine* a triangle not to be a figure, not to be composed of lines and not to have three sides. Of course one could imagine our using the word 'triangle' differently. It could be used to refer to shrimp in garlic sauce. But so long as it continues to have its present meaning all triangles, real or imagined, will, of necessity, have three sides. [p. 23]

One could react to this claim of Waismann's by objecting that although what he says about ordinary everyday terms like 'cat' may well be true, the terms of empirical science can, like the terms of mathematics and logic, be precisely defined. Waismann replies to this objection by pointing out:

'But are there not exact definitions at least in science?' Let's see. The notion of gold seems to be defined with absolute precision, say by the spectrum of gold with its characteristic lines. Now what would you say if a substance was discovered that looked like gold, satisfied all the chemical tests for gold, whilst it emitted a new sort of radiation? 'But such things do not happen.' Quite so; but they *might* happen, and that is enough to show that we can never exclude altogether the possibility of some unforeseen situation arising in which we shall have to modify our definition. Try as we may, no concept is limited in such a way that there is no room for any doubt. We introduce a concept and limit it in *some* directions; for instance, we define gold in contrast to some other metals such as alloys. This suffices for our present needs, and we do not probe any farther. We tend to *overlook* the fact that there are always other directions in which the concept has not been defined. And if we did, we could easily imagine conditions which would necessitate new limitations. In short, it is not possible to define a concept gold with absolute precision, i.e. in such a way that every nook and cranny is blocked against entry of doubt. [p. 120]

To prevent anyone from confusing *open texture* with vagueness, Waismann further observes:

Vagueness should be distinguished from *open texture*. A word which is actually used in a fluctuating way (such as 'heap' or 'pink') is said to be vague; a term like 'gold', though its actual use may not be vague, is non-exhaustive or of an open texture in that we can never fill up all the possible gaps through which a doubt may seep in. Open texture, then, is something like *possibility of vagueness*. Vagueness can be remedied by giving more accurate rules, open texture cannot. An alternative way of stating this would be to say that definitions of open terms are *always* corrigible or emendable. [p. 120]

Care must be taken to insure that no one confuse the concept of *family resemblance* with the concept of *open texture*. Far too often these two concepts are confused. Sometimes they are even equated. They should not be. The family resemblance aspect of our ordinary empirical concepts is a feature of their *actual* use. If we simply *consider* the various things we call 'games', we can see that there is no characteristic or set of characteristics which they all have in common. We can see that Wittgenstein is right without using our imaginative powers. We do not have to imagine the world to be any different than it is at present. But the concept of open texture cannot be explained to anyone without calling on him to use his imagination. The explanation of the concept of open texture always involves what philosophers call a *Gedankenexperi-*

ment. A *Gedankenexperiment* is a thought experiment; a use of one's imagination. When one engages in such a thought experiment, one ignores the way things are and considers what it would be like or what one would say if things were different from the way they actually are.

Further Considerations about Meaning

Another point which must be appreciated in order for one to understand the way a language like ours works is that the meaning of one word always involves the meaning of other words, which in turn involve still others. No word in our language can be understood in isolation from most other words in our language. Odell makes the point in the article on natural language interfaces thus:

> A word in a natural language is like a piece from a jigsaw puzzle. The role of any individual piece can be grasped only in the context of the complete puzzle. Without the rest of the pieces a given piece is meaningless because it has no purpose or function. "But couldn't it be given a purpose or function?" One could, of course, drill a hole through it, run a string through the hole and use it as a necklace. But then it is no longer functioning as it was *meant* to function. Strictly speaking, it is no longer a jigsaw puzzle piece, even though one might recognize it as such and so describe it. A word in a natural language, like a piece from a jigsaw puzzle, loses its function and its meaning when it is separated from all the other words (pieces) which comprise the language (puzzle). [p. 27]

Another salient characteristic of natural languages is that they accommodate humankind's irrepressible creativity. The flexibility of natural languages explains how poetry, novels, and other linguistic art forms can exist. If natural languages were inflexible and formalistic, these art forms would not exist.

Great novelists, poets, journalists, and academicians are recognized by their ability to use language in ways no other has done before them. Innovative uses of language are extremely varied and they embody an important aspect of natural language use. Metaphors, puns, similies, jokes, analogies, and other creative uses of language are as necessary to fine literary fare as are garlic and salt to the culinary art.

Previously, it was established that the sentence about the bull's impending charge could be used to accomplish, among other things, the acts of warning, stating, and promising. These speech actions are ones which involve conventions and intentionality. No person could promise if the practice were nonexistent, and it is not possible to promise without meaning to do so, even though, of course, one can promise with no intention of keeping one's promise. J.L. Austin, in *How to Do Things with Words*, referred to these kinds of speech actions as *illocutionary* actions, and he distinguished them from their consequences or what he referred to as *perlocutionary* actions. [pp. 98–131] The things that we say can be said to amuse, annoy, irritate, convince, delight, deceive, perplex, etc. To do any of these things is to have accomplished a perlocution, but it doesn't matter whether you did it with or without intention. The perlocutionary consequences of our actions are what they are independent of whether or not we intend them. I may very well annoy you by saying that a bull is about to charge and not have any idea that I have done so. Or I may want very much to annoy you by saying what I say about the bull. We do very often use language in order to amuse, irritate, delight, etc. others, and we often do so when we are using language creatively.

Much of what has been established in the present chapter regarding the nature of meaning and language is best summarized by the following set of principles originally formulated by Odell in his article on natural language interfaces.

1. Communication through a natural language is, in a large part, a function of context. *Where* and *when* something is said largely determines *what* is said. (I will refer to this as the *Context Principle*.)
2. What we mean is also a function of *how* we say it. Where or upon what word or words we place an emphasis (*intonation contour*), as well as how we move various parts of our bodies (*body language*), will frequently affect what we mean. (*Emphasis Principle*)
3. The range of things (speech acts) a given sentence can be used to accomplish is limitless. (*Multiple Speech Acts Principle*)
4. What a sentence *means* (a proposition) is often quite different from what we *mean by* it, which is sometimes a statement, sometimes a warning, sometimes a request and sometimes something else. (*Intentionality Principle*)
5. What a given string of words means is not a function of the formal characteristics that string possesses. "Why not?" can be used to make a request, even though its *form* is that of a question. (*Non-Functionality Principle*)
6. What most, if not all, general empirical terms *mean* in a natural language, as opposed to what we might *mean by* them on some specific occasion, cannot be specified *formally*, that is, in terms of necessary and sufficient conditions. They are family resemblant in nature. (*Family Resemblance Principle*)
7. Since most of the general empirical terms of a natural language are family resemblant in nature, it follows that in order to get at their

meanings, i.e., the concepts they express, one must specify the set of overlapping and criss-crossing characteristics which determine the similarities and differences relevant to the question of whether or not some imagined or existing case falls under the concept in question. (*Overlapping and Criss-Crossing Definitions Principle*)

8. Even if we legislate sets of necessary and sufficient conditions to govern what they mean, we can't be sure that our legislations will preclude the existence of contexts where we will be uncertain what our words mean; that is, we can still imagine cases where we wouldn't know whether or not a given word applied. The words of natural language are open textured. (*Open Texture Principle*)

9. The concept expressed by any given word in a natural language is inextricably tied to the concepts expressed by nearly every other word in the language. While the words themselves are no doubt *discrete*, the concepts they involve, or are tied to, are *continuous* with other concepts. (*Continuity Principle*)

10. A very large number of speech acts which can be implemented in a natural language involve expressing one's emotions. A natural language incorporates the distinction between a genuine and a non-genuine expression of an emotion. Expressing concern, and expressing genuine concern are recognizably quite different. (*Sincerity Principle*)

11. The meaning of a great many speech acts is intentionally creative and non-standard. We often use language in inventive and innovative ways to amuse, clarify, convince, annoy, insult, etc. Punning, poetry, word play, and pre-eminent prose all depend on our ability to use language with a certain impunity.* (*Creativity Principle*) [pp. 28–30]

If these contentions are true, then communication through a language like English is largely a function of context (where and when) and emphasis (how). Such languages are organic and flexible. Meaning could be formally described only if there was a set of *discrete* contexts such that every speech episode (use of language) necessarily took place in a context belonging to this set and if everything we said was said with the *same* intonation contour. But, as Odell further observes:

> Contexts are not discrete entities. They form a continuum. We cannot say when one leaves off and another begins. And, the nuances in meaning that are possible through voice inflection, facial expression, eye contact, etc., are, like contexts, *non-denumerable* and *unspecifiable*. What all of this means is much of the

---

* The eleventh principle is an addition to the original list, and appears in a revised but as yet unpublished version of the paper on natural language interfaces.

communication that takes place in a natural language cannot be captured in a formal program. [p. 31]

Does this mean that we cannot hope to provide an analysis of what any of our words mean? Does it mean that we cannot determine when certain words have the same meaning, or that a given word type has a different meaning on one occasion from what it has on another? The answer to these questions is No.

Analyzing Meaning and Determining Difference of Sense

We can provide an analysis of the meaning of any given word, but we must recognize that doing so is not providing à set of conditions both necessary and sufficient. As an alternative to the procedure practiced by Carnap, the positivists, and even some antediluvians today, one can claim that the proper way to do a conceptual analysis of an expression is to search out and specify what is the set of overlapping and criss-crossing characteristics which determine what are the similarities and differences that are relevant to the question of whether or not some imagined or existing case is an instance of (falls under) the concept in question.

One does this by examining the many, many uses that an expression has. Some of the characteristics which can be discovered in this way are more consequential than others. Some are even necessary conditions in the sense previously explained. For example, if it is not an activity, then it is not a game. Many other characteristics are relevant as well. Some of them are associated with some instances, some of them are not. Ultimately, however, such an analysis will always be incomplete because there is no way to take into account all the ways in which a context can affect what one means by some particular use of some expression.

Odell and Kress have provided a criterion for determining difference of sense or meaning which is quite consistent with all the observations we have made about language. Their criterion does not purport to be both a necessary and a sufficient condition for difference of meaning but rather only a sufficient one. What they claim is that "no single case of multivocality [difference of meaning] can be found where our criterion fails to yield the conclusion of multivocality."*

We will state their criterion and then explain it. Here is a version of the criterion:

An expression *e* has a different sense in sentence Sa than it has in

---

* "A Paraphrastic Criterion for Difference of Sense," J. Kress and S. Jack Odell, in *Theoretical Linguistics*, January 1983.

sentence Sb if: (1) there is a word or phrase f which is a metaphrase of e in Sa; (2) there is a word or phrase g which is a metaphrase of e in Sb; (3) there are no sentences in which either f or g is a metaphrase of the other; and (4) neither Sa nor Sb is odd.

A metaphrase of an expression is simply a different expression or a phrase which can be substituted for the original expression in any sentence without either changing the truth value of that sentence or producing an odd or meaningless sentence.

Consider the following sentence:

The reporter caught the hottest show in Vegas.

The word 'caught' can be metaphrased with 'attended and viewed'. To say that the reporter attended and viewed the hottest show in Vegas is to say precisely what the original sentence said. If the original sentence is true, it will have to be true that the reporter attended and viewed the show. And clearly this result is not odd or meaningless.

Now consider a different sentence:

The reporter caught a cold.

The word 'caught' can be metaphrased with 'came down with'; saying that a reporter came down with a cold amounts to saying that he or she caught one. The truth of the one claim insures the truth of the other, and there is nothing odd or meaningless about claiming that a reporter came down with a cold.

Now that we have example metaphrases for the 'caught' of each of our sentences we can ask if the meaning of 'caught' is different in our example sentences. According to the criterion, 'caught' can be said to have a different sense in two different sentences if there exists a metaphrase of one and a metaphrase of the other which cannot metaphrase (replace) each other in any sentence. If I substitute 'came down with' for the 'caught' of the first example sentence the result is:

The reporter came down with the hottest show in Vegas.

This is certainly an odd result. If we substitute 'attended and viewed' for the 'caught' of the second example, the result is the nonsensical sentence that follows:

The reporter attended and viewed a cold.

And, in keeping with the criterion, nothing that one 'attends and views' will have to be something that one sensibly also 'comes down with'. Therefore, the 'caught' of the first sentence has a different meaning from the caught of the second one.

At the end of the last chapter we observed that a journalist who masters the contents of that chapter could not help being a better, more effective journalist. The same claims can be made for the present chapter. Mastery of its contents puts one in the position to analyze what others mean and to express one's own meaning much more clearly and unambiguously. An expertise in the subjects covered in this chapter tunes one into the various nuances and pitfalls that exist in our language and prevents one from falling into the traps that are omnipresent in language. One of the main lessons of much of contemporary philosophy is the recognition of how deceptive and misleading language can be. The philosopher Wittgenstein spent most of his philosophical career trying to dispel the philosophical myths that have resulted from inattention to language.

Still there are those among us who try to belittle the accomplishments of the analytical movement in philosophy with the charge that it is much ado about nothing. They charge that when a philosopher draws a fine distinction what he has done is "just a matter of semantics." No slogan could be more unfair or further from the truth. This chapter itself speaks out against the absurdity of this charge. But in order to prevent anyone's having any future doubts about the validity of this charge we will take up the gauntlet and defend contemporary philosophy.

It's Just Semantics

It is not altogether clear what it means to say what the title of this section says. Part of what it means is clear enough, however. It is pejorative in force. The speech act that one intends to carry off with it is deprecatory. What is said by it is something like, "You aren't really saying anything about the nature of things, you are just playing word games". Underlying this form of objection is the view that the kind of concern which philosophers exhibit regarding language is a trivial concern. Worthwhile intellectual endeavor, according to this scenario, has as its goal the understanding of things, not words. These discreditors of philosophical analysis claim that philosophers ought to follow the example set by anthropologists, biologists, physicists, physicians, and other respectable scientifically oriented professionals. Philosophers, this scenario continues, should concern themselves, as they did in the past, with things like life, truth, beauty, knowledge, wisdom, and the good. These things, the detractors assert, are the proper objects for philosophical study. Leave language to the linguists. They exhibit the proper sort of perspective on the study of language. They simply describe it. The problem with the philosophy that is practiced today, continues the detractor's scenario, is that it proceeds beyond description and attempts to draw conclusions about things from the study of words. Words, these critics allege, are one thing, things are another. And, they assume, that the twain shall not meet.

But the assumption about the impossibility of joining the two is altogether unfounded. It is certainly true that words are one thing, and things another. But it is also true that concepts or the meaning of words are still another sort of thing. And they provide the bridge from the word to the thing.

The words involved in the expressions 'possible for' and 'possible that' are words which we use to mark an important conceptual distinction. And this distinction spills over into the world. The realities which these two expressions demarcate are quite different, but the demarcation, which is the recognition of that difference, resides in the concepts these words incorporate.

If you are a prisoner on death row being visited by a journalist who has been devoted to getting from the governor a stay of your execution, you are going to be very interested in what he has to say in answer to your request to know whether or not the governor is going to grant your stay. If the reporter answers you with, "It's possible", you will, because you studied the first part of this chapter, respond with a question. You will ask, "Do you mean that it is *possible for* him to do so or do you mean it is *possible that* he will do so?" Your appreciation of this difference makes it impossible for the reporter to mislead you on this matter. If he is a compassionate individual, he is apt to be trying to do so when he says what he does. Every governor has the power to do so. All of them *can* do so. But this is not what you want to know. What you want to know is whether or not this particular governor has any intention of doing so. Is there *evidence* that he will do so? Clearly we are talking about what the words mean, but we are also talking about your life or death. The matter is not trivial. At least, not to you. And if this does not convince you, perhaps our use of this distinction to clarify and undermine scepticism in the chapter on epistemology will.

We also saw at the beginning of this chapter how significant Austin's distinction between *by mistake* and *by accident* could be to our being properly informed about an event with international ramifications. And in some sense every intellectual exercise is just semantics. But this is not a trivial fact. It is of the utmost importance. Every time we argue, inquire, confirm, think, postulate, encourage, or convince, we make use of language. In that sense we engage in semantics. But where would we be if we did not engage in these activities?

Consider, for example, cognitive thought. Much of what we mean to be talking about when we talk about cognition would be impossible without language. Suppose I ask you to consider, for example, the proposition that a million-sided polygon is a greater-sided figure than is a million-sided polygon minus a thousand sides. Can you entertain this thought or proposition without language? Just try it! You might very well be able to visualize a figure with many sides alongside one with fewer sides. But this is not to grasp that a million-sided figure is a greater-sided figure than a million-sided one minus a thousand sides. Your image will be the same if you try to imagine a thousand-sided figure being greater-sided than a thousand-sided figure minus a hundred sides. Your powers of imagery are too limited for this discrimination. But your language is not. And it is through language that the distinction must be grasped.

Suggested Reading

Alston, William P. *Philosophy of Language*. Englewood Cliffs, N.J.: Prentice-Hall, 1964.

Austin, J.L. *How to Do Things with Words*. Cambridge, Mass.: Harvard University Press, 1962.

Carnap, R. "The Elimination of Metaphysics through Logical Analysis of Language." In A.J. Ayer, ed. *Logical Positivism*. New York: Free Press, 1959.

Caton, Charles E., ed. *Philosophy and Ordinary Language*. Urbana: University of Illinois Press, 1963.

Chappell, V.C. *Ordinary Language*. Englewood Cliffs, N.J.: Prentice-Hall, 1964.

Davidson, Donald, and Harman, Gilbert, eds. *The Logic of Grammar*. Encino and Belmont, Calif.: Dickenson, 1975.

Fodor, Jerry A., and Katz, Jerrold J. *The Structure of Language*. Englewood Cliffs, N.J.: Prentice-Hall, 1964.

Grice, H.P. "Meaning." *The Philosophical Review* (66 (1957).

Hayakawa, S.I. *Language in Thought and Action*. New York: Harcourt, Brace, 1949.

Kress, J.R., and Odell, S. Jack. "A Paraphrastic Criterion for Difference of Sense." *Theoretical Linguistics*, January 1983.

Linksy, Leonard. *Referring*. New York: Humanities Press, 1967.

Lyas, Colin. *Philosophy and Linguistics*. London: Macmillan, 1971.

Nagel, Ernest, and Brandt, Richard B., eds. *Meaning and Knowledge: Systematic Readings in Epistemology*. New York: Harcourt, Brace & World, 1965.

Olshewsky, Thomas N., ed. *Problems in the Philosophy of Language*. New York: Holt, Rinehart and Winston, 1969.

Palmer, F.R. *Semantics: A New Outline*. Cambridge: Cambridge University Press, 1976.

Rorty, Richard. *The Linguistic Turn: Recent Essays in Philosophical Method*. Chicago: University of Chicago Press, 1967.

Searle, John R. *Expression and Meaning.* Cambridge: Cambridge University Press, 1969.

Urmson, J.O. *Philosophical Analysis: Its Development between the Two Wars.* Oxford: Oxford University Press, 1956.

Waismann, Frederick. "Verifiability." In A.G.N. Flew, ed. *Logic and Language.* First Series. Oxford: Blackwell, 1960.

White, Alan R. "Conceptual Analysis." In Bontempo, Charles, and Odell, S. Jack, eds. *The Owl of Minerva.* New York: McGraw-Hill, 1965.

CHAPTER 3

Epistemology: Journalism and Truth

The day to day practice of journalism consists primarily in reporting to the public what are considered by the journalists to be the important and consequential events and episodes of the last few hours. But it also consists in ferreting out and reporting on events and episodes which, although they took place some time ago, are nevertheless of interest to the public. The ideal journalist is a person who engages in this activity with enthusiasm, integrity, and dedication. Whether or not a journalist has enthusiasm is a personal psychological matter and does not fall within the scope of this book. Integrity is an ethical issue, and will be dealt with in Chapter 4. What it is that the journalist ought ideally to be dedicated to, and whether or not the ideals can be realized, is the subject of the present chapter.

Ideally the journalist should be dedicated to informing the public regarding the facts in an objective and impartial manner. He should be a devoted truth-seeker. The ideal journalist would be someone like the philosopher Socrates. Like Socrates, the ideal journalist would never be content with an easy answer, any sort of compromise, a biased account, an inadequately evidenced conclusion, in short, anything short of the truth. The ideal journalist is one who seeks to know what the facts are, and then impartially informs the public, allowing the chips to fall where they may.

The key concepts in this account of the goals of the ideal journalist are *facts, objectivity, knowledge, evidence,* and *truth*. These concepts form the nucleus of the network of concepts associated with that branch of philosophy known as epistemology. Epistemologists have throughout the centuries devoted considerable attention to these concepts, and it is to their endeavors we now turn to seek enlightenment.

What Is Epistemology?

Epistemology is a branch of philosophy. It is one of the four major branches or areas of philosophy. The other three are axiology, logic, and metaphysics.* It is that branch of philosophy which is concerned with knowledge. For this reason it is also called the theory of knowledge. It has branches and they are, according to most philosophers, induction, truth theory, philosophy of mind, philosophy of language, and philosophy of science. Philosophers who engage in this branch of philosophy are called epistemologists. They ask and attempt to answer questions like the following: "What is knowledge?", "What are its limits?", "How many ways of knowing are there?", "Is there a difference between factual and mathematical knowledge?", "Can creatures other than humans know things?", "What does thinking consist in?", "Can machines think?", "What is truth?", "What are facts?", "What is science?"

The epistemological topics of most interest to journalists are inductive procedures, factual knowledge, truth, evidence, confirmation, and objectivity. We will treat all of these topics in the present chapter. We will begin by examining the various kinds of knowledge there are. In this way we will clarify what we mean by factual knowledge. We will then look carefully at philosophical scepticism, which is the view that no factual knowledge is possible. If no factual knowledge is possible, and if journalism is concerned with gathering and disseminating facts, then journalism is not possible. We will attempt to meet the challenge of scepticism. We will follow this with an account of inductive method (canons of induction). This will be followed by an analysis of the nature of evidence, which will be followed by an examination of theories of truth. Confirmation will be covered in the section on evidence, objectivity in the section on truth.

Kinds of Knowledge

When philosophers talk about types of knowledge, what they are really talking about is kinds of objects which knowledge can be about. Consider the following sentences:

1. I know that I exist.
2. I know that my friends exist.
3. I know that my computer terminal exists.
4. I know that God exists.
5. I know that spirits exist.
6. I know that werewolves and vampires exist.
7. I know that I am in pain.
8. I always know when my friends are in pain.

* Logic is sometimes classified as a branch of epistemology.

9. I know beauty when I see it.
10. I know that God is good.
11. I know that my computer terminal is made of metal.
12. I know that some spirits are good.
13. I know that vampires are terrorized by the sign of the cross.
14. I know that I went to the dentist last month.
15. I know that I am going to the dentist tomorrow.
16. I know that if I were to claim (1), I would be claiming what is true, but if I were to claim (6), what I would be claiming is false.
17. I know that the universe is as Einstein says it is.
18. I know that triangles have three sides.
19. I know that fifty things minus two things is forty-eight things.
20. I know that there is a vampirelike appearance in my visual field.

These sentences can all be used to make knowledge claims. Few of us would be willing, however, to claim some of these things, because they are *about* things which we believe to be nonexistent. But for the purpose of discussion let us imagine that each of them has been claimed. To claim (1) is to make a knowledge claim about one's own existence. The *object of knowledge* here is self. The same object of knowledge can be asserted for (7), (14), and (15). But (14) and (15) can each be said to have an additional object of knowledge as well. The additional object of knowledge in (14) is the past. In (15) it is the future. The objects of knowledge in (2) are other persons. The objects of knowledge in (8) are the feelings of other persons. Philosophers refer to this kind of knowledge as knowledge of *other minds*.

The kinds of objects talked about in (3), (4), (5), and (6) are, respectively, physical objects, God, spirits, and superhuman creatures. The object of knowledge in (9) is beauty. God is again the object of knowledge in (10), but this claim is also about the good. Claim (16) is about truth and falsity. Seventeen is about the universe. Eighteen and nineteen are about mathematical entities. Twenty is about an appearance in a person's visual field. Such appearances are referred to by philosophers as *sense data*. But what about (11), (12), and (13)? Why, one is apt to ask, have we included them at all? Are their objects not already in the list? They are, but there is a good reason for including them on our list. They are required to illustrate the distinction between *knowledge that something exists* and *knowledge that something has certain properties*. It is one thing to know that something exists. It is quite another to know that something has certain properties. Some philosophers have argued that some knowledge of the latter sort is necessary for knowledge that something exists.

Having distinguished these various kinds of knowledge, we are now in a position to state one of the oldest and most venerated theses in epistemology: scepticism.

Scepticism

In case the reader is wondering why a journalist should be interested in scepticism, the answer is twofold. In the first place, as has been pointed out, the justification for the first four chapters is to make good applied philosophers out of perspective journalists. The study of scepticism will help accomplish this. Perhaps no part of philosophy is more sophisticated conceptually than is that part of philosophy devoted to scepticism. The challenge of the sceptic is one which nearly every great philosopher has attempted to meet. (Many of these philosophers have themselves become converted to scepticism.) The study of scepticism is one of the very best ways for the beginner to sharpen his conceptual tools. Many useful philosophical distinctions were initially drawn by philosophers when discussing scepticism. The distinction we drew in the last chapter between *possible for* and *possible that* is a good example. It was first made use of by G.E. Moore in his attempted refutation of Bertrand Russell's scepticism.*

The second reason for recommending the study of scepticism to the journalist is that he is bound to encounter a variety of arguments regarding the impossibility of objectivity. Objectivity and scepticism are intimately connected. One who has worked his way through the maze that comprises the pros and cons of scepticism will not be easily misled by the many fallacious claims that are laid down in behalf of claims like the claim that no journalist can ever be objective, or no journalist can ever really be sure of anything he writes. The latter claim is just an instantiation of scepticism. A good journalist should be in a position to put such claims in their proper perspective. He should know what can and cannot be asserted regarding the possibility of knowledge and objectivity, and the best way for him to acquire this knowledge is to be exposed to the philosophical debate concerning scepticism.

Philosophical scepticism, as opposed to ordinary everyday scepticism, is the view that no one could ever know anything at all about any object that falls into one or more than one of the various classes of kinds of objects isolated in the previous section. If, for example, one holds that no one could ever know anything whatever regarding any other person's thoughts, feelings, or perceptions, one is said to be a sceptic regarding *other minds*. All of us are sometimes sceptical about what another person is thinking. Often we find ourselves doubtful regarding

* "Four Forms of Scepticism," in Moore's *Philosophical Papers* (New York: The Macmillan Company, 1959), pp. 196–226.

what is going on in someone else's mind. Still we are of the impression that we do *sometimes* know what another person is thinking or feeling. The philosophical sceptic we described a couple of sentences ago says that we are mistaken in this impression: no one could ever know anything of this sort. The sceptic does not just assert this view; he (or she) defends it with an arsenal of arguments. We will consider some of the more cogent arguments for this position a little later on. Right now we will describe *classical scepticism*.

One can be sceptical regarding any of the classes of things we isolated in the previous section. Most human beings qualify as philosophical sceptics regarding superhuman creatures and spirits. Many of us are philosophical sceptics regarding God. Scepticism regarding God's existence and nature is called *agnosticism*. The agnostic is one who holds that no one could ever know anything whatever about God. The classical sceptic is agnostic but he is also sceptical about a good many things besides God. The classical sceptic (Sextus Empiricus, David Hume, and Bertrand Russell are classical sceptics) is, in fact, sceptical with respect to all but two of the categories we isolated. As far as he is concerned, we can only claim to know things like (18), (19), and (20). We can, according to this brand of scepticism, only be said to know things which are *a priori analytic* or about *sense data*. We need now to explain exactly what these sorts of knowledge are.

There is *factual* knowledge on the one hand and *a priori* knowledge on the other. When we talk about factual knowledge we are talking about knowing that certain propositions are, as a *matter of fact*, true. When we talk about knowledge of the *a priori*, what we are talking about is our knowing that certain propositions are *necessarily* true. Simply stated, factual knowledge is knowledge of facts.

But then what are facts? A fact is any of the following: an existent state of affairs, an episode in time, a convention, a belief, a conscious process. Objects, for example, persons, places, or things, are not facts. All of the following assertions express factual propositions: "It is a fact that Jones was here last night"; "It is a fact that Reagan had a debate with Anderson"; "As a matter of fact, Nixon was guilty of fraud."

The following assertions can all be said to express *a priori* propositions: "Triangles have three sides"; "Carnivores eat meat"; "5 precedes 6"; "Everything which is magenta is colored"; "A bachelor is an unmarried male"; and "Inventing clichés is impossible." But the distinction between factual and *a priori* knowledge has not gone unchallenged. Some philosophers, for example, Quine, argue that it cannot be maintained.

While we agree that one cannot state the necessary and sufficient conditions which govern the distinction, we feel that the distinction can be defended. We cannot state the necessary and sufficient conditions which have to be met in order for us to refer to something as a piece of furniture; nevertheless, we can recognize things which are furniture and differentiate them from things which are clothing. One way to convince another that one is cognizant of the difference is to produce examples of each. Much of what we said in the chapter on meaning and analysis is relevant to this point. (A good example of what it is to give an analysis in terms of *necessary* and *sufficient* conditions is provided in that chapter's section on the logical positivist's theory of meaning.)

To hold that a proposition is *a priori* is to hold that its truth is independent of the facts. The examples we provided of such propositions are also said to be *analytic*. To hold that a proposition is analytic is to hold that understanding it amounts to recognizing that it is true.

Propositions about *sense data* (experiential propositions) fall into the class of factual propositions. They are the only factual propositions which the classical sceptics will allow that we can have knowledge of. *Experiential propositions* are best understood in contrast to what are called *propositions about physical objects*. Consider that you have in front of you a plain ordinary everyday piece of white paper. Now consider the sentence, 'There is a piece of paper in front of me'. This sentence can be used in a number of ways, e.g., to make a claim (assert a proposition); as a line in a play, poem, or novel; as an example of a declarative sentence in English; as an English equivalent of a sentence in a foreign language. In the present context we are only interested in the first of these possible uses.

Now consider another possible claim: "There is in my visual field at the present moment what appears to be a piece of white paper." This claim is weaker than the first one. The truth of the former depends upon the piece of paper actually being in front of you. To *know* that it is true is to *know* that there is in front of you a piece of paper. If there is no paper there then a claim that there is has to be false. But the paper does not have to be there in order for the other claim to be true. All that is required for the second claim to be true is that you seem to see the paper. Even if you are hallucinating and you claim the second of these things, what you claim is still true. Not so with the former, and as we shall see, this fact about hallucinating provides the sceptic with a reason in favor of claiming that no one could ever know anything about a physical object. The second claim exemplifies what it is to express an experiential proposition.

We want now to look at the main arguments which classical scepticism uses to support its conclusions. But before we do so we need to explain the difference between *deductive* and *inductive* reasoning. When philosophers talk about deductive reasoning, they are talking about *valid* argumentation. We have discussed this topic in the chapter on logic. For now let an example of deductive reasoning suffice. If one claims that some object must be three-sided because it is a triangle, his claim is deductively grounded. His conclusion is indisputable if the object in question is a triangle.

But when one claims, as journalists must constantly do, that some event took place in the past, on the grounds that certain witnesses are willing to attest to it, one's claim is nowhere nearly so well grounded. One does not even have the testimony of one's own senses to rely upon. What makes this reasoning *inductive* is that the reasons provided in favor of the claim (premises) could all be true when the claim (conclusion) is false. This state of affairs can never occur when a bit of reasoning is deductive in character. If the thing we spoke of a moment ago is, in fact, a triangle, then it must have three sides. Most of the reasoning journalists engage in is inductive. The classical sceptic claims that no conclusions based on inductive reasoning can qualify as knowledge. It follows then that if this is right, journalism is a discipline without a proper foundation.

Arguments in Favor of Scepticism

We want now to understand why the sceptic maintains that we can only know *a priori* and experiential propositions. As journalists we claim knowledge regarding propositions falling into most of the classes we previously isolated. We are, unquestionably, interested in factual knowledge. That journalists are interested in factual truth is obvious. A journalist who confessed that he was not interested in getting at the facts would not be read. If we did not want to know the facts, we could invent our own news.

The sceptic has some powerful arguments, and, if they are valid, we might as well close up shop. Fortunately, the arguments are not invulnerable. We shall see that there is a fatal flaw.

The sceptic argues against knowledge of the past and knowledge of the future by pointing out that our claims to knowledge of both is *inductive*, and that such claims always fail to qualify as knowledge. What is meant by this is that, unlike *deductive knowledge*, it is factually grounded, and that what is factually grounded is, with the exception of what is grounded in the current contents of one's cognitive fields, never knowledge.

The sceptic says that all of us would agree that when we *know* something, that which is known must be certain. This is what it is to know something. If there are any grounds for doubt regarding any claim, then the claim cannot be said to qualify as knowledge. The sceptic claims that if it is possible to doubt p, where p is some proposition, then one cannot be said to know p. This contention, which originated with Descartes, and which we will refer to as the *Cartesian principle*, plays a fundamental role in the sceptic's argument. It is, moreover, a principle well grounded in our language. All of us would consider the following dialogue odd:

> *First newscaster:* I'm not sure whether or not I ought to announce that the tenth Irish hunger striker has died. I know you are convinced, but I'm not.
> *Second newscaster:* Don't worry about it. I agree it's not certain that he did. Even I have some doubts. I know, however, that he died.

It does not make any sense to claim, as our second newscaster does, that there are doubts about p, that p is not certain, but that p is known to be true.

The sceptic further claims that since we can never *directly* experience the future, every claim about it involves an inductive inference of the following sort: In the past certain things caused certain other things to transpire, so these same things will cause the other things to occur in the future. Against this the sceptic claims we cannot be certain that the future will resemble the past.

But even if this were so, it would still seem quite reasonable to conclude, on the basis of what we know about the past, that it is highly likely that given certain conditions, certain other things will transpire. Not so, says the sceptic. We cannot, according to him (or her), know anything about the past, from which it would have to follow that we can know nothing about the future. The reason for this is that all claims to knowledge of the future involve predictions that the future will resemble the past. If we cannot know the past, then we cannot know the future.

Against the claim that we can know the past the sceptic argues that claims about the past involve memory, and that whenever memory is involved in a claim-making context, it is always possible for doubt to creep in. Whatever people think they remember or are under the impression that they remember, could always have been different from the way it is recalled. If one *remembers* something having happened, then that thing had to have happened or it is not really remembered. But one can be under the impression that one remembers something which, in fact, never happened. The sceptic's point is that what anyone *directly experiences* when one remembers something which actually happened and what one *directly experiences* when one is only under the impression that one remembers that something happened, are *indistinguishable*. Since they are indistinguishable, it is always possible that when one claims that something happened in the past, one is under a mistaken impression. From which it appears to follow that any claim about the past could be mistaken.

But even if we were to admit this, we would not have to concede some of the sceptic's more radical contentions. Surely nothing would suffice to show that the sceptic is correct when he claims, as he does, that no one could ever know that one's *own* self exists. Even Descartes, who popularized many sceptical arguments while building a case for scepticism regarding the possibility of knowing various kinds of object (knowledge which he ultimately reinstated), never doubted that one could know that one's own self existed. In fact, Descartes claimed, that *nothing* was more certain than one's own existence. According to Descartes, one might even be confused enough to doubt that triangles have three sides, but never that one existed.

Descartes is himself somewhat confused on this matter. The fact that *someone is uncertain* about p does not imply that p *is uncertain*. Nevertheless, Descartes' point that even the act of doubting is an affirmation of self (the doubter) remains plausible whether or not he is right about this detail. Even if he is wrong in thinking that the existence of self is more certain than *a priori* propositions, he nonetheless provides reasonable grounds for certainty regarding the existence of self.

Hume was the first to refute Descartes on this matter. Russell provides a contemporary version of the refutation. Russell's version of the Humian argument goes as follows. Whenever we talk about ourselves we are talking about an entity which is assumed to have been born on a specific occasion, to have occupied time for a specific number of years, to have had certain experiences in the past, and to be existing in the present. (Another way of putting this contention is to say that the word 'self' means or has reference to not only some presently existing and conscious entity, but also some entity which existed and was conscious in the past.) If this is true, then the sceptic can claim that, since he has shown that we cannot have knowledge of the past, we cannot have knowledge of self. Since knowledge of self is essentially tied to the past, whatever problems exist regarding knowledge of the one carry over to our knowledge of the other.

While this might seem to be inconsistent with the sceptic's claim that certainty can be attained for experiential claims, it is not. The sceptic can claim, as Russell does, that what is certain about such claims is that a conscious something is having an experience. So long as one does not go on to infer that that conscious thing which is having the experience is, in fact, some specific person with a specific birthday who has had a large number of experiences in the past, such a claim can be said to be certain.

Against the possibility of knowledge of physical objects the sceptic voices several arguments. We will consider three of these. They are what has been traditionally referred to as the *argument from illusion*, the *dream argument*, and what we call the *differing persons and perspectives argument*.

Simply stated the argument from illusion involves nothing more than the recognition that what we appear to see is sometimes other than it appears. We are all familiar with how a straight stick in water can appear bent, how two curved lines, which are equal in length, can appear unequal in length, and other such illusions. The sceptic reminds us of these phenomena. He also reminds us that humans hallucinate. Lumped together, these phenomena are presented as the argument from illusion.

The sceptic also reminds us that when we dream we also take it that certain objects are present when they are not. He is not talking about nightmares either. He is talking about those altogether realistic dreams all of us have had on occasion, where one wakes up and for a time after waking has doubts as to whether or not what one dreamed actually happened.

The differing persons and perspectives argument involves calling attention to how a penny rotated away from us can appear elliptical rather than circular in shape, how a round earth can appear flat as a table top, how two persons can see what they agree is the same thing very differently.

All of these phenomena and others are cited to convince us that we can never be sure what are the properties possessed by any physical object, or even that it exists. As the sceptic does when attempting to make sceptics of us all where the past is concerned, he (or she) asks us to recognize that what we directly or actually experience when we observe that a stick is straight or a penny is round is indistinguishable from what we actually experience when we experience the stick, submerged in water, as bent, or the penny, when rotated, as elliptical. The same stick cannot *be* both straight and not straight, but since each of the stick's appearances, as they are experienced, are indistinguishable one from the other, it follows that there is no better evidence that it is straight than there is that it is bent. Likewise, the same penny cannot be both round and not round, but there is *evidence* of equal weight for attributing each of these properties to the penny.

On the basis of these considerations the sceptic concludes that we can never know what are the real properties that any given physical object possesses. He bases this conclusion on the alleged fact that for any given physical object there is always equally cogent evidence both for concluding that it has a certain property and for concluding that it has the contradictory property.

These same considerations are also appealed to as support for the sceptic's claim that we do not know that physical objects exist. The argument goes like this. In order for us to know that any given physical object exists we must be able to attribute to it at least one property. Otherwise it is impossible for us even to conceive of that thing. But no property can be established for any given physical thing because any attempt to do so leads to the attribution of the contradictory property.

The phenomena of hallucinating and dreaming enter at this point to provide additional grounds for scepticism regarding the existence of physical objects. When we dream and when we hallucinate we take it that there are physical objects present when, in fact, there are none present. The fact that we are deceived in these cases supposedly shows that what we *directly* perceive must be indistinguishable from what we *directly* perceive when we are *actually* in the presence of a physical object. Since what we directly perceive is no different whether or not an object is present, it follows, the sceptic continues, that we can never be sure that a physical object is present; and so we do not know that there are *any* physical objects.

A contemporary sceptic, Peter Unger, offers an argument of a different sort to this same conclusion.* He claims that the concept of "certainty," like certain other concepts in English, e.g., "flat," is *absolute*. Absolute concepts do not, according to Unger, admit of degrees. Although we do say things like "that thing is flatter than that other thing", we do not really mean what we say. According to Unger when we say that something is flatter than something else what we really mean is that that thing more closely approximates being flat than the other thing does. But neither of them *is* flat.

He then tells us that knowing that p is true implies that one is certain of p. If, for example, I know that there is a piece of white paper in front of me, it follows that I am certain that there is a piece of white paper in front of me. For Unger, being certain of p is a *necessary* condition for knowing p. According to Unger, if one cannot be truly said to be *certain* that something is the case, one cannot be said to *know* that it is. Since it is always possible to doubt that some physical object is present or that it has certain properties, because of the possibility that one is hallucinating or having an illusion, it is less certain that one is seeing a physical object than that triangles have three sides. But to say that one thing is always less certain than another, is, on Unger's analysis, to say that it is *never* certain. Such claims can only be said to be approximations of certainty. They cannot ever be said to constitute knowledge.

Another argument which runs through Unger's defense of scepticism is what we shall refer to as the *incompleteness of evidence argument*. What this argument alleges is that whenever anyone makes a claim about

* "A Defense of Skepticism," *The Philosophical Review*, 1971, Vol. LXXX, pp. 198–219.

any physical object — for example, "There is a piece of paper in front of me"—the evidences for it are incomplete. No matter how much evidence one cites in favor of this claim, there remains further evidence which could be collected in favor of it. Every hour one remains in the presence of the paper adds to the evidences for its truth. The more people we get to examine it the greater is the likelihood that there really is a piece of paper present. But since there is always more evidence that could be gathered in favor of the claim, it can never be certain. It can only become more certain. So if Unger is right, and the concept of "certainty" is absolute, what this means is that such a claim can only approximate certainty. Such claims can never attain the status of knowledge.

In a paper presented in 1970, Odell showed what is wrong with the incompleteness of evidence argument, and in doing so he gave expression to an original argument, which he referred to as the *test of time argument*. That argument can easily be construed as an argument for scepticism about the external world. Because of the reasons which will be presented in the next section of this chapter, Odell never claimed that one could found scepticism upon it. Still it is worth looking at. Here is what Odell said:

> An analogy will be helpful here. Consider the case of a bridge. The relation between a bridge and its supporting beams is akin to the relation which obtains between an empirical statement and its evidence. The mere fact that it is always possible to add further support to a bridge does not provide one with a valid ground for claiming that it is not altogether adequately supported. Whether or not a bridge is adequately supported is to be decided in terms of what it is meant to do. The kind of support required is a function of the load the bridge is expected to bear. Not every bridge is expected to meet the specifications met by the Golden Gate Bridge. A criterion of whether or not a bridge is adequately supported at the time of its construction (call it time t1) is whether or not it meets certain standards. If it meets these standards, which are relative to the kind of work load it is expected to bear, then it is adequately supported, and the fact that we could at t1 add further support is irrelevant. But if at some subsequent time t2 it suddenly collapses and it has not been weakened in the meantime, then it was *not* adequately supported at time t1. Hence, the claim that it is adequately supported at time t1 is, it appears, always subject to the test of time.
>
> In my own present circumstances it seems to me that I am clearly justified in claiming that there is a piece of paper in front of me, and also that I am not mistaken when I say that there is. In fact, it seems to me that I am now in a position to say that my claim is

completely certain in so far as I have met all the requirements that I or anyone else can be expected to meet. The bridge engineer can check to see that all requirements have been met. I have done so with respect to the paper. Short of absurdity, there is nothing more I can do. But, like the engineer's bridge, there remains the test of time.

What I want to maintain as regards any physical object statement, S, is that one can always *specify* some subsequent state of affairs which would, in spite of any evidence in its favor, constitute cogent grounds that not-S. "You claim that there was a piece of paper in front of you this morning, that you wrote upon it, even burned a part of it, and that there were others present who saw it. Here are six people who were with you and claim that they saw nothing, and what is more, the sugar cube you had in your coffee this morning was LSD."*

The point of the above remarks is that it is wrongheaded to claim that physical-object statements are never known with certainty, on the grounds that for any physical object there is always (except, of course, in cases where the physical object and all who observed it are obliterated) some additional evidence, as yet uncollected, that would count as evidence in favor of the existence of that object. Nevertheless, one could go on to maintain that the existence of such objects can never be known with certainty because one can always *specify* evidence which would, if it should materialize, count against that certainty.

Against Scepticism

Much can be said to dispel the force of scepticism. One approach is to counter separately the various components of the sceptic's attack. One can argue against the illusion and differing perspectives cases by pointing out, as we did in Chapter 1, that J.L. Austin is correct in claiming that the sceptic has confused the visual sense of "looks" with its evidential sense. In other words, the sceptic has committed the fallacy of equivocation. Here is the way Austin puts it:

Well now: does the stick 'look bent' to begin with? I think we can agree that it does, we have no better way of describing it. But of course it does *not* look *exactly* like a bent stick, a bent stick out of water — at most, it may be said to look rather like a bent stick partially immersed *in* water. After all, we can't help seeing the wa-

---

* "Incorrigibility and the Test of Time," read at the Western Division meeting of the A.P.A., April 1970.

ter the stick is partially immersed in. So exactly what in this case is
supposed to be *delusive*? What is wrong, what is even faintly surprising, in the idea of a stick's being straight but looking bent
sometimes? Does anyone suppose that if something is straight,
then it jolly well has to *look* straight at all times and in all circumstances?*

The quotation from Odell's paper on incorrigibility provides us
with one objection to Ungar's program for scepticism. Another serious
weakness in his approach is his claim that one's knowing some proposition entails that one is certain of it. This view can be counterexampled (a
procedure which is explained in detail in Chapter 1) with the following
case. Suppose you have several journalism students preparing for an
exam on journalistic history. One of them asks the others if any of them
knows the answer to a question about H.L. Mencken. No one knows
the answer but one of them points out that another student who is not
present will know the answer to this question and any other question
one might have regarding journalistic history.

The student says, "Ask Tim, he always knows the answers. I have
never known him to miss." One of the the other students observes,
"Don't be put off by the fact that after he tells you the answer, he will
tell you to check it out with someone else, he always says he's unsure."
All of us know people like this who, for various reasons, lack confidence. The *test* of whether or not someone knows the answer to some
question is not whether or not he feels confident, but rather if what he
says is right.

Other objections to various aspects of the sceptic's program could
be expressed, but rather than continue in this vein, we will isolate an
essential element in the sceptic's attack and concentrate our counterat-
tack on that flank. But in order to do this we must first of all recall a distinction introduced in Chapter 2. It is the distinction between *possible
for* on the one hand and *possible that* on the other. It exemplifies as well
as any example could the significance of what has been called the *analytic approach* to philosophy.

If someone tells you that it is *possible for* your editor to fire you,
you will not be too surprised. You might wonder why anyone would
tell you anything so obvious, but you certainly will not become concerned because of it. Should, however, someone point out to you that it
is *possible that* your editor is going to fire you, you have sufficient cause
for alarm. G.E. Moore sometimes used the distinction presently under
consideration to argue against scepticism, but he *marked it in terms
of* the words 'might' and 'can', words which are used by speakers of En-

---

* *Sense and Sensibilia*, p. 29.

glish to do the same work as is also done in English with the words 'possible for' and 'possible that'.

To say that your editor *can* fire you is, ordinarily, to say that he (or she) has the authority to do so. To say that he *might* do so is to say that there is some *reason* (evidence) for thinking that he will do so. If he says he might, you have ample grounds for concern. The reason we used the word 'ordinarily' where we did in the sentence about *can* is because in some contexts a sentence like, 'Your editor can fire you,' can be used as a warning, and thus provides grounds for alarm. If you have constantly engaged in actions which exasperate your editor, and a friend of yours is aware that you are about to do so again, he may caution you in this way, rather than by saying, "He might fire you". As we pointed out in Chapter 2, one should never fail to understand just how very important is the role that context plays regarding what one means by some word, string of words, or sentence.

The sceptic is arguing that nothing is certain if its denial is possible. It cannot, he contends, be certain that there is a piece of paper in front of one if the claim that there is not a piece of paper there is possible. What Moore contends in his attack on scepticism is that the sceptic can only conclude what he wants to conclude if we allow him to unpack the 'possible' in his contentions as 'possible that'. But, according to Moore, he is not justified in doing so. The 'possible' of his contentions unpacks as 'possible for'. In other words, the claim that it is not certain that there is a piece of paper in front of one has to mean, if it is to be taken seriously, that it is *possible that* the paper is not there.

Claiming that it is *possible for* the paper not to be there is consistent with the claim that it is certain that it is there. One can claim both things. To claim that it is *possible that* the paper is not there is to claim something which is inconsistent with the claim that one is certain that the paper is there. To claim that it is possible that the paper is not there is to claim that there is *evidence* that it is not there. But this is just what Moore will not allow the sceptic to claim. According to Moore, the possibility that one is hallucinating, having an illusion, seeing the paper from a misleading perspective, or seeing it differently than someone else would see it, are all possibilities which are consistent with certainty that the paper is there.*

The fact that people are subject to hallucination, dreams, misleading perspectives, in no way establishes, according to Moore, that some *particular* person is hallucinating or dreaming when in the presence of a *particular* physical object. In order to show that some particular person might be (as opposed to *is*, as all humans are, subject to) hallucinating or

---

* In short, the sceptic's argument can be said to contain an equivocation on the word 'possible'. Once again we see just how fundamental are the applications of logic.

dreaming, one would have to produce *concrete evidence* that he is. What this means is, according to Moore, that the sceptic must show, in order to maintain that *no one* could *ever* know that any physical object exists or has certain specifiable properties, that there is *always* concrete evidence that one is hallucinating or dreaming.

Since in most instances there is no evidence whatever to this effect, the sceptic has to be mistaken. And the fact that, no matter what evidence one has in favor of some claim about a physical object, it is always possible to specify evidence which would count against that claim, does not provide the required *evidence* either. Actual concrete evidence has to be provided against any given claim. The specification of possible evidence is not sufficient. The onus is on the sceptic to prove that the possibility of hallucination or illusion does, in fact, constitute *evidence* that one is possibly *never* seeing what one thinks one sees. Until this is established, we can forget about *universal scepticism* and concentrate on the formulation of *canons of induction*, i.e., proper procedures for the acquisition of factual knowledge.

Canons of Induction and the Nature of Evidence

In this section we will be concerned with methods or procedures of confirmation. Every journalist is engaged in an activity which very largely consists in the practice of confirmation. In this section we will attempt to systematize, in so far as it is possible, that practice. Confirmation cannot be systematized in a purely formal manner. No one can provide a definition of confirmation in terms of necessary and sufficient conditions, because, as we saw in Chapter 2, no human activity can be so defined. (This application of one of the things covered in the chapter on analysis illustrates our contention that certain philosophical analyses are of fundamental importance to any journalist, and that they should be mastered prior to the discussion of themes close to the journalist's daily endeavors.)

The fact that we cannot provide an adequate formal definition of confirmation does not mean that we cannot develop a useful set of empirical *canons* (methods of induction). As long as we recognize that the principles we adopt are at best only guidelines or rules of thumb, and not a set of necessary and sufficient conditions, we cannot err. The great English philosopher John Stuart Mill attempted to prescribe valid inductions in terms of five canons, which have come to be known as *methods*. They are the *method of agreement*, the *method of difference*, the *joint method of agreement and difference*, the *method of residues*, and the *method of concomitant variation*. Regarded as rules of thumb and not as a set of essential conditions, these methods can prove quite useful. We will consider them separately.

Standard logic textbooks present these methods as techniques for isolating causes. The *method of agreement* is usually illustrated by having the reader imagine several individuals all of whom have become ill because of what they have eaten. We are asked to believe that John, Mary, Fred, and Sally all ate at the same place and that three of them have contracted food poisoning. It is then pointed out that John, who is one of the victims, ate, let us say, tomato soup, french fries, turnips, and parsnips. Mary is said to have had tomato soup, turnips, collards, toast, and marmalade. She also became sick. Fred is said to have had tomato soup, french fries, a salad, meatloaf, and mashed potatoes. He became ill. Sally had potato and leek soup, parsnips, french toast, and a garden salad. She did not get sick. It is then pointed out that the cause of the food poisoning must be the tomato soup (assuming, of course, that one and only one of the foodstuffs is the cause). We reason quite rightly that the cause must be present in each case where the effect is present. Here eating the tomato soup can be assumed to be the cause, because it is the variable with regard to which all the cases *agree*.

The *method of difference* can be illustrated with the same sort of case. Suppose that on another occasion the same individuals are taken ill after having eaten at the same place. Assume John got sick but the others did not. Suppose he ate a hamburger, french fries, and a toasted cheese sandwich. Suppose Mary and Sally both ate no toasted cheese or hamburger, but did eat french fries. Suppose Fred ate french fries and a toasted cheese sandwich but no hamburger.

Assuming that one of the foodstuffs caused John to get sick, it is reasonable to infer that his sickness was caused by the hamburger he ate. We infer this on the grounds that any foodstuff which was present when the effect or sickness was not, could not have caused the sickness. By the process of elimination we infer that the hamburger must have caused John to become ill.

These methods can be extended to cover cases that do not involve the determination of cause. Their application to the journalist's daily activities can be exemplified by the following case. Suppose a reporter to be concerned with who will be selected by the new President to become Secretary of State. Suppose further that he is aware that five men are being considered for the post, and that the front runner is described as being an ex-soldier, an athlete, a scholar, a man of the people, a public servant, and a man whose career has been often associated with the new President. If the reporter follows a hunch that a certain candidate, Mr. Magnificent, is the front runner on the grounds that he is an ex-soldier, athlete, a scholar, a man of the people, and a public servant whose career has been associated with the new President, he has applied the *method of agreement*. From the fact that this particular candidate has all the relevant properties doesn't *prove* that he is the front runner. No inductive procedure can prove its conclusion in the sense in which a deductively valid argument establishes its conclusion. A good inductive procedure can only establish its conclusion as *highly likely*. In the absence of other evidence, it would be safe to assume that Magnificent is the front runner. Of course it could turn out that one or more of the other candidates is equally likely the front runner. One or more than one of the others could have all the relevant characteristics as well.

Applying the *method of difference* to the present case would consist in eliminating candidates on the grounds that relevant characteristics are missing. If in checking out the characteristics of the candidates, our reporter eliminates each of them except Magnificent on the grounds that they do not have all of the relevant characteristics, our reporter has applied the method of difference.

Since one or more of the other candidates might, like Magnificent, possess all the relevant characteristics, our reporter must continue to apply the method of difference until he has eliminated all the other candidates. If one proceeds by first determining that Magnificent has all the pertinent characteristics (method of agreement) and then continues by ruling out all the others on the grounds that each of them lacks at least one of the pertinent characteristics (method of difference), one has applied the *joint method of agreement and difference*. Usually, one has to apply this method in order to confirm anything inductively. In the present case applying the method of difference tells us only that Magnificent is a possible candidate. In order to be sure Magnificent is the next Secretary of State we must also eliminate all the other candidates by the method of difference.

If we imagine someone inferring that bad hamburgers must be responsible for a rash of food poisoning at some fast-food establishment on the grounds that the extent of the sickness a victim experienced was proportionate to the number of hamburgers eaten, we imagine a use of the *method of concomitant variation*. One who reasons in this way is not simply concerned with the presence or absence of cause and effect, but with the degree to which they are present. If we suspect that one thing is the cause of another because it is present in all and only those cases where the other is present, then the greater the correlation between its variations in degree and those of the effect, the higher the probability is that it is the cause.

Although this method does not have a natural application to the front-runner case, one can easily enough illustrate it in the natural course of events involved in the gathering and disseminating of the news. The extent of the violence perpetrated on the inhabitants and buildings of some outpost in Israel can be the basis for inferring that it was the work of a certain terrorist organization. This conclusion is inferred on the ground that only this particular organization has the arms and manpower sufficient to inflict so much damage in so short a time. A journalist who inferred that a large corporation was dumping a caustic agent into various streams on the grounds that the extent of its effects was greater in the immediate vicinity of this corporation's plants than anywhere else, would be appealing to the method of concomitant variation.

The fifth canon, *the method of residues*, is not easily illustrated in terms of examples of the sort previously used. Most introductory-textbook writers either omit it on the grounds that it is derivable from the others, or they illustrate it with examples from science. If one attempts to isolate the cause of some effect, call it *a*, by first of all subtracting from the data in question all those factors whose causes are known and then searches for the cause of *a* among the remaining possible causes, one applies the method of residues. If a sports reporter reasons that some offensive guard, Wilde, is directly responsible for a team's having scored the winning touchdown by arguing in the following way, the reporter can, at least roughly, be said to have applied the method of residues.

The reporter sees the other offensive guard and the center cause a collision between the two blocking backs, and sees the wide receivers, the flankers, and the ends engaged in trying to free themselves of defensive coverage. The reporter also observes that the tailback is busy faking a run, and notices that someone throws a tremendous block which enables the quarterback to sneak across the goal line. Our reporter concludes that it must have been Wilde who did it even though not seeing Wilde do it. The reporter draws this conclusion on the grounds that he has eliminated or subtracted from the phenomenon to be explained (the touchdown) all those aspects whose causes are known (the collision of some members of the team, the drawing out of position of the defensive halfbacks, etc.), and so it can be inferred that the touchdown was the direct result of the one remaining possible cause, namely, Wilde.

There are a number of standard objections to Mill's methods, not all of which are valid. It is often claimed that Mill's methods are unsatisfactory because they do not give a complete account of induction or scientific method. This objection is wrongheaded because it assumes what in fact is a mistake, namely, that a complete account could be given. Discoveries in science come about in a variety of ways. There are no prescribed ways for reasoning inductively. To legislate such procedures would have the effect of preventing many future discoveries in science, as well as most of the reasonable inferences we make daily.

Still the proper application of these methods requires some care.

There are a number of objections to the method of agreement, not the least of which is the one usually made through the case of the determined boozer. Suppose someone trained in these methods to be seeking a justification for remaining a boozer in spite of the fact that every morning he has an awful hangover. On Monday, he (or she) drinks bourbon and water and has a horrendous hangover on Tuesday, Tuesday he drinks scotch and water and experiences a gruesome hangover on Wednesday. He turns to cognac and water on Wednesday and again on Thursday morning experiences a terrible throbbing in his head. That same day he imbibes an Irish whiskey and water. The result is the same as before; he wakes feeling rotten. On Friday he takes up rye and water with the same result. Saturday night he indulges in shots of tequila with a water chaser. He wakes on Sunday at death's door and concludes that God must be trying to tell him something, namely, that consumption of water causes one to feel really terrible the next morning, so from now on he had better take his "likker" straight.

This comical example of the failure of the method of agreement can be countered, however, with the observation that the failure is not really due to the method of agreement, but rather to an improper analysis of the contents of the example. Alcohol is the culprit, and each of the substances accompanying the water contains alcohol. Still, the example does illustrate the importance of exercising care when applying Mill's methods. Carefully applied, these methods can, however, be extremely useful.

Evidence

The most important thing to grasp about the concept of *evidence* is that it is *context bound*. What constitutes evidence that something is the case in one context, i.e., under one set of circumstances, need not be evidence of that same thing under other circumstances. If, for example, a reporter who is seeking an interview with a distinguished writer who has just finished a new work hears what appears to be typing sounds coming from the writer's study, the reporter is certainly warranted in inferring that the writer is present in the study. But suppose the reporter knows that this writer hates to be interviewed; that it is his (or her) practice to escape out a back window whenever any reporters are in the neighborhood; that he deceives unsuspecting reporters by playing a recording of someone typing. Under these circumstances the reporter would be stupid indeed to take the sound of the typing to be evidence that the writer is still on the premises.

The concept of evidence is not alone in this respect. There are many other concepts which are context dependent.* Consider the concept of *explanation*. A sentence used to express an explanation under one set of circumstances will be no more than a neutral description under a different set of circumstances. Consider the sentence, 'He is six feet five inches tall and weighs over three hundred pounds.' Now consider a context where someone asks someone else why he is afraid of Johnny Godzilla. In this context, the above sentence will certainly serve to explain why one is afraid of Godzilla. Given his description, anyone would be afraid of him. But, on the other hand, if you are trying to locate Godzilla to give him one thousand dollars in prize money, another person's responding with the above sentence would explain nothing; it would simply describe Godzilla and make it easy for you to locate him.

In the case of evidence, the phenomenon, event, or episode cited as evidence has an independent existence as a phenomenon, event, or episode. Whether that event, episode, or phenomenon *is* evidence depends upon *where*, *when*, and *how* it takes place. In our example, the sound of typing exists as a physical phenomenon; whether or not it is evidence of anything depends upon the circumstances that surround its existence. Its *evidential status* is a function of whether or not it is apprehended by agents, and what *background knowledge* those agents possess. But it does not have to be apprehended directly to constitute evidence. The sound of typing could be evidence of something even when recorded. A bit of plastic tape can contain everything, both visual auditory, that is needed to establish that something is the case.

It must be recognized, however, that the claim that evidence is *contextually circumscribed* is not equivalent to the claim that it is relative or subjective. On the contrary, what is evidence for one person is ordinarily also evidence for others. We have already seen that the background knowledge that an observer possesses will in part determine whether or not some existing phenomenon is or is not evidence. If the reporter in the case about the famous writer has *seen* the writer escape from his study via the back door, nothing emanating from his study would constitute for this reporter evidence that the writer is in his study. Other reporters present who lack this knowledge would be quite right to take the sounds emanating from his study to be evidence that he is in. They would not be justified in taking these sounds to be a *guarantee* that he is in. They are, however, justified in assuming that he is *probably* there. They are certainly not at fault if they choose to remain around outside with the hope that he will eventually allow them an interview. They

---

* According to John Searle, the meaning of every contingent sentence is in some way context dependent. He refers to the contextual factors as "background conditions," and illustrates their contribution to meaning in his article "Literal Meaning," in *Expression and Meaning* (Cambridge: Cambridge University Press, 1979), pp. 117–136.

cannot be faulted by their editors for remaining on the spot. They are justified in claiming that "Although he wasn't there, we had evidence that he was."

Some philosophers have claimed that one cannot have evidence that something is the case unless that something *is* the case. Or, as it is sometimes put, q cannot be evidence of p unless p is true. What the above considerations show is that these philosophers are mistaken.

Truth

Given what we have established about evidence, one might infer that the concept of *truth* involves contextual considerations. This is a correct inference. Whether or not a given assertion or claim is true does often depend upon the circumstances which surround the claim. What can be asserted as gospel in one set of circumstances may very well be completely out in left field under different circumstances. Still, one is apt to object that there are facts, and true statements or claims describe those facts.

This observation is a highly credible one, and one which seems to fit all our intuitions about the nature of truth. This view that truth is a correspondence between what we say and the facts is referred to by philosophers as the *correspondence theory*, and it has had many champions. Aristotle, Locke, Russell, and the early Wittgenstein all held versions of the theory.

The reason for its widespread acceptance among philosophers and ordinary people is that it seems so right. If there is a specific cat on some specific mat and someone points to it and says, "The cat is on the mat," *what is said* (the statement, assertion, or claim) is true, we maintain, because there is a correspondence between *what is said* and *what exists*. We want to say, in general, that whenever there is a correspondence between the statement made and the facts pointed to by it, truth exists, and that when there is a discrepancy between the two, this gives rise to falsity.

But, then, what exactly is meant by 'corresponds'? Various answers have been proposed for this question. Wittgenstein in *Tractatus Logico-Philosophicus* (London: Routledge & Kegan Paul, 1922) explicated the correspondence relation in terms of the picturing or mapping relation. According to this version of the correspondence theory (the picture theory), the assertion, "The cat is on the mat," mirrors, depicts, or maps a specific *state of affairs*. In the case of written speech it is possible to be much more pictorial and write, for example, $\frac{\text{"Cat"}}{\text{mat}}$. Hieroglyphics are even more pictorial, and may to some extent explain why we are so inclined to accept the correspondence theory.*

There are, however, some insurmountable objections to this explication of the correspondence theory. As long as we stick to assertions like, "The cat is on the mat," their truth is easily accounted for in terms of the mapping relation. *What is said* can be said to describe or map *what is in the world.* In such cases, the thing described is a presently existing state of affairs (arrangement of objects, namely, the cat and the mat). If those objects are arranged differently, then the assertion that the cat is on the mat is false. But what about assertions like, "All men are mortal," "Bachelors are unmarried males," and "Triangles have three sides"? Unfortunately, for the theory in question, the truth of such assertions does not consist in their mirroring, mapping, depicting, or in any way corresponding to some presently existing state of affairs. The truth of the assertion about the mortality of humans depends as much on what happened in the past and what will happen in the future as it does on any presently existing state of affairs. Besides, what could possibly be meant by a presently existing state of affairs corresponding to any general truth? When we say that triangles have three sides and that three plus two equals five, we are clearly not describing some existent state of affairs to which we could point if we wanted. One can point to a bachelor and at the same time point to an unmarried male, but in doing so one has not singled out a state of affairs sufficient for the claiming that *all* bachelors are unmarried males. So much for the picture version of the correspondence theory.

But if correspondence is not to be understood in these terms, how are we to understand it? Because of these and other difficulties too numerous to mention philosophers have proposed other theories to account for truth. There are two other traditional theories of truth: the *coherence theory* and the *pragmatic theory.* The former is associated with Hegel and other idealistic and rationalistic philosophers, for example, Bradley, Leibniz, Spinoza, and more recently, Brand Blanshard. It has even been advocated by some logical positivists: Carl G. Hempel and Otto Neurath. The pragmatic theory is associated with the American Pragmatists, Peirce, James, and Dewey, but it was also advocated by Schiller. We will look at each theory separately, starting with the coherence theory.

According to the coherence theory what makes a given assertion true is its coherence or fit with *what is known* or at least with *what is accepted.* The model on which this theory is based is pure mathematics. In a deductive system every acceptable statement must cohere with

---

* In a primitive language, we recognize the conceptual underpinnings of our present-day languages.

every other one. The system consists of a set of propositions or possible statements each one of which is consistent with every other one. In mathematics the test for truth of a given proposition is whether or not it is provable within the system. For example, the truth of, "Three plus two equals five," is tied to the truth of all other propositions of arithmetic. It coheres with the claim that two plus two equals four and two plus one equals three. We know that one of these claims is true because we know that the others are true. The advocates of the coherence theory claim that although it is based on a mathematical model, it can be extended to cover our common-sense conceptions as well as those of empirical science. They point out that claims about the past can only be accepted as true because of their coherence with various other claims or reports about the past. The claim that all men are mortal can be said to be true only if all men in the past have been mortal, and the only test of this is the various reports we have concerning the human beings of the past. This assertion's truth is not arrived at by comparing the claim with some fact or facts. The only thing we can compare such a claim with is other recorded claims. In science, when we reason, for example, that one account is true and another is false, we are, according to this theory, only asserting that the preferred account is most consistent with whatever else we happen to accept.

Such a theory of truth is apt to be quite seductive to a newsman who is every day of his life engaged in ferreting out the news, and who must constantly make judgments regarding what to report as truth. The reporter often finds himself in the following kind of situation: There are some reasons for thinking that some event has transpired and other reasons for thinking that it has not, and the reporter must make some kind of decision before press time. If the reputed event's occurrence coheres with everything else the reporter has heard, knows, and expects, and its nonoccurrence does not, he (or she) is apt to feel quite justified in concluding that the event did take place.

There are many objections to the coherence theory, but none more cogent than the classical one, which is that it fails to distinguish between *what might serve* as a procedure for arriving at the truth and what it *means* to say that something is true. Our reporter is justified in inferring that the event occurred, but may be mistaken, because it could turn out that, as a matter of *fact*, it did not occur.

The pragmatic theory is that what is *useful* to us is what is true. It is sometimes put in terms of what works best. According to this view, a true belief is one which is instrumental in some respect. Those who hold this view are apt to hold that the belief that God exists is a true one because of its *instrumental* value. Belief in God causes men to take moral issues seriously, and this, in turn, benefits everyone. It also provides one with a kind of Linus's blanket as protection against an alien environment in which we frequently experience the discrepancies between our desires and wants on the one hand and a cold and merciless reality on the other.

Although there are many objections which can be brought against this theory, we will mention only one because it is, we believe, sufficient to show that the theory is mistaken. It is one thing to *justify* a belief; it is quite another to show that it is true. One can even, as we shall see in the next chapter, justify the telling of a lie. The fact that a lie has, in some circumstances, better consequences than the truth would have shows only that it is justified. It certainly does not show that the lie or the beliefs it gives rise to are in any sense *true.* Even something as obviously false as a lie can "work" or be "useful" in some circumstances.

In the present century a few other theories of truth have emerged. The principal ones are the *semantic theory* of Alfred Tarski, and the *speech act theory* of P.F. Strawson. The former theory is just an updated formalistic version of the correspondence theory, and, thus, stands or falls with it. The latter theory maintains that saying of some utterance that it is true is simply to carry out the *speech act* of *agreeing* with what is said. On this account, "The cat is on the mat," and, "It is true that the cat is on the mat," contain the same *descriptive* content. All the latter adds is an assessment or appraisal of what was asserted by the former. According to this account, we would not ordinarily say the latter unless someone had already said the former. Saying, "That's true," like saying, "I promise," is doing something other than describing. In the case of the former we could accomplish the same thing by saying, "I agree." On this account, "That's false," means roughly, "I disagree."

No doubt we do use the expression, 'That's true', in accordance with the dictates of this theory, sometimes referred to as the *nondescriptive theory*, but this is not the only way we use it. When we say, for example, that no assertion can be both true and false at the same time, we are *not* talking about the possibility of agreement or disagreement concerning them. When, moreover, we say about certain propositions that they are necessary truths, we are, most assuredly, describing them.

In order to do justice to our notion of truth we must at some point bring into the account reality or facts. For this reason, it should be clear that some version of the correspondence theory is going to be required. The problem we had with the depiction rendition of the correspondence theory is that it made all ascriptions of truth turn on whether or not they mirrored some presently existing state of affairs. This view takes the notion of a fact too strictly. In order to make the correspondence theory work, one must extend one's conception of what is to count as a fact. But one must also extend one's conception of correspondence.

We propose the following extentions: (1) think of correspondence as *representation*, and (2) think of facts as not only presently existing arrangements of objects, but also as past and future arrangements of objects, conventions, beliefs and intentions, and other states of consciousness.

Language is, among other things (many of which we considered in Chapter 2), a symbolic system for the *representation* of reality. Reality is a lot more than simply presently existing arrangements of objects. An acceptable theory of truth must take all aspects of reality into account. When we speak of the facts of mathematics, we are certainly not speaking about any presently existing phenomena. And this is true in spite of the fact that we do wish to describe reality in mathematical terms. It is also a fact that when someone knows something, that something must be true, otherwise, the person does not know it. But here we are not speaking about presently existing states of affairs. We are instead speaking about linguistic facts, i.e., *conventions*. One who knows this about 'knows' knows a *semantic rule* of the language.

In the case of mathematical facts, it is not altogether clear *what* it is we are speaking about. Some maintain that here, as in the case of linguistic facts, what we are speaking about (representing) are conventions. Others claim otherwise. They claim that what is represented by, for example, "three is greater than two," is a necessary truth. We will not attempt to decide this issue, for it is far too complicated to pursue in a book of this sort. But one thing is clear, and that is that whatever mathematical facts are, they are not arrangements of objects (states of affairs).

Some will object that this account of the matter does not take into account the *fact* that the concept of what it is for something to be a fact is ill conceived; that facts are not something objective and mind independent; that facts are in *fact* "theory laden" — which is to say that what we ordinarily take to be facts about the world are really our own perceptions of that reality, and hence, mind dependent and subjective. This view assumes that creatures from other worlds might very well see things radically different from the way we do.

But even if this were true, and it might be, it would not show that there are no facts, or that our concept of truth is flawed. Even if what is a fact for us is, in part, a function of how we as human beings process information, this does not show that nothing can be said to be objective or factual. When we talk about facts, we are not speaking about transcendental entities which are completely independent of the way we apprehend the world. We are only talking about those things which can be said to exist independently of any *given* perceiver, those things all rational agents count as facts. It is these things which the good journalist must seek to know. We do not care at all whether or not the journalist seeks to know what Kant called the "thing-in-itself."

Suggested Reading

Ackermann, Robert. *Theories of Knowledge: A Critical Introduction*. New York: McGraw-Hill, 1965.

Ammerman, Robert R., and Singer, Marcus G., eds. *Belief, Knowledge, and Truth: Readings in the Theory of Knowledge*. New York: Scribner's, 1970.

Austin, J.L. *Sense and Sensibilia*. Oxford: Oxford University Press, 1962.

Ayer, A.J. *Logical Positivism*. New York: Free Press, 1959.

———— *The Problem of Knowledge*. London: Macmillan, 1958.

Chisholm, Roderick. *Theory of Knowledge*. Englewood Cliffs, N.J.: Prentice-Hall, 1966.

———— *Realism and the Background of Phenomenology*. New York: Free Press, 1960.

Landesman, Charles, ed. *The Foundations of Knowledge*. Englewood Cliffs, N.J.: Prentice Hall, 1970.

Malcolm, Norman. *Knowledge and Certainty*. Englewood Cliffs, N.J.: Prentice Hall, 1963.

Moore G.E. *Philosophical Papers*, New York: Collier, 1966.

———— *Some Main Problems of Philosophy*. London: Allen and Unwin, 1953.

Nagel, Ernest, and Brandt, Richard D. *Meaning and Knowledge*. New York: Harcourt, Brace & World, 1965.

Russell, Bertrand. *Human Knowledge: Its Scope and Limits*. New York: Simon & Schuster, 1948.

———— *The Problems of Philosophy*. New York: Oxford University Press, 1959.

Swartz, Robert. *Perceiving, Sensing, and Knowing*. Garden City, N.Y.: Doubleday, 1965.

Weinberg, Julius R., and Yandell, Keith E., eds. *Theory of Knowledge*. New York: Holt, Rinehart and Winston, 1971.

White, Alan R. *Truth*. Garden City, N.Y.: Doubleday, 1970.

Will, Frederick L. *Induction and Justification: An Investigation of Cartesian Procedure in the Philosophy of Knowledge*. Ithaca, N.Y.: Cornell University Press, 1974.

CHAPTER 4

Morality: Journalism and Ethics

After a lapse of many years journalists are once again taking a serious interest in ethical questions. Vietnam and the various events and episodes which surrounded it, and Watergate with all its political intrigues and shady dealings have had a tremendous impact upon the press. These blots upon the national character accompanied as they were by insidious efforts to muzzle the press have produced a renewed interest within journalism for ethical issues. And this has led to a new interest in journalistic ethics within journalism programs. As Merrill has observed elsewhere:

> At any rate, an interest in journalistic ethics is beginning to reappear in journalism education programs, in textbooks and other literature related to mass communications. And one hears increasing reference to press ethics in public speeches and lectures — and even at newspaper and broadcasting conventions and conferences. Names of philosophers are slowly filtering into journalism classes: Kant, Spinoza, Nietzsche, Hobbes, Sartre, and Dewey are beginning to share time with Katz, Lasswell, Osgood, Deutsch, Doob, Parsons, and Lerner. Sociological and psychological emphases, though still potent, are beginning — albeit slowly — to be joined by philosophical emphases in journalism.*

No one would disagree with the proposition that it is important to society for its journalists to be moral or ethical. The kind of journalists which we treasure are persons of good character who are incorruptible and altruistic. It should be made clear, however, that the study of ethics and value theory will not in itself produce highminded and virtuous newspersons. The study of ethics cannot, and should not be expected to, make up for an unethical upbringing. The immoral or amoral person is not going to be transformed into an ethical or moral human being simply by being introduced to ethics.

* *Ethics and the Press*, ed. by John C. Merrill and Ralph Barney (New York: Hastings House Publishers, 1975), p. viii.

This is not to say that there are no good reasons for adults to study ethics. Quite the contrary; since most humans are, or at least seek to be, moral or ethical but are confused about or ignorant of what the real issues are, a forum for clarification and analysis is needed. Philosophy can provide that forum.

In a recent study conducted by the Hastings Center, a number of educational objectives are identified: (1) stimulating the moral imagination; (2) recognizing moral issues; (3) developing analytical skills; (4) eliciting a sense of moral obligation and personal responsibility; and (5) tolerating — and resisting — disagreement and ambiguity.* With the exception of (4), which is largely the result of a proper upbringing, all of these goals can be facilitated by exposure to ethics. In addition, even the most ethical of humans can fail to distinguish between *factual* issues and *value* issues. One who is grounded in ethics and value theory will tend to be, as Sidney Hook has pointed out, one who is sensitive "to the presence of moral issues in what is sometimes regarded as purely factual inquiry."* Since journalists mould public opinion through the information they convey, it is extremely important that they become sensitive to such issues. Hook offers the following by way of exposition:

> The furious controversy over the implications of inquiries concerning genetic group differences is a case in point. Nothing significant in the way of civil rights and equal opportunities follows from any of the reported findings of differences in native capacities of different groups. Suppose in an individual family the IQs of the children range between upper and lower limits of 15 or 20 or even 30 points. Would anyone in his moral senses conclude that therefore this difference justified discrimination against any of the children with respect to their food, clothing, shelter, recreation, health care, and dignified treatment as human beings? There is a distinction between not having the relevant knowledge that would make a difference to our treatment of individuals and not knowing what difference any specific piece of relevant knowledge would make. The crucial questions in the treatment of religious ethnic, and racial minorities are moral, and those who have thrown obscurantist blocks in the path of inquiry into questions of differential genetic capacities out of fear of the social consequences are fundamentally confused.†

* *The Teaching of Ethics in Higher Education*, A report by the Hastings Center (New York: The Hastings Center, 1980).

† "Philosophy and Public Policy," in *The Owl of Minerva*, ed. by C.J. Bontempo and S.J. Odell (New York: McGraw-Hill, 1975) p. 83.

Journalists are becoming more concerned with those ethical questions that involve the profession itself. Most practicing journalists take the view that protecting one's sources is ethically necessary. Such a view is, however, in conflict with the current legal doctrines which refuse to make exceptions out of journalists. Like other citizens they are prohibited from concealing information relating to criminal activities. In the last few years several journalists have chosen to be incarcerated rather than reveal their sources. Were they right in doing so? We will examine this issue in terms of the conflicts that exist between what is *legal* and what is *ethical*.

We will also illustrate how various ethical theories (existentialism, rationalism, utilitarianism, relativism, situationalism, emotivism) can be applied to the reporting and analysis of public policy issues. When, for example, is it proper for the news media to identify a rape victim or an alleged sex offender? Should the reporter be allowed to report on matters related to an ongoing police investigation that might jeopardize the capture of a criminal? Is it right for the press to publicize a suspect's previous criminal record? Is it ever permissible for a journalist to give favored treatment to a public official in exchange for obtaining important information from that official? Is it permissible for a reporter to lie to the public? Is it right for newspeople to accept free trips and other economic benefits? Should the press impose restraints upon itself when covering certain kinds of events? In other words, even though the press thrives on sensational events, would not society benefit if journalists ignored terrorist attacks and kidnappings (assuming that the publicity that coverage of such events generates tends to perpetuate the crime)? Should there be any government restraints on the press? Is it morally imperative for the press to seek objectivity? Such questions raise important issues for journalists and for society.* We will examine these questions from the perspective of the classical ethical theories.

Although the above questions are specific with respect to journalism, they are mere instantiations of more general questions which have been the concern of philosophers for centuries. Ethics is that branch of philosophy which addresses such issues, and it is no less difficult and demanding than Kant, Aristotle, Hume, Spinoza, Mill, or Sartre. In a very real sense ethics is the works of these thinkers. For this reason we will begin our discussion of the above issues by looking at certain classical ethical theories. In order to do so, we must begin with an introduction to certain terminology.

Ethics is that branch of philosophy which addresses the question,

---

* The author of this section acknowledges a debt to professor Michael Petrick for his many contributions to this discussion.

"Which human actions are and which are not morally permissible?" Ethics as a branch of philosophy is not concerned with which actions various cultures consider moral and which ones they consider immoral. The study of the actual ethical practices that various societies engage in is called "descriptive" ethics, and it is the concern of anthropologists. The philosophical discipline called "ethics" is divided into two subsections, *metaethics* and *normative ethics*. Normative ethics is concerned with determining what we *ought* to do under various circumstances or how we *ought* to conduct our lives. Metaethics is concerned with the evaluation of ethical theories, and with the correct analysis of words like 'good', 'right', 'correct', 'proper', 'bad', 'wrong', 'incorrect', 'improper', etc. It asks questions like, "How does one go about validating an ethical theory?" "What is the difference between a teleological and a deontological ethical theory?" "What do we mean when we say such things as 'That's good', 'He is a very good person', etc." We will be concerned with the applications of both these areas of ethics to journalism.

We will proceed by examining and thus coming to appreciate the various theories or approaches to ethics which have been proposed throughout human history. Our first step in this endeavor will be to explain a pair of key terms. We must distinguish between theories or approaches to ethics which are *teleological* and those which are *deontological*.

A teleological ethical theory is any theory which measures the rightness or the wrongness of an action or set of actions in terms of its/their consequences. To say that Hitler's fascist state was evil because of the human suffering it brought about is to judge a set of actions in terms of their consequences, and is, thus, to issue a judgment which is teleological in character. The same thing can be said of Roskolnikov's decision to murder his landlady. His judgment is based upon his opinion that murdering and robbing the landlady will result in good consequences for society. He plans to take the money he will steal and invest it in his future. When he finishes his education, which he plans to pay for with the landlady's money, he will work for society. The type of teleological theory which Roskolnikov's deliberations exemplify is called *utilitarianism*, and we will discuss it in detail a bit further on.

Any theory which judges an action or set of actions in nonteleological terms is said to be deontological. Some deontological theories ground ethical judgments on reason; others ground them in God's will; some appeal to human decision; others claim that the correctness or incorrectness of an action is to be decided in terms of the conventions of society; some hold that an act is right or wrong depending upon whether or not it has an objective though nonnatural property of being good or bad; others try to ground ethics in nature.

Teleological Ethical Theories

Teleological theories come in two flavors. Some are *altruistic*. Others are *egoistic*. Whether or not a teleological theory is altruistic depends entirely upon whether or not it judges an action to be right or wrong in terms of its consequences regarding others. If an action can be said to have had good consequences for others, then it can be said to be "good." If its consequences for others are harmful, then it is said to be "wrong." A theory which judges an action to be right or wrong in terms of its consequences for one's own self is an egoistic one. An egoist is one who claims that any action which ultimately benefits one's own self is right. In other words, if doing x can be determined to be of greater benefit to one's own self than doing y, then one ought to do x.

The most popular and representative teleological and altruistic ethical theory is *utilitarianism*. The most important and influential thinkers to be associated with utilitarianism are Jeremy Bentham and John Stuart Mill. Utilitarian theories are either *hedonistic* or *nonhedonistic*, depending upon whether or not they assess consequences in terms of pleasure. A hedonistic theory is one which considers pleasure to be the ultimate good. Hedonistic utilitarianism holds that an action is good if it maximizes pleasure. More specifically, an action x is said to be better than an action y if x produces more pleasure than y. The often quoted utilitarian maxim is: Act so as to produce in the world the greatest possible balance of *good over evil*. The hedonistic version of this maxim is: Act so as to produce the greatest possible balance of *pleasure over pain*. This has been most often interpreted to mean that when one is faced with a situation where the means to some end are deplorable, one must, nevertheless, utilize those means if the result of doing so maximizes pleasure over pain. Anyone who, like Roskolnikov, thinks that it is permissible to murder someone if society as a whole will benefit, is a utilitarian. If he measures that benefit in terms of pleasure, he is a hedonistic utilitarian.

There are, of course, other ways to measure the benefits of an action. One could, for example, claim that the ultimate good for human beings is self-knowledge. This is just what Socrates, that most remarkable of all philosophers, claimed. Another possibility is to claim that scientific knowledge or knowledge of the universe is the highest goal for humans to attain to. This seems to have been the view of Newton. Others have maintained, along with Epicurus, that the highest good is the absence of pain. Various other positions are possible. Anyone who holds that an action's worth depends upon the consequences it produces, and that this worth is to be determined along dimensions other than the pleasure dimension, is a nonhedonistic utilitarian. An example of a nonhedonistic utilitarian rendition of the utilitarian maxim would be: Act so as to maximize the *amount of self-knowledge* in the world.

There are at least three standard objections to utilitarianism. The first is that since we cannot see into the future, how can we ever determine what the consequences of any one of our actions is going to be? And since we cannot determine what are going to be the consequences of any one of our actions, how can we ever determine what we ought to do at any given time? The second is that two actions could be equivalent in terms of their respective consequences and not be morally equivalent. One of them could involve stealing, lying, even murder. Still the outcome as regards pleasure, self-knowledge, or whatever one chooses to measure benefit in terms of, could be equal. The third and most telling objection (which is closely tied to the second objection) is that utilitarianism permits inhuman or barbarous injustices. An example of this would be the putting to death of one community member in order to make more pleasurable the lives of other community members, as is done in Dürrenmatt's powerful drama, *The Visit*. Roskolnikov's killing his landlady is another case in point. Even the sacrificial killing of innocents practiced by primitive societies can be justified along utilitarian lines. This horrifying practice maximized pleasure by alleviating the collective anxiety based upon its practitioner's belief that failure to do so would anger the gods.

These objections can be met, however, if one distinguishes between what philosophers refer to as the distinction between *act utilitarianism* and *rule utilitarianism*. The act utilitarian is one who judges the rightness or wrongness of an act in terms of its *consequences*. The rule utilitarian is someone who bases his decisions on a *set of rules* which are grounded on the utilitarian maxim. The following dialogue will prove useful for the clarification of this distinction:

> *First reporter:* They claim that they won't ever release the hostages if we report the kidnapping to the public. They will fly them to Cuba.
>
> *Second reporter:* I think that the kidnappers are bluffing. If you ask me, what we ought to do is call their bluff and put out a story about it. This will cause them to release the hostages so that they can get out of the country before they are captured.
>
> *First reporter:* You can't be sure of that. We should do what they request. On the whole, it is best to do whatever kidnappers request. In the past things have worked out better when their demands have been met than they have when their demands were denied.

The second reporter bases his decision regarding what ought to be done on what he (or she) expects the consequences of the action to be. The first reporter bases his decision on a principle (i.e., a rule) to the effect that under such circumstances it is best to meet the demands of the culprits. His justification for following such a rule is in terms of the good consequences which result when one follows such a principle or rule. Unlike the second reporter, he does not try to base his intended action upon his expectations regarding its consequences. For this reason he does not have to make a prediction about the *future*. And so he is not subject to the first of the standard objections to utilitarianism. The justification for his intended action is the principle. The justification of the principle is the alleged fact that following it in the *past* has had good consequences. Hindsight does not require omniscience. Rule utilitarianism also sidesteps the other two standard objections to utilitarianism. Rules against stealing, lying, and murdering are said to be justified because the consequences of not observing them would be disastrous.

This is not to say that there are no problems with rule utilitarianism. It is only to say that the standard objections to utilitarianism can be surmounted by this form of the theory. Unfortunately, a major, perhaps even insurmountable, obstacle blocks its acceptance. Although rule utilitarianism does not sanction inhuman or barbarous injustices, it does allow for all kinds of other injustices.* Suppose that there exist two fathers each of whom has five children. Suppose that one of them gives each of his children five dollars a week and that the other father gives his favorite child twenty-five dollars a week and gives his other children nothing.

Suppose further that it just happens to be the case that the total pleasure that the five children of the former father receives is exactly equivalent to the pleasure that the one child of the latter father receives. Also suppose that the other children of the second father are unaware that their sibling is being favored, and so do not experience any pain. Suppose further that each of these fathers acts in terms of a rule. The first father adopts the rule that each of his children is to get an equal share of what he can afford as allowance money. The second father adopts the rule that his favored child should receive all the money that he can afford to give.

All of us are inclined, are we not, to judge that the second father is unethical and that the first father has behaved in an exemplary way. Yet each of their rules is on equal footing with respect to the utilitarian maxim. Each rule produces the same balance of pleasure over pain. What this shows is, according to most philosophers, that ethics cannot be founded solely upon the principle of utility. At the very least ethics requires an additional principle to insure a fair or just distribution of the good. This principle is usually called the *principle of justice*.

Another problem with rule utilitarianism is that it depends upon

---

* And so is, ultimately, subject to the second objection.

our ability to justify *induction*. Since some philosophers are convinced that induction cannot be justified, these same philosophers are not going to buy a theory which depends upon it.

One final objection needs to be mentioned and that is the integrity issue raised by Bernard Williams.* His point is that there are circumstances where following the utilitarian guidelines forces one to compromise one's integrity. Williams asks us to suppose we have a chemist who has throughout his or her lifetime followed certain principles such as not working for or having any connection with any company which engages in research having to do with biological warfare. We are asked to suppose further that the consequences of the chemist's taking a job with a firm which does research in chemical warfare are apt to be better than they would be if a warmonger were to get the job. According to Williams, to demand that the chemist take the job on utilitarian grounds (assuming that a warmonger has applied) is to insist that he compromise his integrity. Ultimately, what Williams is driving at is that it would be a misuse of our ordinary concepts of what is right and what is wrong were we to describe his refusal to take the job as "wrong". In short, what Williams has shown is that utilitarian theory does not do justice to our common or shared notions of morality and ethics. It ignores an essential ingredient by ignoring integrity. While this has to be conceded, there are, as I will eventually establish, times when the consequences of our actions far outweigh, and thus override, any considerations concerning integrity. I will return to this matter in the final section of this chapter.

Let us now return to *egoism*. Although egoism has had and continues to have a large number of adherents, most philosophers agree that it involves an insurmountable difficulty. It is usually alleged that one cannot *advocate* it without inconsistency. Which is to say that anyone who publically recommends it is being inconsistent. In his remarkably useful and deservedly influential book, *Ethics*, William Frankena points out that

> If one takes a maxim as a moral principle, one must be ready to universalize it. Also, as was suggested earlier, one must be willing to see his principle actually adopted and acted on by everyone else, ... and even advocate that they adopt and act on it ... if he is unwilling to share his basic normative premises, then he does not have a morality in the full sense. Hence, for our purposes, we must regard the ethical egoist as holding that everyone should act and judge by the standard of his own long-run advantage in terms of good and evil ... it has been argued that ethical egoism, as thus con-

---

* "A Critique of Utilitarianism," in *Utilitarianism: For and Against*, ed. by J.J.C. Smart and Bernard Williams (Cambridge: Cambridge University Press, 1973), pp. 93–118.

strued, is self-contradictory, since it cannot be to one individual's advantage that all others should pursue their own advantage so assiduously. As Kant would put it, one cannot will the egoistic maxim to be a universal law. [p. 18]

Recognize that *ethical* egoism is the view that one *ought* always to act in ways which promote one's own self-interest. It is not the view that one *does* always so act. To claim the latter is to assert *psychological* egoism. No one claims that the latter view is contradictory. The claim it involves is probably false but it is not inconsistent.

With this in mind let us turn to ethical egoism and elaborate the inconsistency it is alleged to involve. Quite often the circumstances of life are such that some people's needs can only be met at the expense of not meeting other people's needs. This is a *fact* about our world. It is not, however, a logical truth, and so whatever we say will have to recognize that it is logically possible for the world to be different than it is. We can imagine a world in which every person's needs, desires, etc., are distinct from every person's needs, desires, etc. For this reason the inconsistency I am interested in illustrating is not the same as *logical* inconsistency. At any rate, in our world only one reporter can have an exclusive interview with a celebrity. Imagine a reporter who both advocates egoism and seeks an exclusive interview with the novelist Salinger. Suppose him or her to be in conversation with another reporter:

> *Our egoist:* One ought always to act in a manner which promotes one's own self-interest.
> *The other reporter:* I'm glad you said that because, although you have been working for months to get an exclusive with Salinger, I just met a very good friend of his who thinks he can get me in to see him, and, hopefully, he will grant me an interview. I was going to arrange for you to meet Salinger's friend since you have worked for so long to accomplish this interview. But instead I am going to take your advice and pursue my own interests.

Our egoist's action in recommending egoism to his fellow reporter is inconsistent with his egoism. According to his professed aims his actions are supposed always to promote his own self-interest. But his act of recommending egoism does not promote his own self-interest. It stands in contradiction to his self-interest. The problem here is one of self-reference. It is a problem which is similar to the one involved in someone's saying, "All my claims are false." If this statement is true, then it is false.

There is an important difference, however, because the problem with recommending egoism is not, unlike the similar one presented here, vitiated by acceptance of Russell's theory of types. Russell's theory says that the claim about all one's claims is not itself on the same level with one's other claims. It is a claim about them. Its subjects are the ordinary everyday claims that one makes. It is itself not an ordinary everyday claim. In short, it is of a different *type*. In the case of egoism, the claim is that one should never act in a manner which is not in one's own self-interest. Recommending egoism is, however, to act in a manner which is not in one's own self-interest. The recommendation is of the *same type* as what it attempts to prohibit. What one would be saying is, "Act always in your own self-interest, but sometimes don't."

Although this objection is one of the standard objections to ethical egoism, and is in fact usually taught in most courses in ethics, it is fallacious. What cases like the one about the egoistic reporter actually show is, not that advocating ethical egoism is inconsistent, but rather that it is *sometimes* inconsistent to do so. The view which turns out to be inconsistent is the view that one ought *always* both to advocate and to practice ethical egoism. Now, of course, this does not mean that these considerations do not in themselves constitute some kind of objection to the theory in question. A theory which can only be advocated without contradiction under specific sorts of circumstances is, admittedly, rather peculiar.

The fact that egoism cannot be *recommended* without qualification does not mean that egoism is itself inconsistent. One can in fact practice egoism without any contradiction whatsoever. One simply has to refrain from ever recommending it.

Deontological Ethical Theories

The most influential and important deontological ethical theorist who ever lived was Immanuel Kant. For Kant the question regarding whether any human action is good or bad is to be decided not in terms of its consequences, but instead in terms of whether or not the decision to act originates in a proper or right will. The recognition of duty which issues from a rational will is, for Kant, the only proper basis for decision regarding what we ought to do. Kant maintains that it is *duty*, not the *consequences of our actions*, which must govern our decisions regarding how we ought to act.*

How, one might ask, are we to know or recognize when we are acting in accordance with a right will? Kant's answer to this question is provided by his often-quoted *categorical imperative*. The categorical imperative is, according to Kant, "Act only according to that maxim by which

---

* *Foundations of the Metaphysics of Morals*, Immanuel Kant, translated by L.W. Beck (New York: The Liberal Arts Press, 1959), p. 39.

you can at the same time will that it should become a universal law." What this means can best be understood by considering a case like the following one.

Suppose you have a newsperson on the verge of breaking a big story. Suppose further that he (or she) needs corroboration of some aspect of the story, and that the person who is in a position to verify the lead says that he will do so only if the newsperson will keep his identity a secret even from the newsperson's editor. The newsperson knows that the only way his editor will allow him to use the story is if he identifies for the editor his source. The newsperson figures the source will never know that the editor knows who he is, so he decides to lie to the source. Kant would object most strenuously at this point and assert that lying is wrong because it fails to pass the test provided by the categorical imperative. If our reporter were to ask himself if he could will such an action, he would find, if he were mentally competent, that so willing leads one to contradict himself. He would have to will that anyone in a similar set of circumstances should lie.

But when the implications of these circumstances are spelled out, it turns out that what he is willing is that anyone should lie whenever it is to his advantage. Suppose this bit of willing to be suddenly true of this world. Would it any longer be possible to lie for one's own advantage? Clearly not. For in such a world as we have imagined, no reasonable or mentally competent person would believe any other person. Why should he, since in this society lying has become a practice. In such a society one could not succeed by lying, from which it follows that one could not, by lying, further his own ends. Lying is thus recognized to be an irrational act.

When we were talking about utilitarianism we distinguished between a rule and an act variety. Deontological theories are amenable to the same distinction. In the above case we applied Kant's views to show that a particular action was wrong because it could not be willed to be a universal maxim for all mankind to follow. Our procedure was act deontological. Kant, unlike many he inspired, was a rule-deontological theorist. He asked if we could justify conventional fiats, like the one against lying, and then proceeded by means like the above to show that we can. It should be pointed out, in order to prevent by misunderstanding, that even our procedure was rule governed insofar as it involved an application of the categorical imperative. For this reason one may be misled, as some in fact have been, to describe our type of application of Kant's maxim as rule deontological. But by parity of reason the example of act utilitarianism which we cited in the previous section would have to be said to be an example of rule utilitarianism since it involves an appeal to the utilitarian maxim regarding consequences. The difference between utilitarianism and Kant's brand of deontologicalism is that while the former appeals to a principle which defines 'good' in terms of consequences, the latter appeals to one which defines 'good' in terms of the will of a rational being. Both can be said to be of the act or rule variety depending upon whether their respective maxims are used to justify a particular action or a rule (convention, fiat, principle, practice).

There are several standard or classical objections to Kant's theories. In the first place it only seems to work for the case of lying. Kant tried to show that it worked for most of the other conventional fiats as well. For example, he tried to show that it could be used to show that killing was wrong. But he was mistaken. He argued that when one tried to will in favor of killing, one was engaged in an irrational action. Willing thus, he points out, is akin to decreeing that it would be proper for someone else to kill the willer. Now although this idea is an unpleasant thought to most of us, it is certainly not irrational (i.e., contradictory) for someone to do so. In fact, given what we have done to this beautiful planet on which we found ourselves, it is not hard to imagine someone being perfectly willing, and even rationally justified in, willing that every person ought to kill anyone, including the person so willing, who is found contributing to the further pollution of the earth. Kant's other attempts can all be counterexampled in similar fashion.

The reason the lying case works and the others do not is explicable in terms of the difference betwen *speech actions* and *nonspeech actions*. Lying is ordinarily accomplished by an action that involves speech, whereas murder, stealing, adultry, are not. Some acts of cheating are accomplished via speech, and some are not. The form of cheating which involves speech involves lying, and so can be shown to involve a contradiction. The other forms of cheating do not involve speech, and so do not involve a contradiction.

The problem with egoism is that it cannot be recommended (a speech action) without contradiction. It can, however, as we have seen, be practiced (a nonspeech action). It could not, however, and this is extremely interesting, be willed as a universal practice. The egoist, if he is rational, has to recognize that the realization of this willing would obviate whatever advantages one gains from practicing egoism. Willing egoism is like entertaining the proposition, i.e., having the thought that, a million-sided polygon is a greater-sided polygon than a million-sided polygon minus a hundred sides. Having the thought about the million-sided figure is impossible without using a natural language. The having of the thought is simply engaging in a bit of internalized speech.

The same is true of willing that everyone ought to lie for his or her advantage. The point we wish to make is this: The argument against egoism and the Kantian argument in favor of the fiat against lying are, when undressed, one and the same. And like any other contradiction, it must of necessity involve language. Only statements and some propositions, namely, those which are true or false by necessity, can be said to be contradictory of one another. And, moreover, it does not matter whether these statements are explicit (are actually asserted out loud) or implicit (internalized statements).

Another problem with Kant's theory is that it finds certain innocuous actions to be morally wrong. Remember that the maxim says that one is never to do anything which one could not will that everyone should do. Most of us would not want all of mankind to sell flowers on the streets, but we certainly have no objection to some people doing it. In fact, a lot of us actually prefer that some people do sell flowers on the streets. The theory prohibits far too much.

Still another objection to the theory is that the maxim provides only a necessary and not a sufficient condition for morality. In other words, while it specifies that when the condition cannot be met one is acting immorally, it does not tell us when we are acting morally. And it certainly would not do to interpret it as both a necessary and a sufficient condition. If we were to do so, we would have to maintain that a lot of actions which are ordinarily thought of as morally neutral (or amoral) are morally good. Even though one would not ordinarily will that all people begin their meals by uttering their own name, one certainly could will it without contradiction.

Let us now turn to some of the other deontological theories which we mentioned earlier. The most venerated and advocated of all deontological theories is *supernaturalism*. This is the view that what is right is what God wills, and that what is wrong is what is in opposition to that will. In Western culture there are two main renderings of this theme: that of the Old Testament, and that of the New Testament. According to the former, God's will is conveyed to us via the commandments. If we want to know what we ought to do, all we have to do is consult the commandments. The New Testament rendition conveys God's will to us by describing His behavior while on earth. If you want to know how you ought to act, the answer is given in terms of God's actions. One should do what He said and imitate what He did. In a not too extended sense of the terms one could say that the Old Testament version is a rule-deontological theory, while the New Testament version is act deontological. In the former version, our behavior is said to be appropriate when it corresponds to a set of *rules* which God's will validates. In the latter, our behavior is said to be appropriate if it corresponds to His *actions*, which reveal and are validated by His will.

Both versions of supernaturalism are subject to the same difficulties. They depend upon firm belief in God's existence. And this is a matter of considerable controversy. Many, if not most, philosophers find it extremely difficult to believe in God's existence. In fact, there are many philosophers who do not believe that the concept of an omnipotent, omniscient, and omnibenevolent God is intelligible. These philosophers claim that the properties referred to in defining or describing God are inconsistent with one another. How, for example, can an all-powerful and all-good God permit the existence of evil on this planet? Either He is all powerful and allows evil to exist because He is not all good, or He is all good and evil exists because He is powerless to prevent it.

A possible reply to this kind of criticism is that God allows evil to exist so that we may recognize the good. Without evil to contrast with the good, we would not, according to this rejoinder, understand and recognize the good. Unfortunately for its proponents, this rejoinder does not work, and it does not work for two reasons. In the first place, one could respond by asking, "But why so *much* evil?" Do six million Jews have to die in order for us to understand what evil is? We may lack the omniscience reputed to God, but surely we are not so obtuse as this would imply. A much more telling objection to the rejoinder in question is, however, that God with his power could simply have planted the concept of evil within us. He could have caused us to grasp the concept without causing us to encounter the phenomena itself. We understand what it is for something to be a unicorn in spite of the fact that there are none.

In short, the main obstacle to the acceptance of supernaturalism is that it requires one to believe on the basis of *faith* alone in the existence of an unobservable entity the very concept of whom is obscure.

Twentieth-Century Deontological Ethical Theories

The twentieth century has produced two original and influential ethical theories: *existentialism* and *emotivism*. Both are deontological. We will begin with existentialism. The major figure in this movement is a French philosopher by the name of John Paul Sartre. It is his brand of existentialism which we shall take as our model in what follows. The existentialist claims that for the human species, "existence precedes essence." What this means is best understood if we consider what it means to claim the converse. To claim the converse is to claim that the nature or essence of mankind exists somehow prior to or independent of the existence of individual human beings.

Historically, this essence has been said to have a prior existence in one of two ways. It has been said to exist as a concept in the mind of God, and it has been said to exist as a plan in nature. The former view (supernaturalism) has been by far the most common one. It is the view of most religions. It is the view of Christianity. It is the view that God, the *creator*, had in his mind the concept or idea of man, reputedly in his own image, and that he fashioned a *creature* in that likeness. The question as regards what a man ought to do or be (the fundamental question of ethics) is answered in terms of God's will. On this view there are ethical absolutes. Whatever God wills is an absolute. Any question concerning what a man ought to do is given in terms of what God wills.

Because of the kinds of objections we considered when we examined supernaturalism, existentialists of the Sartrian variety assert that it is preposterous to believe in the existence of God. And since this is the case, man is free to determine his own nature unless, of course, some other basis can be said to account for his essence. The only other possibility would seem to be the one referred to above, namely, *nature*.

According to this account, mankind has a nature or essence. Mankind is viewed as an instantiation of a formal system emanating from nature itself. The Hegelian version of this view depicts nature as a rational spirit or mind which both actualizes and comes to know itself. Nature is viewed as rational and deductive, and so are its products. If we want to know what we ought to do, all we have to do is consult reason. Kant's theory of morality is, of course, another version of this view.

The existentialist rejects this account of morality. He urges us to recognize how really limited is the power of reason; to see that valid deductions are all trivial and uninformative; to understand that if mankind did have a nature, we would be able to point to and explain what that nature is, but we are unable to do so.

The existentialist may very well be right about the power of reason. Many contemporary thinkers would agree with the view that reason is quite limited in scope; that our understanding of the world and our place in it, including how we ought to conduct our lives, does not fall within the province of reason. Nevertheless, while it is no doubt true that human beings come in a wide variety of psychological flavors, this fact alone is not a sufficient grounds for holding that human beings do not have something like a nature.

These considerations conjoined with the existentialist's contention that God does not exist are certainly not adequate to show that man is free to be whatever he wills to be. This is, however, just what the existentialist wants to conclude.

What existentialists conclude is that since we are free to be what we want to be, we in effect choose our essence. This is what existentialists mean when they say that our existence precedes our essence. We appeared on this planet quite by accident and so we came to exist. Since that time we have been actively defining ourselves. There are certain restrictions which are imposed on us. We cannot jump over tall buildings in a single bound, we cannot choose our parents or our birthdays, we cannot choose our heights or our looks. But with the exception of restrictions like these, which are involved in what the existentialists call the "human condition," we are utterly free to choose what we ought to do and become. In choosing for ourselves what we ought to be or do, we also, according to the existentialist, make a similiar choice for all mankind.

The existentialist claims that since God does not exist, there are no absolutes and objective criteria for right and wrong. Whatever we choose will be right. So long as we are willing to believe in God, we have an external criterion for what is right and what is wrong, namely, His will. Without God man must decide for himself what is right and what is wrong. His decisions can be based either in reason or in fiat. According to the existentialist, reason is an illusion. Mankind is inherently irrational. Humans pretend to be, even convince themselves that they are, ruled by reason. But they are not.

Men are, however, free to make decisions and to follow through on these decisions. But without God to approve of these decisions, it follows that *any* given decision will be as valid, proper, or acceptable as any other. The supernaturalist who is faced with two or more possibilities for action can say that one of them is right and that the others are wrong. The decision is based on something external, independent, and objective, namely, God's will. The existentialist cannot appeal to anything objective and independent. Whatever one decides to do will be right. For the existentialist, human will is everything. If two of us have a debate about the length of a certain desk we can always decide who is right by appealing to an objective and independent criterion: a yardstick. But, according to the existentialist, there is nothing external and objective to appeal to when we debate values. In short, there is no yardstick for value.

This view is at best somewhat unpalatable.* Since it does not recognize any criterion for proper action other than what the agent selects, this means that nothing is prohibited. The Nazis' decisions are on a par with those of the saint. Since whatever anyone wills is right, the Nazis' decision to exterminate the Jews is right. Unpalatability is not, unfortunately, sufficient grounds for refutation. If God's existence cannot be established and formal or deductive grounds cannot be provided for acting one way rather than another, it would almost have to follow that one action is just as valid or proper as any other.

But, it could be argued, is not utilitarianism a viable alternative to God's will and the demonstrable nature of human reason? Granted that there are problems with utilitarianism, still should not we try to work out the snags since it is our best — perhaps even our only — hope?

Existentialists are not much impressed with this kind of reasoning. They claim that our acceptance of the utilitarian maxim that ethical matters should be decided in terms of beneficial consequences for the greatest number, does itself require certification or validation. And since

---

* Odell's view of existentialism is somewhat at odds with that of his coauthor here, John Merrill. See Merrill's *Existential Journalism* (New York: Hastings House, 1977).

they hold that there is no God and that such principles as the one about consequences cannot be grounded in deductive reasoning, they could insist that utilitarianism cannot be validated. Like any other principle, it could, however — if God could be said to have willed it — be validated. In place of the Ten Commandments, God could have burnt the utilitarian maxim on the stone.

Another popular twentieth-century deontological theory is *emotivism*. And, although it is the product of a tradition very different from existentialism, the two are, as we will demonstrate, consistent with one another. Existentialism is the product of an antiscientific, antianalytic tradition. Emotivism is a product of logical positivism which is highly scientifically and analytically oriented.

The original emotivists claimed that when we say things like, 'That's good", "That's bad", "He is a good human being", "That's the right thing to do", *all* that we are doing is expressing our feelings regarding some person or thing or some person's actions. According to this view, when a newsperson editorializes that the actions of some politician were wrong, he (or she) is, whether aware of it or not, only saying that he disapproves of the actions of the politician. Most newspersons would, of course, disagree with this analysis. They would offer a variety of reasons in favor of their claims, some of which would be utilitarian, some of which would be deontological. But, according to the emotivist, they would, if pressed, eventually have to concede that what they really meant to be saying was that they disapproved.

The emotivist claims that ethical words simply constitute a subset of the class of evaluative terms. In addition to the ethical terms, this class contains aesthetic terms: 'beautiful', 'pretty', 'sublime', 'grand', 'splendid', 'sexy', 'ugly', 'dumpy', 'disgusting', etc. To say that a woman is gorgeous is, on this view, to say that one enthusiastically approves of her. The emotivists distinguish between statements which are *descriptive* and statements which are *expressive*. Descriptive ones are said to be true or false, descriptive of some external or natural property, and experientially verifiable. An example of a descriptive statement would be, "That's red." If I say this about an object which is red, what I say is true. If I say it about a blue object, what I say is false. What I describe is an external property of the thing, and the statement can be verified. All one has to do to verify it is to look at the object in question.

"That's good" and "That's beautiful" do not, so the story goes, describe an object. They are not true or false in the sense that they attribute a verifiable property to some object. They simply *express* our feelings regarding an act or object. Of course if they mean "I approve of it," then there is a sense in which they are true or false. If I do not have the appropriate feeling, then they are false. If I do, then they are true.

But they are neither true nor false in the sense that they attribute an observable property to something. These philosophers hold that expressive statements can be sincere or insincere, but not mistaken. One either has or does not have the appropriate feelings.

Emotivists eventually modified their position on this matter to take into account the fact that it would be peculiar to assert that something was, for example, good or great and further assert that you would not recommend it. If you tell me that a movie is great, I infer that you are recommending that I see it. Of course, you may caution a person who is squeamish not to see a violent movie which you feel is great, but when you claim that it is great, you are in effect saying that most people should see it. For these reasons the latter-day emotivists (Charles Stevenson is an example*) claim that "That's good" means "I approve, do so as well."

What the emotivists are saying is that nothing *is* good in the sense in which things *are* three inches long or red. Matters of value are nonobjective. They are subjective and personal. They can be discussed and debated, and one person can convince another that he is mistaken. Yet, no emotive statement can ever be demonstrated to be mistaken. On this account of the matter there are no absolutes. Like the existentialists, the emotivists claim that there are no yardsticks for determining values. So, even though these two types of philosophers approach things very differently, the upshot of their respective views regarding ethics is the same: a *personal* as opposed to a *cultural* relativism.

A personal relativism insists that everything turns on the individual's decision. A cultural relativism holds that the values of any given society are such only because they are accepted. The distinction we drew earlier between act- and rule-oriented theories can be used to illuminate the difference between these two relativistic approaches. The kind of personal relativism exemplified by existentialism and emotivism is of the act-deontological variety. Cultural relativism exemplifies a rule-deontological type. The personal relativist holds that what is valuable is what the individual decides is valuable. The cultural relativist claims that what is valuable is what society *legislates* to be valuable. Neither kind of relativist believes in the objectivity of values. Ultimately, one choice or law is as valid as any other.

Objectivity and Ethical Theory

At this point one is apt to feel inclined to protest loudly against *any* form of relativism on the ground that there are certain actions which anyone in his right mind would judge to be wrong. What about the

* *Ethics and Language*, Charles L. Stevenson (New Haven: Yale University Press, 1944).

treatment of the Jews by the Nazis? One wants to be able to claim that what the Nazis did to the Jews is *horribly* wrong. Only an inhumane monster could possibly condone it. In other words, we feel that there must be some objective basis on which to ground the claim that what the Nazis did was wrong.

While it is no doubt true that most of us are horrified by the behavior of the Nazis, this fact alone does not establish that what they did is absolutely and objectively wrong. The fact that something horrifies us cannot be taken to be sufficient evidence that it is morally wrong. Is an earthquake or a tornado, each of which is extremely horrifying, morally wrong? Although the answer to this question is no, still there is, one might argue, an important difference between Nazis and forces of nature. Nazis, unlike forces of nature, do what they do with the *intention* to injure, and destroy. True, but what is one to say about the man who in the act of defending his children mangles an intruder with a burst from a twelve-gauge shotgun? What he has done is horrifying, but we do not feel that it is *clearly* wrong.

In short, what we are saying in response to this line of objection to relativism is that the reason we *feel* that certain actions are so clearly and objectively wrong is because they are so horrifying to us, but the fact that they are so horrifying to us does not *show* that they are morally wrong.

Another form of relativism which needs to be mentioned is what has been called *situationism*. Unfortunately, the term is not always used with the same meaning we will assign it here. It is sometimes used to refer to a kind of act utilitarianism. Situationism as we shall be using the term can be said to refer to an ethical position which is both a cousin of existentialism and quite commonly adopted by practicing journalists. The situationist, like the act utilitarian, holds that ethical issues cannot be decided in the abstract. Both hold that decisions regarding how we ought to act must be grounded in the concrete of actual situations. Both claim that we can only see what is to be done when we are faced with particularizing circumstances. Abstract and theoretical considerations are at best only vaguely suggestive hints for how we ought to conduct our lives. They do not completely dismiss ethical principles. Rather, they emphasize the exceptions to such principles. The difference between the two views is twofold. In the first place, one can be a situationist in our use of the word and not be a utilitarian. One could be an egoist or even one of the various kinds of deontological ethical theorists. In the second place, the situationist we are interested in discussing is distinquished by his (or her) relativism. As Merrill has pointed out elsewhere:

The journalistic situationist may well be the one who believes that

Cola Journ Rev.
v 32 p 41-5 Jul./Aug. 93

New York
p. 18 Mar. 15 93

WJR Ja/F 93
q. 14

Amer. Journ Rev.
q. 26 - 30 April 93

The Unesco Courier
p. 12.15 Sept. 90

Cola Journ. Rev.
44-45 Nov/Dec 91

Journ. Edue. I Bound Per) Tu 2nd floor
V 47 #1 Spng 92 - date 1 Tu
1 Tu
1 Tu

Journ Quarterly

ress" V.69 #1 - date 1 Tu
Bound Per. / 2nd floor 1 Th
3 TT
ess" Circulation desk 1 Tu
1 Th
3 MWF
d Typography I 3 TT
ress" 1 Tu
Periodical Holdings Th
ress" 1 Tu
ress" 1 Tu
ress" 1 Tu
ress" 1 Tu
ress" 1 Tu
1 Th

he should tell the truth *as a basic principle*, or that he should not generally distort his story, but who will, after due consideration of the situation in which he finds himself, conclude that it is all right to distort *this particular story*, or even to lie. Do the circumstances in this case warrant a departure from basic — generally held — moral guidelines: this is the rational question which always confronts the situationist. He is one, then, who takes special situations into consideration in making his ethical decisions; he is a relativist to be sure, but a rational relativist, one who *thinks* before breaking a basic ethical rule. [*Ethics and the Press*, p. 14]

The situationist looks for grounds upon which to base his decisions. Ultimately, however, he recognizes that there is no principle or set of principles to which he can appeal, not even the utilitarian maxim. He recognizes that any attempt at justification through principles involves an act of *legislation*.

No philosopher is altogether satisfied with any form of relativism. But unless we can come up with some objective criterion for value we are stuck with a choice among its various forms.

The existence of an ethical code can, however, be demonstrated to be necessary in some sense. Odell and Zartman have demonstrated elsewhere that certain principles are *necessary presuppositions* for the existence of a natural language.* In a similar vein it can be argued that ethical principles are necessary preconditions for the existence of a social community. Without any ethical principles it would be impossible for human beings to live in harmony and without fear, dispair, hopelessness, anxiety, apprehension, and uncertainty. Hobbes, in his great treatise on the state,† recognized this even though he did not put it in these terms. He talked about mankind in the state of nature and claimed that:

> Whatsoever therefore is consequent to a time of war, where every man is enemy to every man, the same is consequent to the time wherein men live without other security, than what their own strength, and their own invention shall furnish them withal. In such condition, there is no place for industry, because the fruit thereof is uncertain, and consequently no culture of the earth; no navigation, nor use of the commodities that may be imported by sea; no commodious building; no instruments of moving, and removing, such things as require much force; no knowledge of the

---

* "A Defensible Formulation of the Verification Principle," S. Jack Odell and James F. Zartman, *Metaphilosophy*, January 1982, Vol. 13, No. 1.

† *Leviathan*, Thomas Hobbes, reprinted in *Modern Classical Philosophers*, compiled by B. Rand (Cambridge, Mass: The Riverside Press, 1952).

face of the earth; no account of time; no arts; no letters; no society; and which is worst of all, continual fear, and danger of violent
death; and the life of man, solitary, poor, nasty, brutish, and
short. [p. 82]

Hobbes is correct in his view that civilized existence is impossible
without some rules of conduct. This is not to say that Hobbes or we
want to maintain that human existence in any way requires the existence
of an ethical code. We do not even hold that there is any ultimate value
to be placed upon civilized existence. Whether or not civilized existence
is to be preferred to uncivilized existence is not a question which has to
be answered in order to establish an objective basis for an ethical code.
All one has to show for this end to be realized is simply that harmonious human existence (what we commonly call 'community') requires
an ethical code.

One has to proceed with caution at this point because it is extremely
easy to make a mistake. To avoid refutation one must explain carefully
what one means by 'requires' in this context. Since one can imagine
human beings who differ from present humans in that they are by nature given to loving each other and treating each other with immense respect and consideration, it follows that one can imagine a community of
humans which sustains itself without an ethical code. And so it would
be a mistake to think that the existence of an ethical code is required as a
matter of logical necessity for the existence of a community. It is not a
matter of logic.

What we are saying is only that insofar as human beings are the
way they are, and so long as they remain this way, an ethical code is
necessary in order for them to coexist as a community. Without some
sort of ethical code, humans as we know them cannot live in harmony.
So although there are no absolutes in ethics, there is a sense in which
one can say that there are *objective* values. The relativist says that all
values are relative to some individual or group of individuals. In opposition, we claim that the need for an ethical code is independent of any
given culture or society. No society or community could exist (given
that human beings are the way they are) without an ethical code.

Now, of course, it is one thing to assert that an ethical code is a
necessary presupposition for the existence of a community. It is quite
another thing to be able to specify exactly which principles — i.e., what
ethical codes — are necessary. In fact it could turn out that although *an*
ethical code is required for the existence of community life, *many* different, even incompatible ones, would accomplish this end.

There is considerably more to be said on this subject but most of it
will have to be said elsewhere. All we wish to say further at this point is
that any ethical code which meets the criteria expressed here must con-

tain principles which promote community life. Principles like, "One ought not take the life of another except to prevent a greater tragedy," "One ought not to take another's possessions except to prevent an unfortunate event from taking place." The principles of an acceptable system will have to have their exceptions built in. They will be formulated so as to contain or be understood to contain a *ceteris paribus* clause. Specifying all the exceptions and spelling out all the extenuating circumstances is no easy task. In the case of the above principle regarding the taking of a human life one would have to specify what constitutes a greater tragedy. For the second principle above, the one about taking another's possessions, one would have to specify what sorts of events would be more unfortunate than a person's having his possessions liberated.

Applications of Ethical Theory to Journalism

Early in this chapter we isolated some of the main ethical issues characteristic of journalism. We will now examine these issues in the light of what we have learned about ethical theory.

We will begin by considering the question regarding whether or not a reporter ever has the right to lie to the public. Odell has argued elsewhere* that the answer to this question is that in certain circumstances he (or she) not only has the right to do so, he is morally culpable if he does not. Odell makes this point by asking us to consider the following case:

> Suppose you are a local television newsman on a small island community just off the Florida mainland. Suppose further that the only route to and from the island, other than the waterway, is a two lane bridge. There are many residents on the island. A large number of fully occupied condominiums exists on the island. Most of the people who live in the condominiums do not have boats, and, in fact, there are very few boats on the island. You know that a tropical storm is brewing, but it is not supposed to be very severe. Your phone rings. It is the weather service to tell you that a terrible error has been made, and not only is the storm much worse that it was supposed to be, it is already very close to the mainland. It will, in fact, hit the island shortly. There isn't time to fully evacuate the island. It is clear that a lot of people are going to die. You must make an announcement, but you realize that telling the truth will cause a panic. There will be a run on the bridge. This

* "A Review of Teaching Ethics in Journalism Education by Christians and Covert," in *Teaching Philosophy*, April 1981, Vol. 4.

will cause a traffic jam, which will in turn make it impossible for anyone to escape via the bridge. And since it is virtually certain that any one left on the island will die, it is equally certain that nearly every resident of the island will perish. You can't suppress the news because then no one will attempt to get off the island. The only thing to do is lie. You are compelled by the circumstances to do so. You have to tell them that there is a severe storm on the way, and that everyone should evacuate the island. So far you haven't had to lie, but in order to prevent panic you must also say that there is ample time for an orderly evacuation. Now you are lying, but you *are obliged* to do so because this is the only way you can *see* to insure that some will escape.

In stating this case no appeal is made to an ethical theory. The case is meant to illustrate the point that one is sometimes morally obliged to lie. It also shows that when certain circumstances obtain we recognize what must be done. Appeal can, however, be made to ethical theory. And it would naturally arise in a context where one asked what justifies our reporter having acted the way he did. The justification we advocate, in keeping with the theory set out in the previous section, is that certain kinds of behavior are necessary if society as we know it is to persist. To allow all these people to die so that the reporter can remain a truth teller would be an incredible breach of the *common* good. Society would come apart at the seams if we allowed such self-indulgence. The integrity of the reporter cannot even be an issue in this context. Further analysis of the case reveals other information nicely describable in terms we have learned from ethical theory. The course of action which this case establishes as the only proper one for our reporter is no doubt *teleological* in character. The consequences of his not lying are so horrendous one cannot imagine his doing otherwise. What this shows is that there are *situations* where the weight of the consequences is so overpowering as to vitiate all other considerations, including considerations having to do with *integrity*. And so his decision can be recognized to be *act utilitarian* in nature. More importantly, it needs to be understood that cases of this sort are responsible for whatever credence teleological theories, and specifically utilitarian ones, and even more specifically act-utilitarian ones, possess.

The confidentiality issue is, as was suggested previously, an instance of a more general question: "When one's principles or ethics conflict with the laws of one's land, is one wrong to follow one's principles?" An answer can be given in terms of the distinction we drew earlier between what is *legally permitted* and what is *ethically correct*. One could argue that when a reporter refuses to divulge a source, and in so doing breaks the law, the reporter may, nevertheless, be morally right. If he (or she) has given his word not to reveal his source under any circumstances, the breaking of that promise is unethical even if it is legal. For the most part the law of the land reflects the ethical code of that land. But it does not have to and it sometimes does not.

This fact can easily be grasped if one considers what so often happens after revolution and the seizing of political power by those outside the establishment. What usually happens is one of two things, both of which illustrate and ground our claim. Either the revolutionaries change the existing laws, altering some and dropping others so as to guarantee what they conceive to be the basic ethical rights of each person, or the laws are changed to fit the political objectives of those seizing power at the expense of certain individuals or some group or groups of people. The former alternative is instantiated and evidenced by both the American and the French revolutions; the latter alternative, by the Nazis seizing power in Germany. It is also illustrated by many of the conquests of one nation by another. And both of these phenomena can be evidenced to have existed side by side in the case of the Russian revolution.

Injustices can only be rectified so long as men are willing to break existing laws for the sake of ethical principles. The continuance of the community depends upon it. Principles which guarantee just distribution of what we all value are, as we have seen, necessary for the existence of a harmonious society. The upshot of these considerations is that a reporter's refusal to divulge sources even when it means incarceration, can, in general, be justified, even applauded.

One should not conclude from this that every reporter is always justified in concealing a source. There are going to be times when the price of keeping a promise of any kind is too great. One would certainly not be justified in concealing the source of one's information when it is learned that the source not only knows where "the bomber" is going to strike next, but so many details about past bombings not to, in fact, turn out to be the bomber.

No set of exact rules can be formulated which will always tell the reporter what to do. What we can do, and, we hope, have already done to some extent, is to have both stimulated our audience's moral imagination and developed its analytic skills, to have sensitized it to ethical issues, and to have established an objective basis for ethical judgment. If we have succeeded in this, the reader should be able to work out the answer to such questions as, Ought I conceal this source? The recommended program may sound like situationism, and in some ways it is like that, but it is very different insofar as it does not condone relativism.

At the beginning of this chapter we identified certain other journalistic issues: When is it proper for the news media to identify a rape victim or an alleged sex offender? When does a reporter have the right to report on an ongoing police investigation? When does a reporter have the right to publish a suspect's previous arrest record? When may a journalist give favored treatment to a public official in exchange for important information? When is it all right for a newsperson to accept free trips and other economic benefits? When is it proper for the press to impose self-restraints or suppress certain news? When is it proper for the government to restrain the press? Is it morally imperative for the press to seek objectivity?

Each of these questions can be discussed in accordance with the model provided by our discussion of the confidentiality issue. We will, however, say something specific about each one of them. Because the questions at the end of the list are more complex, perhaps even more important, we will provide a somewhat more detailed discussion of them.

In general identifying rape victims serves only to whet morbid appetites. If, however, publishing the victim's identity makes it possible for the public to assist in finding the victim, who is wandering about Manhattan in a severe traumatic state, one is certainly on good ethical ground in doing so. Identifying an alleged sex offender cannot, in general, accomplish anything other than to prejudice the case. But suppose the offender is alleged to have perpetrated serious sex crimes, has not been apprehended, appears to be in a given part of the city where he is known, and is thought to be seeking other victims. Under these circumstances the right thing to do would be to warn the inhabitants of that section who to be on the look out for. Similar circumstances would justify publishing a suspect's previous criminal record, especially if such knowledge seems necessary to warn the public. Suppose further that the suspect has just escaped from a maximum-security prison and that on his last escape he raped and killed two teenage girls.

The reason we have police is to help maintain or promote the *community*. Therefore, any action on the part of the press which can definitely be said to jeopardize the efforts of the police in maintaining the order necessary for the existence of the community is to be ethically deplored. If, however, there is just cause for scepticism that reporting on such matters will indeed affect the outcome of the ongoing investigation, then, of course, the reporter is free to follow conscience.

Of course there are going to be times when it is to the advantage of the community to possess certain information, and if the trade-off in favored treatment to an official of the government for this information is nothing more than occasional acknowledgment in the press of a willingness to serve the public, it is hard to find fault or culpability. It is not impossible to do so, however. In fact, Williams's contentions regarding integrity can be very nicely applied to this issue. A reporter who shows a willingness to compromise in this kind of situation is apt to show a similar willingness in less harmless contexts. Nothing is of greater value to the community than citizens of firm and uncompromising character who as a matter of principle refuse to engage in such practices no matter how harmless the *consequences* appear to be.

The only time it is proper for a reporter to receive free trips and other economic benefits is when they make it possible to provide coverage of some event or phenomenon which could not be covered otherwise. To accept anything beyond expenses is, although commonly practiced, quite unconscionable. Favoritism of the worst sort is often the upshot of this practice. Clearly, this issue is tied to the one just discussed. The same considerations regarding integrity apply here as well as above.

The issue regarding restraints, whether self- or governmentally imposed, is one of the most interesting issues in journalistic ethics. And although we will not be able to cover it in the detail it warrants, we will try to show how ethical theory can facilitate our understanding of the complexities involved.

The impending-storm case already quoted to establish that lying is sometimes morally correct has application to the present issue. If it is morally proper to lie to the community under certain kinds of circumstances, it is clearly proper to suppress information under the same kinds of circumstances. In fact, lying is a form of suppression. Whenever you lie to someone, you suppress the truth. And sometimes when you suppress something you *mislead*, and so, the end result is the same as when you lie. No doubt it is important to distinguish between lying and suppressing. Nevertheless, one needs to recognize how insidious are some of the uses we make of this distinction. Far too often people hide behind this distinction and claim that while it is true that they failed to mention something, still they did not say anything which was untrue. What is so often the real issue in such cases is not whether or not we have been *lied* to, but whether or not we have been *deceived*. And this gets lost because drawing the distinction in such contexts has the force of a diversionary maneuver. Humans often use language in the same way that the octopus uses his ink.

We now return to the discussion of the relevance of the impending-storm case to the suppression issue. It matters not whether the newsperson on the island imposes the restraint from within or whether some official of the government imposes it from without. The common good demands that the newsperson both suppress certain facts and lie. In short, what the situation demands is that the public be deceived. There are lots of other cases which illustrate the need for restraint and suppression. News organizations have to recognize that they are instruments of the community and as such are responsible for its well being. Actions which in any way jeopardize the community must be avoided.

So far we have only presented grounds in favor of news suppression. We want now to argue against too liberal an interpretation of these grounds. To establish, as Odell's case does, that there are times when morality countenances suppression of the news is not to establish that morality countenances such action in general or for the most part. Quite the contrary. Suppression is a form of deceit and so cannot be accepted as the rule rather than the exception. Deceit in circumstances like those which obtain in the impending-storm case can be sanctioned, even lauded, yet no community (in the sense in which we use the term) could exist which practiced general deceit. Here we can apply what we learned from Kant to show that one could not consistently will both that human beings should for the most part deceive one another and that the community as we know it should continue to exist.

So far we have seen that sometimes there are good reasons in favor of suppressing the news. We have also seen that there is an inconsistency involved in overly generalizing this activity. The question which must now be addressed is, "When if ever is it proper for the government to restrain the press?" We have argued that it is sometimes ethically necessary to suppress the news. We have argued that it is necessary for the press to impose self-restraint whenever such suppression benefits the community and wrong to do so when it jeopardizes the community. We would impose the same guidelines upon government, but with a certain proviso. Only in cases where the media refuses to restrain itself and where the publication of certain information threatens the community should government intervention be allowed. To empower the government to supervise the press is to invite disaster. It is to fertilize the soil for dictatorships. Government intervention can be tolerated only as a last resort.

Another issue we wish to address in this chapter is the objectivity issue. No person in his right mind would disagree with the proposition that objectivity is important for journalism. But is it morally imperative for the press to seek it? We want to claim that in fact it is; that an editor who said he or she was concerned with presenting only one side of the news would be pursuing an unconscionable course; that any newsperson who knowingly slants a story in a specific direction is morally culpable.

Someone will no doubt demur at this point with, "How can you possibly insist that journalists be judged morally culpable if they don't seek objectivity?" They will claim that no person can be objective, and thus, that it is outrageous to demand objectivity of journalists.

If these critics were right in claiming that objectivity is impossible for anyone to attain, then, of course, they would be correct in their demurrer. But they are not right. Objectivity is not impossible. The reason these critics claim what they do is that they confuse what we will refer to as *epistemic* objectivity with what is ordinarily referred to when we demand that someone be simply "objective." What they do is commit what we described in the chapter on logic as a fallacy of *equivocation*.

What the critic has in mind when he talks about objectivity can be inferred from the arguments used to convince us that we cannot be objective. It is argued that we are all products of our particular cultures; that none of us is free from cultural bias; that we all apprehend things differently because we all have our own sensory fields; that when we look at some object or witness some event we tend to see it differently when our perspective changes; that we are prisoners of our particular up-bringings; that the beliefs of our peers, parents, and teachers tend to become our own beliefs.

One can concede all of this and still insist that our journalists be objective. We need only point out that what we call for when we demand that our journalists be objective is not that they do the impossible and transcend their sensory apparatuses and their cultural backgrounds, but only that they strive to be *impartial*. We simply ask our journalists to act from proper motives. We ask them to be altruistic, to have our best interests at heart. We expect them to refuse to act in favor of any particular interest group, political party, or corporation. And we expect this kind of self-restraint from them even when such favoritism personally benefits them or their particular media agency. Society has every right to expect its journalists to act impartially. Journalists who refuse to be objective in this sense are of no worth whatever to society.*

As a final exercise in the application of ethical theory to journalism we would like to concentrate upon a recent media event with obvious ethical dimensions.

In 1981 the *Washington Post* was involved in a scandal featuring one of its reporters. This scandal, which has been referred to as the "Jimmy Story," involved a reporter's lying to the public in order to further her own career. She fabricated a story about a black ghetto child who was supposedly taught how to use drugs in his home. She won a Pulitzer Prize for the story, but had to return it after it was discovered that she had invented the story.

Nearly everyone would agree with the proposition that what this reporter did was wrong. But how would one justify this assessment? Let us consult the theories we have considered in this chapter. The super-naturalist answer would be that what the reporter did was wrong because it breaks one of God's commandments. The Kantian answer would be that it was wrong because the categorical imperative estab-

---

* Please note that in Chapter 8 (Metaphysics) Merrill presents the case that journalistic objectivity is impossible if defined in a certain way. Also a distinction is made in Chapter 8 between the realist and the idealist perspectives on objectivity. For a journalist, in the real world, the operative word in his quest for objectivity is 'desire' — desire to be as objective as possible.

lishes that it is wrong for one to lie for one's own advantage. One cannot, according to Kant, will such a course of action without contradicting oneself. The answer according to egoism is that what the reporter did was wrong because the action had bad consequences for her. Had she been able to bring it off, so that she received the prize and was able to keep it, she would have been right to lie to the public. In retrospect, since we know that the consequences were bad for her, we can see that the egoist's answer would have to be that what she did was wrong.

The act utilitarian's answer likewise depends upon what are the consequences of the reporter's lying to the public. The difference between egoism and act utilitarianism concerns what consequences are considered in appraising the action. If the act is appraised in terms of its effects on the actor, it is appraised along egoistic lines. If it is appraised in terms of its consequences for society, then it is appraised along act-utilitarian lines. The act-utilitarian answer, in the present case, would be harder to determine than the egoistic one because it depends upon how we assess the actual consequences.

If the reporter's lying can be said to have harmed the public because, for example, it caused the public's confidence in the media to erode, then it would be said to be wrong. If, however, her lying can be said to benefit society, because it makes us more critical of what we read and because it focuses attention on what is, in fact, a grim state of affairs, it would be said to be right. The rule-utilitarian answer would be that it is wrong because permitting reporters to lie to the public would in the long run have negative consequences. Eventually we would lose all faith in the media. The existentialist answer would be that lying to the public cannot be said to be objectively wrong. What we consider right or wrong is altogether subjective. The answer of emotivism is similar. Whether we decide that what she did is right or wrong depends upon whether we approve or disapprove of her actions, and the fact that most of us disapprove shows only that we share a common heritage. A situationistic position for the "Jimmy Story" cannot be provided. There is no *one* correct answer according to the situationist's position. Different answers are possible depending upon how one assesses the situation.

The answer according to the theory advocated in the present chapter is that her action is wrong in an objective but not absolutistic sense of the word 'wrong'. It is objectively wrong because by allowing such an action to become a practice any journalist would ultimately contribute to the breakdown of community. So, what is cited as a reason for saying that her action is wrong is pretty much the same on this account as it is on the rule-utilitarian account. Both theories are concerned with the consequences that the action has upon society. The difference is that the utilitarian theory does not recognize and allow for adjustment along the lines suggested by the principle of justice. The account advocated in the present chapter *does* recognize that there will be cases, different from the "Jimmy Story," which will involve assessment in terms of equal and just distribution of benefits. Harmonious existence in a community is possible only where such distribution is possible.

Which among these various positions is the right one to take regarding the "Jimmy Story" is a question we will leave to the reader. Review the criticisms which have been previously advanced against the various ethical theories considered here, and then attempt to resolve the issue for yourself. If you have mastered the subject matter of this chapter, you should at least appreciate the difficulty involved in justifying what most of us believe, namely, that the reporter who wrote the "Jimmy Story" acted unethically.

Suggested Reading

Bok, Sissela. *Lying: Moral Choice in Public and Private Life*. New York: Random House, 1978.

Brandt, R.B., ed. *Value and Obligation*. New York: Harcourt Brace Jovanovich, 1961.

Christians, Clifford G., and Covert, Catherine. *Teaching Ethics in Journalism Education*. New York: Hastings Center, 1980.

Ewing, A.C. *Ethics*. New York: Free Press, 1965.

Fletcher, Joseph. *Situation Ethics: The New Morality*. Philadelphia: Westminister Press, 1966.

Frankena, William. *Ethics*. Englewood Cliffs, N.J.: Prentice-Hall, 1973.

Girvetz, H.K., ed. *Contemporary Moral Issues*. Belmont, Calif.: Wadsworth, 1968.

Halselden, Kyle. *Morality and the Mass Media*. Nashville, Tenn.: Broadman Press, 1968.

Hazlitt, Henry. *The Foundations of Morality*. Los Angeles: Nash, 1972.

Hulteng, John L. *The Messenger's Motives: Ethical Problems of the News Media*. Englewood Cliffs, N.J.: Prentice-Hall, 1976.

Johannesen, Richard L. *Ethics in Human Communication*. Prospect Heights, Ill.: Waveland Press, 1981.

Merrill, John C., and Barney, Ralph D., eds. *Ethics and the Press: Readings in Mass Media Morality*. New York: Hastings House, 1975.

Merrill, John C. *The Imperative of Freedom*. New York: Hastings House, 1974.

Paton, H.J. *The Categorical Imperative: A Study in Kant's Moral Philosophy*. New York: Harper, 1967.

Phelan, John M. *Disenchantment: Meaning and Morality in the Media*. New York: Hastings House, 1980.

Rivers, William L., Schramm, Wilbur, and Christians, Clifford. *Responsibility in Mass Communication.* New York: Harper & Row, 1980.

Rubin, Bernard (ed.). *Questioning Media Ethics*: New York: Praeger, 1978.

Thayer, Lee, ed. *Ethics, Morality and the Media.* New York: Hastings House, 1980.

Taylor, Paul W. *Problems of Moral Philosophy: An Introduction to Ethics.* Belmont, Calif.: Wadsworth, 1978.

IMPLICATIONS

Now that Odell has taken us through the philosophical pathways of logic, semantics, epistemology, and morality, let us turn our attention — with an especial emphasis on journalistic concerns — to axiology, rhetoric, political theory, and metaphysics. The following pages will be more journalistic in tone than those of Part I.

Not only will Part II be more journalistic in tone and style, but it will deal less with philosophical basics and more with the implications of philosophical problems for journalism. We hope that Part I has given the reader an introduction to many of the philosophical fundamentals and has familiarized him with some of the philosopher's special terminology. Now the reader is ready to deal with philosophical ramifications of journalism more directly. It is with this in mind that we discuss in Part II such topics as journalistic awards (as related to value) and media evaluation (as related to quality). In addition, on the following pages the reader will find such subjects as journalism education and journalistic authenticity discussed.

In the chapter on rhetoric, the whole area of journalistic persuasion is taken up. Legitimate and illegitimate persuasion are discussed and various propaganda devices presented. To serve as examples of rhetoric, an ethical code and some selections from an international journalistic organization headquartered in Czechoslovakia are discussed.

Chapter 7, dealing with journalism and politics, presents and discusses various theories or concepts of the press and provides some philosophical commentary on them.

In the final chapter on metaphysics — using the term in a rather loose fashion to be sure — many questions are raised and discussed about the raison d'être of journalism. Here at the very end of the book, the reader is brought face to face with the basic rationale for journalism and left to contemplate many puzzling questions. The matter of truth in journalism, as well as its corollary, objectivity, is brought up — this time from a journalistic perspective rather than from a purely philosophical one — and discussed.

John C. Merrill

CHAPTER 5

Axiology: Journalism and Values

When we get into the area of journalistic axiology, we find ourselves entering a precarious terrain of philosophical speculation where eerie mists of judgment obscure our clear vision. Although the subject of value in journalism is plagued with subjective pitfalls which give rise to argument, there is no reason why journalists and journalism students should not make systematic and serious journeys into its winding byways. Basic questions should be asked and contemplated: What is the value of value in journalism? Are some media more valuable (or qualitative) than others? What is the importance of context in a consideration of value? What are the rewards in journalism for value?

And then there are axiological concerns related to the journalists as individuals. How do they value themselves? What is the source of this valuation? How does education affect journalistic value? Is the concept of "professionalism" valuable to the journalist? How does a journalist's political ideology relate to value? And, finally on the personal level, how is the existential concept of authenticity related to value? We shall not try to answer all such questions here, but these and many others are worthy of consideration by the conscientious journalist.

Most journalists are concerned with value in their daily work, whether or not they give much thought to it. They want to do a "good" job — or most of them say they do — in whatever task they are engaged. Even a journalist working for a publication of questionable purpose and quality desires to do a good job, that is, fulfill the expectations — or exceed them — of the publication, even if these expectations are socially not admirable, e.g., making sex and crime entertaining and alluring to the reader.

Even if I write a lurid, sensational, and possible distorted headline, I want to make it a good one, that is, effective in accomplishing the overall purpose of the publication. So, in effect, I will have proved to be valuable to my publication although I have written what most critics might find offensive. So taste inevitably mixes with value in journalism, and the matter of relativity or context further complicates any discussion of journalistic axiology. I, as a journalist, may write a "valuable" head-line for my particular newspaper, all the while recognizing the fact that it is in poor taste — or that, under different circumstances, I would not choose to write such a headline.

Such a stance evidences a pragmatic approach to axiology and pushes into a corner any concern with authentic and idealistic axiology. What I am saying, if I have this pragmatic orientation, is that I am doing what the special circumstances call for even though I do not feel comfortable with it. This is journalistic "adjustment" and it is a quite common stance in modern journalism; in fact, "adaptiveness" is often held up as a great value in itself.

This practical or pragmatic stance, of course, indicates an abdication of personal journalistic authenticity. Such authenticity has been set aside for utilitarian or pragmatic reasons, and individual journalists easily rationalize this by saying, in effect, that they can, or should, do a good job even in a position that has no real personal or social value. Or, if they are more astute in their rationalization, they may somehow think of some pragmatic reasons why the job (e.g., writing for a sex-crime magazine) does, in fact, have some real social value. Such rationalization usually is very flimsy, taking this typical form: "Many people in our society, for psychological or other reasons, actually *need* to have sex ex-ploited for them in journalism. It gives them pleasure or it fulfills a basic need; therefore, what I am doing is valuable." Of course, when a jour-nalist uses this rationale, it is usually justified by what the journalism sup-posedly (no real evidence present) does for someone else. Seldom, if ever, is it justified by what this kind of journalism does for the journalist.

What the journalist is doing in such a case is separating (or trying to separate) himself from value; he is attaching value to his journalism as he perceives its impact on his audience or on society — or more specifical-ly, on some segment of society. But the authentic journalist, one who values his own personhood and integrity, cannot convincingly find value outside his own values. And the case can be made that the journalist who justifies his journalism simply on the grounds of fulfilling a need or desire of the public or some aspect of it is little more than a journalistic hack, giving people what they want (or what he thinks they want, or what will sell) instead of giving them what he sincerely and honestly thinks is a good story (one that would be of real value to them). In other words, he is settling for something less than authentic and long-term value in journalism, and is retreating into the pragmatic mire of the mar-ket mentality instead of progressing into the honest territory of existential value.

The journalist works under the persistent pressures which often cause him to adapt to the social good (or supposed social good) and to institutional expediency. Being a member of a group and accepting institutional responsibility tends to suppress conscience and distort valuative concerns. It is not easy for the institutional journalist to retain his authenticity in the field of axiology. It is too easy simply to accept the values of the employer and give away existential responsibility.

Journalists, at least those concerned with lasting value, are going to have to recognize the great importance of their own values, not only when they are interpreting the news, but also when they are deciding what it is and how they will play it. If, and when, this happens, we will witness a real revolution in journalism, for values are at the very foundation of journalism. As values change, journalism changes.

Few would deny that a concern for value is important for the journalist, and, as we have seen, value is closely tied to personal authenticity. As we become less authentic, we run the risk of losing any meaningful understanding of value and of becoming slaves to expediency and conformity, taking on the valuative colors of the situations in which we find ourselves. What difference, we may ask ourselves, does it really make if we are writing for the *National Enquirer* or for the *New York Times*? And why is not my pornographic (or even trite and pedestrian) publication as valuable as the *Wall Street Journal* or *Commentary*?

Such questions — heard extremely often today — show what is happening in the field of journalistic axiology. They indicate the expansion of a new pragmatism and the advent of a new relativism that is threatening to obliterate value or to make a discussion of the subject all but meaningless. As an intellectual climate develops where everything is equally valuable and equally good — a climate where there is really no hierarchy of values or quality, and egalitarianism has spread its deadly roots even into axiology — we are faced with the prospect that journalism will be practiced in an axiological vacuum. And, of course, if this ever really happens, then we are faced with perhaps an even more profound prospect: the literal death of journalism itself, at least in its serious news/commentary/interpretive core aspects. But enough now of this introductory philosophizing about axiology. Let us turn to more mundane levels of discussion.

Media Quality and Evaluation

Few people would deny that quality in journalism is closely related to value. If qualitative elements did not presuppose value, then there would really be no sense in a journalist's trying for quality — trying to add the dimension of excellence. Surely quality must imply (or signify) value *of some type to someone*. The problem (or one of the problems) is: How do we recognize quality and how do we explain any value it might have?

This is a big question. It is one which journalists (as well as artists, musicians, cooks) have been wrestling with for centuries.

One complicating factor in all this is that value may be quite personal — of a sensitive, emotional, or aesthetic nature — and not really open to measurement on a utilitarian scale. A poorly laid out newspaper page may communicate the same information (other things being equal) as a well laid out page; since it communicates, someone might say that it is as valuable as the more attractive page. But this person would be overlooking aesthetics completely and would be judging on purely pragmatic or utility-inspired reasons.

What makes one journalistic medium have quality and another one not? Let us consider a few things which must be considered in arriving at an answer to such a question:

1. Excellence of technique — aesthetics.
2. Policy built on worth, purpose, or concept.
3. Degree to which the worthy purpose is achieved.
4. Excellence of communicative skills.
5. Aesthetic pleasure — of journalist *and* audience.
6. Reputation among experts in the field.
7. Use as model or example by others in the field.
8. Availability in libraries or in journalism schools.

Other indicators of quality could be mentioned, but these eight are enough to indicate that there are ways of ascertaining quality or value and of establishing the fact that some journalism is better than others. Journalistic contests with their hierarchy of awards and prizes attempt to establish quality and value. But are they successful?

Journalistic Awards

Journalists and their organizations, like most others connected with creative and artistic pursuits, feel impelled to reward outstanding practitioners. Awards proliferate in journalism and its kindred fields, such as publishing and advertising. Who has made the most valuable, the most notable, contributions this year? Innumerable banquets and conferences spawn growing numbers of plaques, certificates, medals, and the like for various contributions. Presumably the donors feel that the winners of such awards have done something of special value.

The growth of prizes and awards probably reflects the increasing desire of journalists to become members of a profession, to publicize their activities, and to improve their image with the public. If we tell the public, in essence, that we (or some of us) are doing things that are noteworthy and valuable, then the public will begin to think that we really are. Award-giving is a form of image-building and a way by which journalists can justify to themselves and to others that they are in a worthwhile and valuable business.

All journalists and journalism educators who have been judges for such contests recognize that they are, by and large, farces. Judging is often done haphazardly, always superficially and hastily, and often without a set of meaningful criteria; often the care with which the entries are presented and packaged affects the judges more than the substance of the entries does, and often the name of the newspaper or magazine from which the entry comes impresses the judges more than does the entry itself.

In many of these contests the judges race through the entries, giving very little serious thought to them. Quite often decisions are made on nonqualitative reasons — for instance, on the basis of political factors. We have seen cases where the jury, actually ignoring quality or value, have given top awards to persons so as to distribute the winners around the state or nation or to give some kind of equity to racial or other demographic groups. On occasion juries, finding that four of the five top winners have been from the same newspaper, have discarded two or three of these and have substituted less valuable contributions from other newspapers. Those who have done much judging of such contests could — and do — tell interesting and often startling stories about the mechanics of award-giving.

All of this is not to say that there are no conscientious judges, or that all journalistic contests are farces. Certainly, however, when one looks around the country and the world and sees the thousands of contests being conducted and the myriad of awards being given, one begins to wonder if the main purpose of the contests is not to publicize certain groups and organizations and to provide still another reason for bringing people together to enhance the image of donors and sponsoring organizations.

It would be enlightening (and surprising) if there were some way to make public the deliberations of award juries in journalism. Let the public — and those who entered the contest — see what goes on at the meetings of the award committees and juries. If this were done, there would be a revolution in such matters. Award committees would have to be more logical, more precise, less political, less arbitrary, and certainly they would have to do their homework more carefully and judge their entries against a common set of meaningful criteria. But, then, journalists who cry loudly about open meetings in government might not themselves be so willing to provide such openness for their own meetings.

What is particularly bad about most journalistic contests is that the jurors are not recognized experts themselves in the areas they are judging. Often the same newspaper-contest judge will make decisions on news stories, editorials, features, and even photography and page makeup. How can this person be qualified to judge all of these areas? Or, for that matter, to judge any one of them? This matter of qualified judges is really at the root of the troubles with the journalistic contests. Little or no thought or attention is given to the qualifications of the judges. People who will simply take the time to do it are often asked to judge. What are their special qualifications for judging editorials, for example? Nobody seems to want to know. Most judges will admit that they have no special qualifications, nor do they have any well thought out criteria or standards against which to judge the entries. They are simply asked to judge, and are left to their own whims, feelings, and values in making their decisions. No wonder there are so many journalists who produce significant journalism who do not take the time and effort to enter contests.

The journalists and the journalistic organizations that sponsor such contests should turn their attention to some basic questions. A few they might ask themselves are:

What is the value (purpose) of this particular contest?

Do we have specific and meaningful criteria for judging in every area of the contest?

Do we have competent judges? How do we define competency for judges? Should not the names and qualifications of judges be made public along with the contest winners? Is it not really as difficult, or more difficult, to pick good judges as it is to pick contest winners?

Is it important that the contestant or medium not be known to the judges?

Most persons who have anything to do with such contests obviously believe that there are distinctions in quality. They want to hold up those who have made the most valuable contributions in certain areas. There is really nothing wrong with this; it is an admirable enterprise — if it is taken seriously and if awards are given by competent judges and for the right reasons. At present there is considerable doubt among journalists (and others) that awards are very meaningful, that judges are very competent, and that evaluative criteria (if used at all) are salient. People who conduct such contests must face this growing skepticism — even cynicism — in the field of journalistic contests.

Media Evaluation

Another, but related field, is that of media evaluation. Media critics and evaluators abound. It seems that everyone wants to be a judge, a critic, an appraiser, an evaluator of the journalistic media. "The *New York Times* is a good newspaper," we hear quite often. "*Le Monde* is a far better newspaper than *France-Soir*," would be an expected comment in France. Such statements as this are common in journalism texts: "*Asahi* is by far the best daily newspaper in Japan." And we hear such judgments as the following everyday: "You can believe the *Wall Street Journal*" or "the *Nation* gives far better political analysis than does the *National Review*" or "You should watch CBS for your news, not NBC."

Most of these appraisers or evaluators are quite haphazard in their method. In fact, most do not have a method — unless you would call *uneducated whim* a method. Lack of a systematic method, an absence of meaningful criteria of evaluation: this is the main problem with most media evaluation.

Why, we might ask, is the *New York Times* a good newspaper? Or why is it (if it is) a better newspaper than the *Washington Post*? Such questions force the evaluator to refer to criteria, to be specific, to define "quality" or "value" — to differentiate intelligently among the "poor," the "better," and the "best."

The world is full of media evaluators and critics — speaking in pulpits, classrooms, streets, clubs, political campaigns, conventions of all kinds, in small select seminars, in legislatures, and at mass rallies. Evaluations are forthcoming from the Eric Severeids of national television and the John Does, chatting at the corner bar or grocery. Nonmedia people, especially since the mid-1970s, are articulating their opinions about the mass media more often, more loudly, and more assuredly.

It has really been a short step from the critical appraisal of the press by the controversial Hutchins Commission* in the 1940s to the many sorties into the area of media criticism triggered by the equally controversial blasts by Spiro Agnew in the late 1960s and early 1970s. The decade of the 1980s is being called the Decade of the Mass Media; it must, as well, be called the Decade of Media Criticism, for the media are being looked at and appraised by all sorts of people ever more frequently.

---

* The formal name of the self-appointed and self-styled commission which studied the American press in the 1940s was the Commission on Freedom of the Press; its chairman was Robert M. Hutchins, then Chancellor of the University of Chicago. A report of the Commission's findings was published in *A Free and Responsible Press* (Chicago: University of Chicago Press, 1947). See especially Chapter 2, "The Requirements," pp. 20–29.

A good newspaper to the Hutchins commissioners would be one that gave "full access to the day's intelligence," that presented and clarified "the goals and values of the society," that presented a "truthful, comprehensive, and intelligent account of the day's events in a context which gives them meaning," that provided a "forum for the exchange of comment and criticism," and that gave a "representative picture of the constituent groups in the society." Little wonder, judging by these fuzzy and largely unachievable standards, the Hutchins Commission found American newspapers basically irresponsible — certainly not what the Commission thought of as "socially responsible."

The typical criticism today is not so exalted and intellectual as that of the Hutchins group. It is more direct, less monumental, and perhaps more meaningful. For instance, we hear that most media are careless with basics — spelling, punctuation, pronunciation and enunciation, names, quotations, statistics. Almost all of us who have ever read a newspaper about a speech we made or a program in which we participated, or about some event at which we were present, know full well the validity of this criticism.

When we take a close look at almost any individual newspaper, we note that it is superficial, not only in its selection of stories and pictures, but in the way it handles each separate story. Glancing down the columns, we notice the haphazard fashion in which unrelated stories and pictures are presented, and also the unsynthesized mishmash of bits and pieces of news and views. And we see, also, that close to two-thirds of the total space is taken up by advertising scattered meaninglessly throughout the pages.

Now, to a basic question: Who should evaluate the press or pass judgment on the press? The answer to this question in the context of the American political and social system, of course, is that anyone and everyone should criticize the press. This is the American way. But, going a step further, this is not to say that everyone is equally well qualified to evaluate or criticize a newspaper or other mass medium. This seems to be a valid statement in spite of the commonly held beliefs that mass communication is everybody's business and is too pervasive and important to be left completely to the rather small group of media people who prepare and disseminate the messages.

But we dare not try to tell surgeons what is good surgical technique, nor do we presume to inject our uneducated opinions into other specialized areas where we grant expertise to the specialists. Journalism may not be a specialty to the degree that medicine is, but there are experts in journalism who are more knowledgeable about aspects of journalism than are nonjournalists. Politics may be too important to be left to politicians (whatever that may mean), but certainly journalism is too important to be left to non-journalists. Although for a number of reasons journalism is not a profession, the most prominent and serious of its practitioners agree pretty well on many of the fundamental aspects of what might be considered good journalism. For example, graphics people and page designers can agree rather closely as to what is good typography and page layout. Leading photographers can at least agree on what is *not* good photography — and this in spite of the possibility that many viewers of the photographs might like them. And journalists who take writing seriously and have concentrated on style and effectiveness generally agree as to what is good writing and what is not.

In other words, serious practitioners in the mass media do have a pretty good idea of what is quality and what is not. They do recognize a hierarchy of value; they do have standards. In spite of the high degree of subjectivity in journalism — as compared to medicine, for example — there does remain a rather large area where there are standards of quality. All is *not* relative in journalism. One person's opinion is *not* just as good as another's; some media people (and journalism educators) *are* more knowledgeable and effective than others. Some stories *are* better written than others. Some TV commercials *are* more creative, artistic, and effective than others. Some radio voices *are* superior to others, and some foreign correspondents *are* more accurate and perceptive than others. Some headline writers *are* more skillful than others, and some photographers *are* more technically proficient and imaginative than others.

Let us look briefly at the matter of evaluation, using *newspaper* evaluation as an example. First, there is the matter of context. Many persons would say that the context is all important. How can you possibly say that the *New York Times* is a better newspaper than, say, the *Columbia Missourian*? The *Missourian* in its context, Columbia, Mo., may be just as good as the *Times* in its context: New York City, the country, and the world. It is doubtful that very many serious students of newspapers would accept this thesis, but the context advocates do have a certain point, and such a position appeals to large numbers of persons who see themselves as tolerant, progressive, and open-minded. The contextualists, if they took their case very far, would find themselves in the position of not being able to compare any mass medium with another as to value or quality; they would logically have to assert that every single medium is ultimately *in its own context* and cannot, therefore, be compared to any other medium.

Context is, of course, important when evaluating media and comparing one to another. No intelligent critic, for instance, would fault Virginia's *Alexandria Gazette* for having no foreign correspondents and being composed of few pages when compared to the *Washington Post's* bulky editions and rather extensive international coverage. No sensible critic would compare a TV network's thirty-minute newscast with the news presentation of the *Miami Herald* or *Time* magazine. Persons who would say that the *National Geographic* was a better magazine than *Esquire* could not be taken very seriously because they, too, would not be taking the context of *kind* into consideration. So, context certainly is important for anyone evaluating the media. But the problem comes when critics carry this matter of context too far — when they become like the person who grew weeds around the house instead of roses because "in their own context" they were just as good.

When one keeps the matter of context in mind and is reasonable in its application, one has a good start as a media evaluator. There is a hierarchy of value or worth, or of quality, in the mass media. Too long have media people — and others — evaded this issue. Too long have they timidly gone along acting as if all newspapers were equally good because *somebody* liked them and they fulfilled *some* purpose. Let us consider some of the reasonable criteria that can be used to evaluate the mass media. And let us deal here with noncontextual evaluative criteria, in this case for *newspapers*. These may be used for any newspaper, regardless of its type of context, regardless of whether it is daily or weekly, communist or capitalist, large or small, urban or rural, general or specialized.* The critic or evaluator would not use only one of these criteria but would try to make use of as many of them as possible in passing judgment.

First, there are at least eight *internal* (using the newspaper itself) criteria that the evaluator would find useful in appraisal:

1. Good typography and makeup techniques. In every country there are typographic and design specialists; these are the experts who, in a sense, define what is *good* practice in this field. They can define good typography and makeup practices and should be considered more important than others in evaluation.

2. Editing and proofreading care. Regardless of where the newspaper is published or how large it might be, a common criterion of evaluation is the care with which it is edited and proofread. Sloppy editing shows up in any language, in any size paper, in any nation, and is considered undesirable.

3. Correct spelling, punctuation, grammar. Although permissiveness has been growing in this area, there are still basic and generally standardized rules for spelling, punctuation, and grammar that educated people in any country understand and respect.

4. Picture reproduction and printing excellence. Some newspapers have clearer picture reproduction than others. Likewise, the general printing quality is better on some papers than on others. Care in

---

* These criteria are adapted from those presented in John C. Merrill and Ralph Lowenstein, *Media, Messages, and Men* (New York: Longman, 1979).

printing is a good criterion to use in evaluation, regardless of what newspaper you are talking about.

5. Balance in editorial/news material. When you are considering general newspapers, this is a useful criterion for evaluation. *Balance* is almost a basic assumption for a good newspaper. The paper will not be overloaded with any one type of subject matter — that is, unless you are dealing with a specialized newspaper.
6. Concern with staff quality. An evaluator of a newspaper, observing and interviewing, can learn a lot about the paper's concern with having a good staff — well educated, skilled, with high morals.
7. Concern with editorial policy. The evaluator could check to see how much emphasis is given to editorial policy. Does the paper seem to have one? Do the staff members know what it is? How well does the paper achieve this policy or reach its goals?
8. Concern with self-evaluation and outside criticism. The assumption here is that a good newspaper will evaluate its philosophy and practices regularly and that it will welcome criticism; the better the paper, the more concerned it is with its quality.

Now, let us turn quickly from the *internal*, or newspaper-related, common evaluative criteria to five others that might be called *external*, or audience-related. These five can be used for checking the reputation or image of the newspaper among readers:

1. Frequency of quotation and allusion.
2. Frequency of library subscription.
3. Reputation among journalists/historians.
4. Reputation among politicians, government officials, and diplomats.
5. Reputation in academic circles.

In addition to the thirteen common evaluative criteria mentioned above, we could add certain others, especially when we are considering newspapers within a libertarian context. Such criteria as these are important: concern for people's right to know; concern for public service; pluralism in news and views; resistance to outside pressures; separation of news and views; headline accuracy; reliance on own staffers; economic stability; ability to bring about desired changes in society; general social utility; and factualness or reliability or accuracy of reportage (credibility with audience).

For newspapers in authoritarian or controlled societies, such special criteria as the following might be added to the eight common ones mentioned earlier: understanding of, and achieving of, purpose or goal; homogeneity of staff; self-criticism and evaluation; dedication to staff improvement; general media system cooperation; elimination of unstabilizing elements; staff dedication and dependability; ability to bring about desired changes in society; and general social utility.

Journalism: A Profession?

Journalism is not a profession. Many journalism students, and many journalists, are horrified to hear that. Being a part of a profession means so much to them that even considering that, as journalists, they are not part of a profession is almost treasonable. Not only is journalism not a profession, but there are many of us who have been saying for years* that we who live in libertarian societies should not *want* journalism to be a profession.

Journalism lacks the first essential of a profession: rules for admission. As Thomas Griffith says in his sprightly book, *How True: A Skeptic's Guide to Believing the News,* even hairdressers have rules for admission to their line of work. Journalism simply does not have any minimum entrance requirements. Anyone can practice journalism; and, of course, this is quite consistent with the theory of the open society and the concept of the value of pluralism in a journalistic system. Journalism in a libertarian society (e.g., the United States) has no licensing or certification mechanisms, signs of a profession.

Journalism has no exclusive body of knowledge. It is an eclectic field, a borrower from many disciplines. Journalism has no mechanism for getting rid of unqualified or unethical practicioners; it has no way that someone can be "de-pressed" from journalism as lawyers can be disbarred from law. Journalism has no elite body or inner circle that reigns over the field; in fact, it does not even have an outer circle of exclusive workers (like the American Bar Association or the American Medical Association) for an elite guide.

No generally accepted code of ethics can be found in journalism. There are many codes scattered here and there among branches and associations of journalism, but none of them is really binding, even on their own members. And some of the codes one would expect to be meaningful, such as the one set forth by Sigma Delta Chi/the Society of Professional Journalists, is about as meaningless and illogical as any ethical code could be. However, it is rather typical of all journalistic codes. (See Chapter 6 below for a critique of the SDX/SPJ code of ethics.)

People enter and leave the field of journalism at will. There is no real roster or list of journalists. I can crank up my mimeograph machine and

---

* See J.C. Merrill, *The Imperative of Freedom: A Philosophy of Journalistic Autonomy* (New York: Hastings House, 1974), Chapter 6, "Toward Professionalism."

turn out my little newssheet, and I am a journalist. The editor of the *New York Times* and the student editor of the Podunk High School *Tiger Rag* are equally journalists, and are equally protected by the First Amendment of the U.S. Constitution. Now, many journalists working for the big and established media recoil from thinking about this; they like to consider themselves professionals and certain others as something else. But all journalists in the United States are "something else"; they are certainly not members of a profession.

The value of journalism would be enhanced if journalism were a profession: this is what many persons believe. If journalism were a profession, then it would be more responsible, more efficient, more skillful, more careful, more accurate, and on and on. And certainly, they say, journalism would command more respect, and probably its practitioners would be better paid. So the trend toward professionalism continues. More and more journalists come from journalism schools, various organizations of journalists are writing their own ethical codes, and there are even voices here and there proposing that journalists in the United States be licensed, as is the case in many countries. All of this is supposed to make journalism more responsible and better accepted by society — and, of course, to give journalism more dignity and status than it has as simply a craft or vocation.

Let us present some caveats. In an open society such as is found in the United States the tradition of open journalism is very strong and is compatible with the spirit of the First Amendment and with the concept of pluralism. Journalism as a profession would shrink this pluralism, would cause a restrictive and elite corps of journalists to evolve, and would tend to squeeze the unorthodox or journalistic eccentrics out. Also, professionalizing journalism would cause journalists to think more about themselves and their vested interests than about the public and their responsibilities to provide this public with a variety of information and perspectives. In short, journalism as a profession would lead to press conformity and would not be compatible with tradition, the Constitution, or the basic philosophy of libertarianism.

This is not to say that journalism will not become a true profession one day. Through increased emphasis on codes of ethics, through peer pressure, press councils, entrance requirements checked by standard examinations, and more rigorous demand for professional journalism education, journalism very well may reach professional status. What is contended here is that this would be undesirable. What keeps American journalism vigorous and diversified (and, to some, irresponsible) is the very fact that it is not a profession. William Barrett, reflecting the existentialist view of professions in *Irrational Man*, states our case very well in these words:

The price one pays for having a profession is a *déformation professionelle*, as the French put it — a professional deformation. Doctors and engineers tend to see things from the viewpoint of their own specialty, and usually a very marked blind spot to whatever falls outside this particular province. The more specialized a vision the sharper its focus; but also the more nearly total the blind spot toward all things that lie on the periphery of this focus.

And Ayn Rand, although not in sympathy with existentialism generally, reflects Barrett's opinion about the dangers of professionalism. Here is part of what she says in *The New Left: The Anti-Industrial Revolution*:

> If there is any one way to confess one's own mediocrity, it is the willingness to place one's work in the absolute power of a group, particularly a group of one's *professional colleagues*. Of any form of tyranny, this is the worst; it is directed against a single human attribute: the mind — and against a single enemy: the innovator. The innovator, by definition, is the man who challenges the established practices of his profession. To grant a professional monopoly to any group, is to sacrifice human ability and abolish progress; to advocate such a monopoly, is to confess that one has nothing to sacrifice.

These are strong and insightful words. They warn those who would push for professionalization in journalism to recognize these dangers and expend their energies in trying to remedy many faults of journalism, but not by making all journalists march to the same drummer. And this can be done by paying more attention to the whole area of axiology, where values generally are enthroned. What is needed is a will to have more vigorous, vital, and pluralistic journalism.

Education for Journalism

Closely related to professionalism and perhaps stemming, albeit slowly and quietly, from the journalist's desire for a kind of exclusivity or eliteness, is education for journalism. Like a profession itself, journalism education narrows the focus and restricts the options and possibilities that lie beyond its values and concerns. Such a narrowing focus in the field of education, if such is really the case, is a dangerous trend in journalism. Many journalists recognize such a danger and many others see journalism education as a positive development and a healthy aid to the achievement of true professionalization.

As we said in the preceding section, any trend toward homogeneity that tends to exclude eccentric persons or elements from journalism, is contrary to a free and open society. Certainly the growing concern with journalism education can be looked upon as such a trend. Any person familiar with journalism education realizes that it has a nationwide effect on young would-be journalists, casting them increasingly into similar molds of thought and action. And this is the case in spite of valiant efforts on the part of individualistic students — and, occasionally, faculty members. University procedures, rules, and regulations — in hiring, promotions, etc. — regarding journalism faculty members force the teaching staff into ever greater conformity. It is little wonder, then, that students coming through the mills of academic journalism education evidence similar values, perspectives, and general orientations. Sacred cows too often find pleasant grazing spaces in journalism education, where they are seldom disturbed or replaced.

Strong defenders of journalism education respond that such is not really the case, that journalism students have ample chance to receive a diversified education, that faculty members are quite different in their concepts and biases, and that there really is no attempt to mass-produce any kind of stereotyped product. However, most will admit the pressures are upon the journalism schools and departments to hire certain kinds of faculty members and that rather imposing obstacles in the form of specific requirements, core courses, percentages of journalism courses versus other courses, and the like, are placed before the student seeking a journalism degree.

Journalism education defenders say that their "ever more rigorous requirements" are good for the student and for the "profession," and that they serve as a kind of natural screening process whereby "unsuited" (unsuitable?) students are eliminated early. An ever tightening and more rigorous journalism education, they say, is what is needed for a more professional journalism. Respect, dignity, and an improved status for journalists and for the profession, they say, will result from a more standardized and disciplined education.

Such words as these are often heard from journalism educators: "What we need is for *all* programs granting journalism degrees to be more or less the same substance, scope, and quality. All journalism students should be exposed to basically the same educational experience so that prospective employers can make some valid assumptions about the qualifications of those they are planning to hire." From such statements and beliefs as this, it is little wonder that accreditation of journalism programs is taking on increasing importance.

Accreditation of journalism programs is but another — and probably the most important — way so far to regiment and police journalism education. Surely it is possible for journalism to be taught and degrees given in nonaccredited departments and schools, but there is a stigma attached to such educational units, and the students who are part of them (as well as the professors) are generally looked upon as second-class citizens by their accredited colleagues elsewhere. And this in spite of the fact that many nonaccredited journalism programs are more flexible, more imaginative, more responsive to the needs of their communities and regions, and more intellectually rigorous than are the accredited ones.

Editors and publishers, broadcast news directors, and advertising and public relations executives are hiring more and more of their new staffers every year from "professional" (accredited?) schools and departments of journalism. It gets more difficult every year, happily attest the journalism educators, for the major in philosophy or history or English to get a job in the communications media. Journalism is truly on the road to professionalization. Of course, there are still media executives who have their doubts about the journalism student's superiority over others, but their number is becoming smaller, and it is not unreasonable to predict that by the year 2000 virtually all journalists hired will be products of formalized (and presumably accredited) programs in journalism and communications.

In addition to the trend toward accreditation, there are other forces tending to standardize coursework in American universities. Educators and professionals are getting closer together, ideologically and physically, and they are sharing their ideas at the growing number of professional meetings each year. Workshops, conferences, and conventions for journalism educators, often sponsored by professionals, are proliferating. Literature dealing with journalism education is having an impact on the development of a more coherent and unified program of education. The same textbooks are being used in ever more common courses all across the country. Increasingly, journalism professors are reaching common objectives and understandings with their colleagues elsewhere, are moving more frequently from campus to campus, and are thereby spreading their educational philosophies and techniques nationwide. In recent years, this sameness of journalism education and values is even spreading across national borders. All of this strengthens the growth of professional journalism education, which, presumably, will in time weld the practicing journalists into a homogeneous professional society. Emphasis more and more is being placed on professional work in journalism. The mavericks, the eccentrics, the nonconformists are more and more being squeezed from journalism faculties and from the ranks of professional journalism. To many this is a good sign and indicates a maturing of journalism.

Daniel P. Moynihan, for one, has noted that journalism lacks what he calls "an epistemology" shared by all "respected members of the profession"; Moynihan feels that if journalism in the United States is to be a profession (and he wants it to be one), there must be basic knowledge agreed upon by all the "professionals." Presumably, this will only occur in a system where professionalism has progressed to the extent that all journalists will be produced by a common education so that a standard body of knowledge and theory of ethics have been agreed upon.

In spite of what has been said about the trend toward more conformity in journalism education, there are still certain factors which militate against a rapid homogenization. Chief among these factors, perhaps, is a basic dichotomy in the professoriate. Although some try to deemphasize its importance, there is an obvious division in most journalism faculties.

The theoretical, more academic faculty members with their scholarly credentials (often the Ph.D.) are on one side, and on the other are the nonscholarly, the more "professionally oriented," with much practical experience. There are the so-called "Chi-square" professors, the doctoral faculty members who mainly teach graduate-level courses and apply their "scientific" skills to a variety of rather esoteric media studies — or they teach such courses as communication theory and research. And there are the "green eyeshades" teachers, who emphasize techniques such as news reporting, newspaper makeup, headline writing, advertising copy preparation, and the like.

These two basic groups have been rather contentious for years, and this, it is fair to say, has served to keep some degree of pluralism or diversity in journalism education. We probably should say, also, that there is perhaps another group of faculty members — the "hybrids" — who have some journalistic experience, and also an academic eclecticism and liberal arts orientation which places them somewhere in limbo between the "trades" teachers and the "communicologists" (the researching theoreticians). These hybrids teach a variety of courses which are often not wanted by the other two groups — such courses as Comparative Press Systems, Ethics of Journalism, History of American Journalism, Book Reviewing, Journalism Law, and Mass Media and Society.

So it is probably safe to say that these three faculty factions have done much to retain healthy tension and often debate in journalism education and have postponed a certain unanimity and agreement which will accompany a further professionalization of very many students.

Pressures, however, are building up against this tension created by the three groups. Within journalism education itself there is increasing talk about the need to eliminate these disagreements and have more cooperation among the groups. Also, more and more retired (or disgruntled) editors and journalists of one kind or another are entering journalism education to begin a second career. This is causing the balance of faculty to begin to shift from the academically oriented professor to the professionally oriented. As this happens, journalism programs will further reflect the perspectives of the professionals, will emphasize the need for their students' conforming to these, and journalism education will follow more than lead, conform more than experiment. And, of course, this is exactly what most practicing journalists think journalism *should* be doing: preparing students who can step quickly into the real world of journalism, who can do things the way they are expected to do them, with a minimum of boat-rocking. This philosophy represents the conformist school of education, the product school of pragmatic education. It is a popular one with many journalists who are business and organization oriented — especially media executives. But it is one which does not find favor with more individualistic and open journalists with a liberal arts tradition.

Journalism education does increase and encourage conformist journalism, and, in the view of many thoughtful persons, will lead to more responsible journalism. A responsible journalism, however difficult it is to define, obviously is a more socially valuable journalism. Therefore, the proponents of more professional or conformist journalism education have a kind of utilitarian rationale for their position. Conformist it may be, but this is the conformity of responsible journalistic activity and is of great value to society.

Others of us are not quite so sure. Believing also in responsible journalism, we have some problems with equating a growing monolithic *concept* of responsibility with the real thing, and we are still willing to leave each journalist to define responsible journalism and to set standards of behavior.

That journalism and journalism education are indeed becoming more monolithic, more conformist, more professional we have no doubt. But even as we watch the journalists, the journalism professors, and journalism students closing ranks, we are encouraged to see that some students and professors manage to fight the system, to develop and retain their authenticity and autonomy, and to survive the educational treadmill in spite of its deadening aspects. There are still many who, fortunately, recognize the fact that value is not simply made up of activities which help a group of colleagues or the amorphous public, but also lies within the individual journalist as the potency of the will and the recognition of the importance of personal integrity and authenticity.

Value and Authenticity

The journalist who values his authenticity and his integrity has one dedication: to selfhood. Certainly, denying selfhood and depreciating one's own individuality is a strong tendency in collectivistically oriented human nature. Not everyone considers the individual of prime value. But there are many who do, and these enthrone personal authenticity and attempt to oppose the persistent pressures which too often push them toward accepting the social good and institutional or professional expediency.

It is not easy for professional journalists, dedicated as they might be to institutional values, to retain their authenticity. In his book *Media Power*, Robert Stein has written that "journalists are going to have to rely on their own values more than less, not only in interpreting the news but in deciding what it is." Stein is appealing to journalists to value their own opinions to a greater degree and to be more honest and authentic.

Value ultimately resides in the individual journalist. Journalism is for the journalist, not the journalist for journalism. Whatever value journalism may have to a society, it derives from the individual authenticity of practitioners. The journalist is valuable, important, sacred if you like, *qua* person, and should salvage as much of the essence of personhood (authenticity) from the encroaching embrace of modern society as he or she can. This embrace threatens the very self of journalists as well as the selves of those to whom they direct their messages. William Barrett talks of this threat to self in his *Irrational Man: A Study of Existential Philosophy*, which we quoted earlier:

> The last gigantic step in the spread of technologism has been the development of mass art and mass media of communication: the machine no longer fabricates only material products; it also makes minds. . . . If here and there in the lonely crowd (discovered by Kierkegaard long before David Riesman) a face is lit by a human gleam, it quickly goes vacant again in the hypnotized stare at the TV screen.

It is indeed difficult, if not impossible, for journalists to serve two masters: the institutionalized "profession" and themselves. They must either prize one and deemphasize (or even scorn) the other, or find themselves circling slowly in the eddies of passivism and frustration with no values at all to direct them. Institutionalization, indeed, can be looked on as a value for the journalist; but it is a value only in its pragmatic social meaning, not in its psychophilosophical existential meaning.

In concluding this chapter, we must stress the *value of the person*, the authenticity of the individual journalist. The journalist of greatest value may be the one who is something of a Nietzschean superman — a person who has learned to transcend self, to rise to, and beyond, one's highest potential. Such a person would be a "higher man," a law unto himself, a center of virtue, and a powerful, happy center of exuberant self-confidence and self-expression.

A key concept of Nietzsche, consistent with his existentialist orientation, is his passionate belief in the worth of the individual and his view of the hero as the person who does not submit to authority — or at least fights constantly against it. Karl Jaspers reinforces this position; the true person, the valuable person, he writes, is the one who on his own initiative gains possession of the mechanism of his life; and if he does not, says Jaspers, he simply becomes a machine that surrenders to the nonhuman apparatus of institutions.

So, in conclusion, we have seen that in axiological concerns the journalist must constantly seek to determine value and quality in journalism; must be aware of the complexities of qualitative hierarchies in the broad world of journalism; but most of all, must be sensitive and appreciative of the value of his or her own personhood and authenticity — out of which all value flows.

Suggested Reading

Barrett, William. *Irrational Man: A Study of Existential Philosophy*. Garden City, N.Y.: Doubleday, 1958.

Griffith, Thomas, *How True: A Skeptic's Guide to Believing the News*. Boston: Little, Brown and Company, 1974.

Harris, S.J. *The Authentic Person*. Miles, Ill.: Argus Communications, 1972.

Jaspers, Karl. *Man in the Modern Age*. Garden City, N.Y.: Doubleday, 1957.

Merrill, John C. *Existential Journalism*. New York: Hastings House, 1977.

Merrill, John C., and Fisher, Harold. *The World's Great Dailies*. New York: Hastings House, 1980.

Rand, Ayn. *The New Left: The Anti-Industrial Revolution*. New York: New American Library, 1971.

Stein, Robert. *Media Power: Who Is Shaping Your Picture of the World?* Boston: Houghton Mifflin, 1972.

CHAPTER 6

Rhetoric: Journalism and Persuasion

Journalism, through the media of mass communication, is thought of mainly as being in the news business. This is certainly true. But journalism is also in other businesses — entertainment, for one, and persuasion for another. In fact, it might be said with considerable validity that journalism informs, entertains, and persuades. All other functions normally ascribed to journalism can be subsumed under these three. In this chapter we are concerned with the third, the persuasive, function of journalism.

We are bombarded daily by journalistic messages intended to persuade. This rhetorical element in mass communication is very large and very effective. It appears not only in advertising, on editorial pages, and in documentaries of broadcasting, where probably the most overt examples of it can be found, but also in the so-called neutral zones of journalism: the news columns and news programs.

Somebody is constantly trying to persuade us through some journalistic channel; rhetoric sweeps in on us trying to pull us this way or that, to make us accept some position in such areas as religion or politics, or to sell us some commodity or piece of merchandise, or to get us to accept some idea or ideological position.

Arguments, and we use this term for language and pictures intended to persuade anyone of anything, drone constantly in our ears and flash unceasingly before our eyes. Many of these are fallacious, those which *should not* persuade a rational person. Of course many of these fallacies do indeed persuade, but that is another matter.

Some rhetorical fallacies are very crude and obvious; they fool very few people. But many are highly sophisticated, and often lead the wary down paths they do not care to tread. The dealer in fallacies, the rhetorician who is purposely attempting to dupe the audience, is most often known as a *propagandist*. Rhetorical journalism, then, is journalism designed to persuade, and this becomes propagandistic when the persuader makes use of dishonest, biased, or irrational tactics.

It is difficult for the journalist *not* to be a deceptive rhetorician, especially if he (or she) has strong convictions and values which he desires to spread to others. It is a short step, indeed, from rational promotion by open and direct means, fortified with evidence, to the indirect, distorted, and devious verbal tricks of the rhetorical con artist. Often the journalist is advised to keep value judgments out of his writing, implying that if he does this he will automatically eliminate any persuasive content his message might have. But messages without the writer's value judgments can be persuasive, and messages with the writer's value judgments can fail completely to persuade.

Journalistic rhetoric, then, is a mixture of straightforward, logical, and truthful persuasion and the con artistry of the propagandist. The problem faced by journalism's audiences is to determine which is which — to try to separate the wheat of honest journalism from the chaff of propaganda.

This detection of propagandistic rhetoric in the rhetorical winds that sweep in upon us is a task beyond the capabilities of most of us. Linguistic analysis is too mentally tiring, too sophisticated an intellectual exercise for most consumers of journalism to participate in very often. Hard as we may try to avoid it, we will be duped by the propagandistic rhetorician. Emotional and nonrational arguments tend to creep in and do their mischief.

Even if message consumers are sophisticated in propaganda devices and in the detection of logical fallacies, they will still find it difficult not to succumb to the skillful tactics of the persuasive journalist who wants to con by deceptive rhetoric.

In this chapter we want to discuss some principles of persuasion — both honest and dishonest — used by the mass media. This will get us into the area of persuasion in some depth, both as a legitimate and ethical journalistic area of concern, and as a devious and unworthy aspect of journalism.

Briefly we shall summarize the basic principles of rational (or honest) rhetoric, outline the principal fallacies used by propagandistic journalists to persuade, present some of the basic devices of propaganda, and specify particular insidious techniques found commonly in the mass media. And then, in conclusion, we shall analyze a code of ethics as an example of what can be done in rhetorical communication.

Legitimate Persuasion

Contrary to the beliefs of some journalists who represent the fastidious segment of reportorial objectivists, there is nothing wrong with persuasive journalism. The desire to persuade readers, listeners, and viewers is a legitimate objective in journalism. No stigma should be attached to the rhetorician in journalism who attempts to persuade audience members to vote for a particular candidate, support a certain bond issue, rally in favor of anticrime legislation, contribute to hunger relief organizations, or to support any number of projects thought worthwhile by the journalist. Nor is there, per se, anything wrong or dishonest in advertising which attempts to persuade people to accept (or buy) products, institutions, ideas, or candidates.

In other words, persuasion is a legitimate and intrinsic part of journalistic endeavor, and no journalist should apologize for trying to get others to accept his positions. It is *how* the journalist persuades that makes the difference. The journalist can persuade forthrightly, honestly, rationally, ethically; or in ways that distort, dupe, confuse, and generally deviate from the open and forthright paths of the honest rhetorician. The journalist can lay out the evidence, the facts; he can be specific and thorough in presentation; in short, he can let the facts and evidence themselves persuade. Or, and this is oftentimes the easier and quicker of the paths, the journalist can purposely withhold certain facts, play up some of them, distort others, and take liberties with the language so as to make his case more immediately potent and the chance of success in persuasion more assured.

In the first case, the journalist is a legitimate persuader, an ethical rhetorician; in the second, an illegitimate persuader, an unethical or propagandistic rhetorician. Now, of course, the question arises: Why should not the persuader use any means at hand? This question gives rise to kindred questions which may be asked: Why should not the ends justify the means? Why should not the persuader use any techniques which will work to help him achieve the goal?

The implication of such questions is important. We face here the pragmatist in journalism again who desires to make use of any and all tools which will cause his or her journalism to "work." This position has strong appeal, and no doubt this rationale is at the base of much propagandistic journalism today. What is wrong with this position is that it takes advantage of the audience, of unsuspecting and trusting people who receive the messages and accept them at face value. The audience members, in effect, are at the mercy of journalism — an institution that leads them to believe that it can be trusted. When dishonest persuasion is injected into journalism, few among the audience are aware of it. Therefore, they are likely to be persuaded to a position they would not accept if they had an honest and more balanced presentation of the arguments and evidence.

Quite frankly, the main problem with propaganda or dishonest rhetoric in journalism is that it takes advantage of generally trusting people who, in a large sense, have no way to protect themselves against it. Of course, people can protect themselves to some degree by wrapping themselves in a protective cloak of skepticism, or even cynicism. They can stop trusting the mass media, can hold all information suspect, doubt all statistics, screen out all opinion, and isolate themselves in their own little world.

They can determine not to be persuaded. They can, quite intentionally, persuade themselves not to be persuaded by any outside messages. They can retreat into a psychologically protective cave where they are content to survive without making many decisions, even if they are groping about in the dark. Cynicism is, indeed, a kind of defense against journalistic rhetoric; but, too often, going hand in hand with this cynicism is ignorance — ignorance of the complex world around us, part of which is composed of the machinery of persuasion.

Persuasion is hard to run from. It is subtle; it is complex; and it does not exist as a discrete communication form. It does not rush upon us in journalistic isolation; rather, persuasive symbols trigger already existing predilections, and our biases are further strengthened. Oftentimes we are persuaded, not by overtly persuasive techniques, but by neutrally presented information not intended by the journalist to persuade us at all. What is persuasive to one is not persuasive to another. Seeing television pictures of bloody corpses on a battlefield may persuade one person to cry out for peace and another to cry out for revenge. Persuasion, yes, but persuasion in different directions. And then there will be some who will not be persuaded by such television pictures at all.

But even acknowledging that persuasion is complex, and to a large degree relative to the individual being exposed to it, we can speak of legitimate and illegitimate persuasion in journalism. Legitimate persuasion, or nonpropagandistic persuasion, is that which is based on the communicator's motivation to be as honest, accurate, and thorough as possible. In other words, the *legitimacy* of the persuasion is basically determined by the *intent* of the journalist who is trying to persuade. Or, to apply another criterion, it is determined largely by the *means* or *techniques* used by the persuader.

The legitimate rhetorician or persuader uses honest techniques; eschews purposeful distortions, omissions, and exaggerations, and concentrates on giving as much of the substantive and evidential information regarding the subject as is humanly possible. This type of persuader is interested in having the audience agree with him, accept a position or product, but the persuader wants it to come to this acceptance *rationally*. The persuader wants the audience to come to a nonemotional conclusion, to accept the validity of the position because of the evidence and the basic rationality of the position. The legitimate persuader wants the audience members to come to *their own* conclusions — not from being duped or tricked by skillful rhetorical devices, but through an appeal to rationality and evidence.

Now there are those who say that this is really impossible, that *all* persuasion to some degree relies on a stacked deck, and thereby is illegitimate. What these people are saying is that all persuaders are in some sense dishonest and will, if the need arises, use those methods which are expedient in that particular circumstance. Unfortunately, these people are probably right. It is difficult, if not impossible, to visualize persuaders *never* lapsing into dishonest tactics. But we do feel that some persuaders are concerned about these dishonest tactics and consciously *try not* to use them in their rhetorical activities. It is a matter of attitude; it is a matter of basic intent. There are journalists who are, in this sense, basically propagandists or illegitimate persuaders, and there are others who are basically legitimate or honest persuaders.

In conclusion, the legitimate persuader is characterized by these traits:

- a desire to be open, frank, and honest with the audience
- a desire to present evidence for the contentions
- a desire to be as thorough as possible in argument
- a desire to be fair to the other side by not distorting information relating to it
- a desire to deserve and retain the audience's trust
- a desire not to distort, exaggerate, hide, or otherwise indulge in dishonest treatment of information

It is not easy in journalism to be a legitimate persuader, but it can be done. The whole matter of ethics and the basic attitude of the journalist toward journalism and toward the audience coalesce at this point. Persuasive, as well as nonpersuasive, journalism is open to the skulduggery of the dishonest practitioner. Many of our colleagues in advertising have said that the totally honest persuader has a practically impossible job, for he or she has given up the use of most of the potent weapons. Few will deny the validity of this observation. But the fact remains that the journalist who wants to persuade can, with considerable effort and guided by a moral consciousness, steer clear of propagandistic methods which undermine integrity and take advantage of the audience's trust.

Illegitimate Persuasion

In contrast to the rational persuasion just discussed, to the forthright persuasion done by a journalist of principle and integrity, there is the reverse: the propagandistic or illegitimate persuasion practiced by the person who believes that the end justifies the means and resorts to means which are designed to be less than open and honest.

The illegitimate persuader does not want his (or her) audience to have the facts that he, the persuader, has. He intends to persuade through his rhetoric and wants to use any means which he thinks will be successful in this persuasion. He resorts to rhetorical tricks, to logical fallacies, to standard and very subtle propagandistic devices, to deception, to dishonest and purely emotional appeals — in short, to any device which he finds pragmatically useful.

Deception is the key word to describe the illegitimate rhetorician. The aim is to deceive if deception is necessary for the success of the persuasion. Inauthentic communication is the order of the day for this kind of persuader; there is no respect for honesty, balance, thoroughness, and truthfulness. Such a persuader is lacking in integrity; he has ceased to be an authentic communicator, and has morally forfeited his right to respect and credibility.

This is not to say that he is not successful, or that he is not often believed and even respected by many in his audience. Often he is extremely effective in his rhetorical campaigns to persuade. He is especially good and successful at fanning the fires of prejudice which already are burning in his audience. Audience members, by and large, are trusting enough, naive enough, ignorant enough, and credulous enough to believe a large amount of what they read and hear. And they are also, to a very great degree, prone to be persuaded and to react emotionally to skillfully designed messages. The illegitimate persuader in journalism knows this very well and indulges in kinds of emotional appeals and logical fallacies which have proved effective with general audiences.

This inauthentic persuader is not interested in the accurate communication of information so that the audience can determine for themselves their own decision; rather the communicator has a preordained decision designed for the audience.

Often such a persuader is called a propagandist, a term which carries a generally negative or unethical connotation. We feel that this is a justified comparison — the illegitimate (inauthentic rhetorician) and the propagandist. They are really the same and are dedicated to pulling, to various degrees, the proverbial wool over the eyes and to getting people to believe as the persuader wants them to believe.

At any rate, the person we are calling the illegitimate persuader does make use of various logical fallacies and resorts to numerous propagandistic tricks to achieve a preconceived purpose. Let us look at a few of these fallacies and then at some of the propaganda devices commonly found in journalism.

What are some of the chief fallacies utilized by the illegitimate persuader? Let us mention a few:

1. *Appeal to authority*: Use of an authority in one field to support a

case in another. The persuader can always find some "authority" who will state or support the persuader's case.

2. *Provincialism*: The fact that there is a tendency for people to identify strongly with certain groups, to think mainly of in-group versus out-group. The persuader thus appeals to this proclivity, couching persuasion in terms of an audience member's in-group loyalty and out-group suspicions and hostilities.

3. *Non-sequitur*: Involves the persuader giving reasons for a situation or for a position that are not relevant or may not be. The persuader jumps to conclusions which do not follow from the evidence, and only the alert audience member will be able to withstand the temptation to go along with the persuader.

4. *Ambiguity*: A very common practice of the illegitimate persuader, using vague or ambiguous terms which often lead to mistaken conclusions. When journalists purposely make use of terms that can be understood (and often are) in more than one way, and make no effort to clarify the meaning, they are using these terms for their own ends and are not concerned about understanding.

5. *Jumping to conclusion*: Using simplistic conclusion technique to win others to a point of view. Usually the technique takes the form of stating that when a first step is taken, then a second will follow — and on and on. It is often referred to as a "slippery slope" or "domino theory" technique.

6. *Ad hominem*: Attacking the person rather than the argument.

7. *Two wrongs make a right*: Because they did X, it is all right for us to do X.

8. *Tokenism*: Making use of a small, often insignificant, gesture instead of an adequate, serious, responsible effort.

9. *Hasty conclusion*: Coming to a conclusion without enough evidence.

10. *Questionable classification*: Incorrect labeling of something on the basis of evidence.

11. *Questionable cause*: Labeling something as the cause of something else on insufficient evidence.

12. *Straw man*: Distracting the audience by substituting another issue for the real one under consideration.

13. *Questionable or false analogy*: Using analogy when situations are really different.

14. *Either-or fallacy*: Something is either this or that; no provision is made for points across the spectrum, or for merging of categories.

15. *Begging the question*: Failure to stick to the question; merging other questions with the one under discussion or leaving it completely for another.

Journalistic Propaganda

Now, with a few of the main fallacies out of the way, let us turn briefly to some of the propagandistic devices which the illegitimate persuader uses in journalism. Certainly many of them are akin to the fallacies just mentioned, and all of them are indicative of the communicator's propensity to persuade and mislead through less-than-honest devices. It might be more accurate to describe these devices as attempts to distort the news. News, of course, is distorted every day in one way or another, even by those journalists who try to avoid distortion. But here we are talking about purposeful distortion of the news to satisfy some desire of the journalist; therefore we must consider these devices as propagandistic or illegitimate persuasive techniques.

Let us mention a few:

1. Selecting certain stories and discarding others. Biased selection and rejection of stories is one of the most subtle ways to build up a pattern of persuasion in journalism.
2. Playing stories either up or down. Emphasizing or deemphasizing stories which are selected is another way of conditioning audiences with persuasive intent.
3. Misleading or inaccurate headlines. Commonly this device is used to affect audiences of newspapers and magazines. By selection and emphasis in the headlines, certain aspects of the stories beneath them can be highlighted, and the impact is great on the readers, especially the casual ones.
4. Presenting an incomplete or superficial story. By interviewing only certain people, presenting only one side or only several sides of a story, leaving gaps in the story, the persuader can bias the story and can render a potent persuasive package.
5. Printing or not printing certain letters to the editor. This device is easily used by propagandistic journalists for persuasive purposes; its potency is obvious.
6. Selecting and using certain columnists, photographs, and even comic strips in the newspaper. Such basic publishing techniques as these can be used, and are used, for propagandistic purposes.
7. Fictionalizing and fabricating stories, often by using the composite technique, whereby segments of different stories or story possibilities are woven together to make a story. This is a dastardly type of journalism, but it is used, as was illustrated by the *Washington Post* reporter in April 1981, when she lost her job and her Pulitzer Prize when her hoax was revealed.

8. Using undisclosed sources. A device widely misused by unscrupulous journalists who desire to distort the news, to withhold important information — sources — from the reader. Reporters can easily, in the guise of presenting the news, publish any of their own opinions and attribute these quotations to an unnamed source; the reader has no way of verifying the statements.
9. Using the "one-man cross section" approach. The journalist quotes one person on some matter and in some area of concern and projects that opinion onto a larger group.
10. Tampering with quotations and quoting out of context. This is a very common device for propagandizing; newspapers can make an enemy look foolish or a friend seem articulate and wise by tampering with quotations. This is one of the most subtle and unethical, and generally undetectable, devices the illegitimate media persuader uses today.
11. Using such an expression as, "The mayor was unavailable for comment." This device can cast suspicion on a person very easily and certainly is a negative statement in its unmodified form.

We could continue a discussion of journalistic propaganda, but will stop with these eleven devices. Certainly there are many others, and the seven well-known basic ones — transfer, name-calling, glittering generalities, cardstacking, testimonial, plain folks, and bandwagon — are relevant to the illegitimate persuader in journalism. All these devices are used every day. They all stem from a desire to mislead, to give faulty or no evidence, to appeal to emotions and to social and in-group instincts, and to the audience's lack of information on certain subjects.

Persuasion in very subtle, and it is certainly more prevalent than most people suspect. Even normally objective persons, who claim to enjoy a kind of neutrality in the world, often find themselves in the persuasive role. Journalists are no exception. For all their talk of objectivity, they probably more frequently than anyone else are found in the role of persuader. Many of these journalists, while mouthing platitudes about the value of pluralism and journalistic autonomy, are busy in their professional groups writing codes of ethics and creeds of journalism which are designed, although not overtly, to make journalists more conformist and less autonomous. These professional standards of one kind or another are really persuasive devices in themselves, planned as subtle — and not so subtle — ways to enlarge the number of journalists who believe alike and act alike. We turn now in the concluding section of this chapter to these journalistic internal persuasive or rhetorical devices: codes of journalistic behavior.

Journalistic Codes and Creeds

As rhetorical devices — and surely that is what they are — journalistic codes and creeds have poliferated since World War II and today can be found adorning the walls of communications-related enterprises throughout the world. As the trend toward professionalization goes forward (UNESCO and its Third World and Marxist subparts began seriously in 1980 and 1981 to push licensing of journalists as part of this trend), we shall be seeing more and more codes of ethics and other guides and sets of standards and assorted creeds. We shall see more agitation for such codes, even on the international level in the 1980s. Behind these attempts at standardization and regulation always lies an elite of some type that thinks it has the answer for the proper exercise of this or that aspect of journalism.

Persuasion is really at the root of these codes and creeds. Journalists must be persuaded that action A is right and action B is wrong; come let us reason together, say the codes, and let us act in concert according to this reasoning. The problem with such codes and creeds, however, is that they are not even efficient in what they try to do — develop a consensus in thought and action; reason: the rhetorical devices of the codes of ethics and the creeds are so nebulous, fuzzy, ambiguous, contradictory, or heavy-handed that the few journalists who do read them are perplexed, confused, bewildered, angered, and scared off. Journalists, of all people, should use the language skillfully, directly, and effectively, and in many instances they do. But when it comes to codes and creeds they seem to retreat into a kind of bureaucratese, or sociological jargon that benumbs the mind and frustrates any attempt to extract substantial meaning from the writing.

For the sake of illustration, we would like to conduct a brief semantic analysis of the Code of Ethics of Sigma Delta Chi — the Society of Professional Journalists. This code was adopted at the society's convention in 1973. It was written (or an older one was rewritten) by a committee of SDX, and has been printed in thousands of copies and distributed throughout the country as representative of the ethical thinking and values of the nation's largest "professional" organization of journalists.

We shall present the SDX Code verbatim below, but in segments, and following each segment we shall make a few analytical comments. Many readers will feel we are nit-picking and are being unfair to this code of ethics. Perhaps we are, but this exercise will illustrate something important about rhetoric — SDX's and ours. It will illustrate how language can be used positively and negatively, clearly and fuzzily, fairly and unfairly to achieve predetermined ends. Whether or not the reader agrees with our critique of the code, it should prove of some interest, and, perhaps, of some value. Such an analysis forces the analyst into such philosophical areas as political and social theory, epistemology, and ethics. Linguistic philosophy, of course, is intertwined in all these areas. Let us take a brief look, then, at SDX's exercise in rhetorical communication:

The Society of Professional Journalists, Sigma Delta Chi

CODE OF ETHICS

Adopted by the 1973 national convention

The Society of Professional Journalists, Sigma Delta Chi, believes the duty of journalists is to serve the truth.

We believe the agencies of mass communication are carriers of public discussion and information, acting on their Constitutional mandate and freedom to learn and report the facts.

We are told immediately that the Society believes that truth-serving is the duty of journalists; we shall see later in the code that this duty is modified considerably. The SDX code writers then say that they "believe" the agencies of mass communication are carriers of public discussion and information. We *know* that these agencies are such carriers. Next we are told that this is so because of their Constitutional mandate and freedom to learn and report the facts. Where can we find any such Constitutional mandate?

We believe in public enlightenment as the forerunner of justice, and in our Constitutional role to seek the truth as part of the public's right to know the truth.

We believe these responsibilities carry obligations that require journalists to perform with intelligence, objectivity, accuracy, and fairness.

The code might just as well have reversed the first sentence above to read, "We believe in justice as the forerunner of public enlightenment," for all the difference it would make. Merely high-sounding rhetoric, full of words, signifying very little. Here again, too, is reference to "our Constitutional role to seek the truth"; there is no such Constitutional role. And next comes the well-worn phrase, "public's right to know." Where does the public get such a right? The next sentence about responsibilities and obligations in the Code is almost too strange to mention: "those responsibilities carry obligations that require journalists..."

One last comment on that sentence: There are no "obligations that require" journalists to perform with intelligence, objectivity, accuracy, and fairness. In fact, it is easily noticed that many journalists perform unintelligently, subjectively, inaccurately, and unfairly. When we read something like this Code sentence, we feel caught in rhetorical quicksand.

> **To these ends, we declare acceptance of the standards of practice here set forth:**
> ***RESPONSIBILITY: The public's right to know of events of public importance and interest is the overriding mission of the mass media. The purpose of distributing news and enlightened opinion is to serve the general welfare. Journalists who use their professional status as representatives of the public for selfish or other unworthy motives violate a high trust.**

The Code writers here declare acceptance of the *standards* — which really are not printed — which they set forth. What do they mean they "declare acceptance"? Does this mean that all journalists — or even SDX members — accept what is said? Then we are told that the "public's right to know of events of public importance and interest" is the overriding mission of the mass media. In the Code's first sentence we were told that serving the truth was the duty of journalists. And, after all, what is really of public importance and interest is determined by the journalist, not the amorphous public; therefore, how is such a "right to know" meaningful beyond the news determination and subjectivity of the press itself? In the next sentence we meet the term "enlightened opinion." Who is to determine what opinion is enlightened and what is unenlightened — especially *a priori*? Does this mean it is unethical to express opinion at all unless you are positive that it is enlightened? Enlightened opinion is often, like beauty, in the eye of the beholder. And in the last sentence in the above segment of the Code, we are told that journalists are "representatives of the public" and beyond that we are informed that "selfish motives" are unworthy. Both statements, of course, are highly debatable.

> ***FREEDOM OF THE PRESS: Freedom of the press is to be guarded as an inalienable right of people in a free society. It carries with it the freedom and responsibility to discuss, question, and challenge actions and utterances of our government and of our public and private institutions. Journalists uphold the right to speak unpopular opinions and the privilege to agree with the majority.**

Now the Code writers drag in another platitude that has little to do with ethics. Of course people "in a free society" will be concerned with freedom of the press; a free society assumes a free press. Then we are told that press freedom carries with it the freedom to discuss, etc.; this is obvious. Whether freedom carries with it the responsibility to discuss, etc., is, however, open to question. Then in the last sentence we are told that journalists uphold the right to speak unpopular opinions. We should think that journalists (in a free society) would even uphold the right to speak *popular* opinions and the privilege to *disagree* with the majority. And what about the right to *agree with the minority*? Is SDX unconcerned about this? This is another rhetorically empty segment of the code.

*ETHICS: Journalists must be free of obligation to any interest other than the public's right to know the truth.

At last, and strangely, we come to ethics in the Code of Ethics. Imagine a subtopic of a Code of Ethics called "Ethics" — but that is exactly what we have here. And directly following this subtitle "Ethics," we hear the old refrain about the "right to know." What is more, we are told that journalists must be free of any other obligation than serving this "right"; and yet, the whole Code is filled with various *other* obligations. Perhaps even stranger, after this introductory sentence following the subtitle "Ethics," the Code writers begin a numbering system 1 through 5 — as you will see as the Code continues; these items 1 through 5 have nothing really to do with the "right to know" introductory sentence, and go off into several unrelated directions. This is an example of rhetorical anarchy.

> **1. Gifts, favors, free travel, special treatment or privileges can compromise the integrity of journalists and their employers. Nothing of value should be accepted.**
> **2. Secondary employment, political involvement, holding public office, and service in community organizations should be avoided if it compromises the integrity of journalists and their employers. Journalists and their employers should conduct their personal lives in a manner which protects them from conflict of interest, real or apparent. Their responsibilities to the public are paramount. This is the nature of their profession.**

Here in the first two of the five items, we are told that nothing of value should be accepted — special seating, books for review, press cards? — and that journalists should, in effect, isolate themselves, from political and community involvement. And then come the last two short sentences of the segment above: one informing the journalists that their responsibilities are paramount and one saying that "this" (?) is the nature of their profession.

3. So-called news communications from private sources should not be published or broadcast without substantiation of their claims to news value.

What about news communications from *public* sources? Does not SDX care about them? And, if we can simply substantiate that they are *claimed* to have news value, then it is all right to publish or broadcast them? This is what the Code says.

4. Journalists will seek news that serves the public interest, despite the obstacles. They will make constant efforts to assure that the public's business is conducted in public and that public records are open to public inspection.

Now we are told that journalists *will* do certain things, such as seeking news that serves the public interest. Do the Code writers mean *should* or *ought to*, or do they really mean that they *will*? It is interesting that journalists will not just make an effort to make available public information; they will make "constant efforts."

5. Journalists acknowledge the newsman's ethic of protecting confidential sources of information.

This is simply not true. Many journalists do not accept any such ethic. And, assuming it were really true, there would be no need for putting it into a Code of Ethics: everyone already would acknowledge such an ethic.

*ACCURACY AND OBJECTIVITY: Good faith with the public is the foundation of all worthy journalism.

This introductory subtitle and sentence is another example of vacuous and platitudinous rhetoric which leads into a list of eight items, many of them having nothing to do with accuracy and objectivity, or with good faith with the public.

1. Truth is our ultimate goal.

This is an unrealistic and fuzzy goal, albeit a worthy one. What level of truth? What kind of truth are they talking about?

2. Objectivity in reporting the news is another goal, which serves as the mark of an experienced professional. It is a standard of performance toward which we strive. We honor those who achieve it.

Objectivity is *another* goal? Why is not objectivity part of the first goal, truth? And what, we might ask, is meant by "objectivity"? A fair question if such a Code is really to mean anything. We are told that it is the mark of an experienced professional; but then in the very next sentence we are told that it is really nothing more than "a standard of performance toward which we strive." Which is it? a mark of the experienced professional, or a standard toward which to strive? Some journalists, however, must do more than just strive for it, for according to SDX, "we honor those who achieve it."

3. There is no excuse for inaccuracies or lack of thoroughness.

SDX Code writers and others know that there really are plenty of excuses for inaccuracies — time pressures, lying or inaccurate sources — and they also must be aware that there is always a lack of thoroughness in news writing. As the general semanticists say, you can never say everything about anything.

4. Newspaper headlines should be fully warranted by the contents of the articles they accompany. Photographs and telecasts should give an accurate picture of an event and not highlight a minor incident out of context.

Now the Code writers are getting into specific journalistic admonitions which seem somewhat out of place in the midst of the foregoing fuzzy rhetoric and semantic thickets. At the least the Code writers have shifted back to the use of "should."

5. Sound practice makes clear distinction between news reports and expressions of opinion. News reports should be free of opinion or bias and represent all sides of an issue.

Sound practice according to whom? To many it is sound practice to integrate expressions of opinion into news reports. We would like to see the news report that is free of opinion; and certainly we know that no news report represents *all* sides of an issue.

6. Partisanship in editorial comment which knowingly departs from the truth violates the spirit of American journalism.

7. Journalists recognize their responsibility for offering informed analysis, comment, and editorial opinion on public events and issues. They accept the obligation to present such material by individuals whose competence, experience, and judgment qualify them for it.

What "spirit" of American journalism are they talking about? All through the history of American journalism use has been made of deception, and outright lying has been common. Is not this part of the "spirit of American journalism"? And, journalists will be interested to know that they accept an obligation to present such material as mentioned in (7) but only if it is presented to them by individuals of competence, experience, and judgment who thereby are "qualified." In other words, "freedom of the press" applies only to those who are competent, experienced, and wise? Certainly SDX does not believe that.

8. Special articles or presentations devoted to advocacy or the writer's own conclusions and interpretations should be labeled as such.

What does this mean? What does the "as such" relate to? If a journalist writes an editorial advocating something, must the editorial be labeled "Advocacy," or if the journalist gives his or her own conclusions, must the article be labeled "the writer's own conclusions"?

*FAIR PLAY: Journalists at all times will show respect for the dignity, privacy, rights, and well-being of people encountered in the course of gathering and presenting the news.

Journalists *will* again, and not *should*? The Code writers cannot quite decide on the perspective of the Code. Why the "at all times"? What about the journalist who is trying to expose the bank president in some fradulent activities — just how far should one go in showing respect for that person's well-being? That is another case of fuzzy rhetoric. Again, this is a lead-in or introductory sentence to five items tacked on after it — to follow in the Code — some of which are not related to this introductory sentence, as you will see:

1. The news media should not communicate unofficial charges affecting reputation of moral character without giving the accused a chance to reply.
2. The news media must guard against invading a person's right to privacy.
3. The media should not pander to morbid curiosity about details of vice and crime.

How do the media tell when curiosity is "morbid" and when it is not? When it is not, presumably it is all right for the media to pander to it. Back under (1), the question might be asked: What about *official* charges? Should the accused be given a chance to reply in these cases? And under (2) we are told the media *must*, while in (1) they *should*; Why the difference?

4. It is the duty of news media to make prompt and complete correction of their errors.

Does SDX really believe this? Every day hundreds of errors of one kind or another are made by media staffed partially by SDXers. Few of these corrections are made at all, certainly not promptly and completely.

5. Journalists should be accountable to the public for their reports and the public should be encouraged to voice its grievances against the media. Open dialogue with our readers, viewers, and listeners should be fostered.

Again the code writers are back to *should*. Just how the journalists are to be accountable to the public is left to the imagination. Also, one wonders how the public is to be encouraged to voice its grievances against the media. And in the last sentence, there is this shift again to "our" from the more impersonal "journalists" in the preceding sentence of that section.

*PLEDGE: Journalists should actively censure and try to prevent violations of these standards; and they should encourage their observance by all newspeople. Adherence to this code of ethics is intended to preserve the bond of mutual trust and respect between American journalists and the American people.

With these two sentences of the "pledge," the SDX Code of Ethics comes to an end. And, if anything, the code ends in an even weaker position than it began. What does the pledge mean? Are all SDX members pledging, for instance, that they will actively censure those who violate the SDX "standard"? Are they really going to try to encourage *all* newspeople, not just SDX members, to observe the Code of Ethics? Presumably they are, for, after all, the Code was adopted by the 1973 national convention.

What is perhaps even stranger about this last section of the Code is the irony of the very last sentence. We are told that adherence to the Code is intended to preserve the bond of mutual trust and respect between "journalists and the people." The operative word here is "preserve." If we already have this mutual trust and respect, then why do we need this Code of Ethics?

This whole Code is rather typical of such codes in journalism, except it is perhaps more poorly written than most. At any rate it brings out the persuasive character of such codes and shows clearly that the intent is to get more conformity into the activities of journalists. Whether it is successful or not, of course, is debatable, for the preconceived motivation is rather obvious. It is interesting that at present many of the so-called Third World countries, along with the socialist world, are agitating through UNESCO for the international community to come up with a global journalistic code of ethics. The motive behind this international persuasive undertaking is also rather obvious, at least to us: the further diminishing of diversity and the increased power of nonpress people over the world's journalism.

Of course, this would not be the position of Third World countries and their supporters for a worldwide code of ethics. Their reason: to make the world's journalism more "responsible." But, as has been pointed out elsewhere in this book, the concept of responsibility is, even more than being extremely semantically difficult, a rhetorical foot in the door of freedom — a foot which permits informational bullies to gain access to, to spread, and, ultimately, to enforce their restrictive standards.

International Rhetoric

Having just mentioned the Third World and its supporters, let us conclude this chapter on rhetoric by looking briefly at an example of *international* persuasion propagated by one of these supporting organizations, the International Organization of Journalists (IOJ), a large multinational group with headquarters in Prague, Czechoslovakia.

The IOJ, incidentally, makes pretensions that it is a nonaligned or neutral organization, certainly not the Marxist group it is generally seen to be by the West. Some of its officers and many of its members, especially those from Third World nations, flit from East to West attending conferences on the mass media sponsored alternately by groups in the two main power blocs. The IOJ has long been very close to UNESCO functionaries, and much of its rhetoric has made its way into UNESCO documents, declarations, and pronouncements.

Published regularly from the organization's Prague office, the *IOJ Newsletter* gives a rhetorical clue to the persuasive (propagandistic) nature of the organization; the reader can quickly detect from the headlines and articles that the IOJ is primarily a *political* entity, more concerned with depicting the West as immoral, depraved, and imperialistic than in trying to improve the state of journalism around the world.

Let us take just two issues of the *IOJ Newsletter* and look briefly at the headlines and stories; they should indicate the major thrust of IOJ ideology and purpose. First, from the March 1981 (No. 5) issue are these headlines:

"West Attacks UNESCO Meeting"

"Working for Peace and a Better Future"

[IOJ and the Union of Finnish Journalists are so working.]

"Eberhard Heinrich Visits IOJ Headquarters"

[Heinrich is president of the Union of Journalists of the German Democratic Republic]

"More Attraction for Readers or Advertisers?"

[Item about free papers of the USA — or complimentary papers, as IOJ calls them. Such papers as the *Bay Guardian* of San Francisco, which do not rely on advertising and therefore can be "freer."]

"Journalists Denied Their Rights? [in Egypt]

"Jean Effel — Gold Pen Winner"

[Awarded by the Association of Hungarian Journalists]

Now, let us turn to the November 1981 issue of the *IOJ Newsletter*. This was the issue which came out after the 9th Congress of IOJ which was held in Moscow (Oct. 19–22). The congress drew nearly 200 delegates (and as many guests and observers), making it, in the words of IOJ President Kaarle Nordenstreng of Finland, "the largest and most representative meeting of journalists ever held anywhere."

Following are a few headlines and passages from stories in this issue of the *IOJ Newsletter*; quotations shall be given without comment, and the reader is invited to react to the rhetorical devices:

"The Most Representative Meeting of Journalists"

[Represented were 96 organizations of journalists from 89 countries, almost all from the socialist world and the Third World.]

"From the Opening Address of the IOJ President Kaarle Nordenstreng"

[The concluding passage from his address:

"It is true that times have turned more difficult, but at the same time our movement has become stronger. In this Hall in Moscow, on the ground of the first and strongest country of modern democratic revolution, we have all reasons to be optimistic. We are the most representative meeting of journalists, and our orientation — democratic journalism — is a leading force in the international information arena."]

"From the Report of IOJ Secretary General Jiri Kubka"

[One passage from the report:

"For us, journalists, it is quite remarkable to note how the pressure has escalated against the Helsinki agreements and the other efforts and initiatives to extend a favourable atmosphere in the world. President Carter's campaign on human rights did not last very long.

"In a country which has not two but three societies — White, Black and Latino — who are thrown into swamps, beaten to death and their murderers let off scotfree, and those who earn forty two dollars a week in wages, in a society in which two thirds of its citizens do not even bother to vote, whose pay rolls include every reactionary thing that existed in the world, one cannot give presidents and presidential advisers the right to interpret the Helsinki agreements and to pronounce judgement on human rights....

"Claims are made for the right to world superiority, world spheres of American interest are proclaimed, and almost as if in the ancient Roman empire every fourth American soldier is stationed outside his country at one of its foreign bases. Instead of human rights the fight is launched against terrorism, but which is meant the national liberation movement in a great many different countries....

"The International Organization of Journalists at the time of its establishment 35 years ago clearly formulated its task — that journalists are committed and responsible. Today we can state with gratification from the tribunal of our 9th Congress that after 35 years this conception of journalism in the world decidedly prevails....

"It is of extraordinary significance for the development of all democratic and progressive principles for the realization of such measures beneficial to most of mankind, which will not divide the world either into north or south, or into white or black or yellow, which will strive so that people not only learn to think, but to think in a certain way, to think not only of their own good but of others, even if they live on other continents.

"Today, this is the view and conviction of the overwhelming majority of journalists in the world and we are certain that this 9th Congress will be the impetus to the further extension of our principles which, as I believe, and as we all wish, should help the journalist's pen bridge the truly serious times in which we now live."]

"Role of Journalists in the Struggle for Peace, Understanding among Nations, Humanism and Social Progress"

[The story with this headline summarizes the 5th International Symposium held Oct. 26–29, 1981 in the capital of the Mongolian People's Republic on the subject capsulated in the headline.]

"Message to Symposium Participants"

[A message to the participants at the Mongolian symposium from Hifzi Topuz, head of the UNESCO Free Flow of Information Section; it was a glowing letter, which concluded with these words:

"At the present time, when the question of peace is of utmost significance in the world, the holding of such a meeting in Asia will once again give Asian journalists a chance to raise their voice in defence of peace."]

"Passages from the Orientation Document"

[Under this headline a few passages from this document, stating IOJ's basic directions of activity for the future in about twenty manuscript pages, are presented. One of these passages is quoted below:

"The duty of democratic journalists is to use honest words to expose this unprincipled deception of the public, to come forward with sympathy and understanding in support of aspirations for the progress of nations which are oppressed nationally and socially. We express our solidarity with all progressive and democratic journalists in all regions of the world who suffer in jails and are persecuted and oppressed by imperialism and reaction for fulfilling their journalistic duties and upholding their democratic convictions. We are proud of our colleagues who despite persecution, imprisonment and torture have remained faithful to the just cause of their people and their mission as journalists."]

"Appeal of the 9th Congress of the IOJ to Journalists of the Whole World"

[In this appeal the Congress called on journalists of the world to support the IOJ goals. A brief part of this appeal follows:

"Here in Moscow, we have become convinced once again that the Soviet Union which lost over 20 million people in the last world war, wants peace, good neighbourly relations with all countries and sincere friendship with all nations. Human, industrial and natural resources are being used to raise the well-being of the Soviet people and to make their life happier. The Soviet Union lays no claim to foreign territory or other peoples' natural wealth."]

Enough of this rhetoric. For those readers who would like to have larger doses of it, they can easily find it in numerous publications of UNESCO and in other issues of the *IOJ Newsletter* and IOJ's main journal, *The Democratic Journalist*, also published out of Prague.

The rhetorical implications of the passages and headlines given above should be clear to the careful reader. The directions in which such rhetoric, cast upon the international scene, are intended to take the receivers of this language are unmistakable. The heroes and villains are set out in bold, clear terms.

Use of certain words like "democratic" and "progressive" and the constant repetition of such trigger words as "peace," "imperialism," "peaceful coexistence," and "democratic journalism" give a certain force — albeit monotonous and juvenile — to these messages and serve well the intent of the international rhetorical communication.

Of course, members of IOJ could deny any rhetorical implication or intention of such passages as cited above, and they often do when they get the chance. And also they can point out that the West and the capitalistic organizations of journalists (two examples: the International Press Institute and the Inter-American Press Association) indulge in similar rhetorical communication — theirs being basically anticommunist. Undoubtedly this is true; we are not maintaining that anyone has a monopoly on global rhetoric. We are simply trying to draw attention to its existence.

Suggested Reading

Ellul, Jacques. *Propaganda: The Formation of Men's Attitudes*. New York: Random House, 1973.

Gordon, George N. *Persuasion*. New York: Hastings House, 1971.

Griffin, Emory. *The Mind Changers: The Art of Christian Persuasion*. Wheaton, Ill.: Tyndale House, 1976.

Hayakawa, S.I. *Language in Thought and Action*. New York: Harcourt, Brace, 1939.

Johannesen, Richard L., ed. *Ethics and Persuasion: Selected Readings*. New York: Random House, 1967.

Kahane, Howard. *Logic and Contemporary Rhetoric*. Belmont, Calif.: Wadsworth, 1976.

MacBride, Sean, et al. *Many Voices, One World*. London: Kogan Page, 1980.

Meyerhoff, Arthur E. *The Strategy of Persuasion*. New York: Berkeley, 1968.

Nordenstreng, K., and Schiller, H.I., eds. *National Sovereignty and International Communication: A Reader*. Norwood, N.J.: Ablex, 1979.

Salomon, Louis B. *Semantics and Common Sense*. New York: Holt, Rineholt and Winston, 1966.

Stevenson, Charles L. *Ethics and Language*. New Haven, Conn.: Yale University Press, 1965.

Stonecipher, Harry W. *Editorial and Persuasive Writing: Opinion Functions of the News Media*. New York: Hastings House, 1979.

Thouless, R.H. *Straight and Crooked Thinking*. New York: Simon & Schuster, 1932.

Wilson, John. *Language and the Pursuit of Truth*. Cambridge: Cambridge University Press, 1967.

CHAPTER 7

Political Theory: Journalism and Ideology

A symbiotic relationship exists between a nation's journalism and its political system. Although perhaps a truism, this is a very important fact to keep in mind as we take a look at the media system of a society by focusing on the philosophy and structure of government. Just as there are varying political concepts and arrangements in the world, there are many types of journalism and ways that they can relate to government.

Journalism's relation to government in a very real sense determines its basic function or purpose in a society. If a country has a political system that is based on a cooperationist philosophy, then it will have a cooperationist journalism that will support government in a partnership role. If a country's political philosophy is essentially a contentious or adversary one, the country's journalism will reflect this antagonisitc/dissident proclivity. In addition to these two rather polarized press-government relationships, theoretically there could be a middle way: journalistic autonomy. In this system, the country's journalism would not function primarily to support or to oppose government; rather, it would have no purpose vis-à-vis government at all. At times it (or any part of it) might be an apologist or supporter; at other times it might be a critic or adversary of government. And, then, on occasion, it might determine not to relate in any way to government.

At any rate, a country's journalism must relate to its governmental philosophy so as not to be dysfunctional. In short, in a closed society a pluralistic and contentious journalism would be socially harmful and counterproductive, and in an open society a journalism espousing a partnership with government would be inconsistent and harmful. Each country, of course, must develop its own government-press philosophy dependent on its peculiar social objectives and national purpose.

Journalism-Government Symbiosis

This is basic: A country's journalism reflects the political philosophy in which it functions. This journalism cannot exceed the limits allowed by

151

its society; on the other hand, it cannot lag far behind. The politico-social context, then, largely determines its journalism, and when journalism functions in accord with this national ideology it is considered socially responsible (in the macroscopic sense).

When one begins to think about journalistic media and their relation to government, it is not long before various theories are developed. We could talk about harmonic versus disharmonic theories; about functional versus conflict theories; about adversary versus supportive theories; about monistic versus pluralistic theories; about self-deterministic versus governmental ("other-directed") theories; about laissez-faire versus control theories. And when we elaborate on these, we begin to see that there are many other ways to label them, and we see that they are usually parts of broader and more inclusive theories.

Other press-government relationships suggest themselves. For example, we can think of the press (vis-à-vis government) as (1) an equal contender, (2) a voluntary servant, (3) a forced slave, and (4) an antagonist or adversary.

In the first case, the press units are independent of government and of each other; there is competition among them, and each is a self-developed-and-managed entity making decisions on a case-by-case basis as to how it will relate to government.

In the second case, the press generally is a servant of government — or it might prefer to call the relationship a cooperating partnership. At any rate journalism basically cooperates with or serves government policy and claims that this is done *voluntarily*. Journalism thus is an instrument of government and will be as long as journalism wills that it be used in this fashion.

In the third case, the press is a forced instrument of government. It is enslaved *involuntarily*. Therefore, it is really a slave, not a servant. It is used by the government; it is controlled, directed, dictated to, censored, and its desires and aspirations are ignored. This is the ultimate totalitarian or ultra-authoritarian situation.

And in the fourth and final case, the press sees itself — and is seen by government and citizens — principally as an adversary of government, a watchdog or check on government. And if it is not this, then it is not doing its duty.

Now, these relationships can be boiled down to a basic trinary typology which might be expressed as (1) press neutrality, (2) press partnership, and (3) press hostility. When relating these three to the well-known and traditional classifications of press theories, we might say that (2) above would embrace what is generally called the communist theory and the authoritarian theory, and (3) above would roughly correspond to what is usually called the libertarian theory. Number one really does not correlate with any of the traditional classifications, although it would mainly resemble the libertarian. However it may or may not be a critic or adversary of government; in fact it may be a critic on one issue and an apologist for government on another.

Regardless of how we might classify all the possible symbiotic relationships of government and media systems, a basic dichotomy always seems to emerge. It presents a simple aristotelian way of looking at differences, and in spite of its dualistic oversimplification and generalized structuring of reality, it is probably still the best way to consider either press theories or political theories.

A Basic Dichotomy

It might be useful to discuss briefly the basic two-valued typology which underlies all theories of the press. It can be called the A-L Model and structures press systems (and political systems) in a dichotomous manner: as either *authoritarian* or as *libertarian*. Actually this A-L model of government-press theories is part pigeonhole and part continuum in approach, for the person using these labels normally recognizes varying *degrees* of authoritarianism and libertarianism. Nevertheless, the basic tendency is to consider various philosophies of government and press as either authoritarian or libertarian.

Press systems, as well as nations and persons, tend to be either authoritarian or libertarian. They are all somewhat schizophrenic, of course, but the basic inclination of each is toward a well-structured, disciplined worldview with explicit patterns of behavior, *or* toward an open, experimental, self-determined, autonomous, nonrestrictive society with a minimum of rules and controls.

Press systems are conveniently labeled authoritarian or libertarian depending on the degree of their self-determinism. The authoritarian system is the one in which the journalistic media have little or no autonomy in the sense of determining their own editorial policies and activities; the libertarian system is the one in which the media are editorially autonomous and operate in an open, competitive atmosphere.

Obviously there are weaknesses in such a dualistic typology, and perhaps it would be somewhat better to use terms like *authoritarian leaning* and *libertarian leaning* in describing government-press systems. Some persons, however, maintain that it is impossible to make meaningful statements about freedom in one country as compared to freedom in another. Freedom, they say, means different things in different societies. Such relativistic concepts would make talk about freedom in the Soviet Union, for example, meaningless when compared to freedom in the United States — at least in any quantitative sense.

Although it is undoubtedly true that meanings assigned to "freedom" (even among Americans) are not identical, no good reason exists why freedom (of the press, for instance) cannot have a rather pure meaning that can be universalized or applied to journalistic systems anywhere. Such factors as how much criticism of government is permitted, how many restrictive press laws are found, and how frequently they are used can be applied universally in order to measure freedom. Ralph Lowenstein of the University of Florida, in his exhaustive PICA studies, has provided a detailed discussion of the way this can be done.

In other words, *extra*-press restrictions and controls do vary from country to country; and in this sense (a very legitimate one) press freedom can take on a core meaning and comparative statements can validly be made about it in countries with disparate governmental philosophies and structures. Press freedom is fundamentally freedom from outside control.

Assuming that there is this basic philosophical dichotomy (A–L) existing among the various national political and press systems, let us turn briefly to the two orientations for a closer look:

Authoritarian Orientation

Authoritarianism is a giant invisible sociological magnet which pulls constantly at people and nations. Authoritarianism implies an authority, and basically it is extremely difficult and painful, if not impossible, for the mass of men and women to be without an authority to direct and lead them. Even for journalists, who theoretically should appreciate and savor the benefits of freedom, self-authority or autonomy is very often a traumatic and unpleasant option. It appears there is a more natural tendency to escape from freedom than to escape from authority.

It may well be that the philosophical base for authoritarianism can be traced back at least to Plato, the first great proponent of law and order, and advocate of submission to an *aristocracy of the best*. According to Karl Popper, Plato recognized one ultimate standard: the interest of the State. Everything that furthers this interest, believed Plato, is "good and virtuous and just" and everything that threatens it is bad, wicked, and unjust. For Plato, actions that serve the State interest would be moral; actions that endanger it, immoral. So, for Plato, the Moral Code would be strictly utilitarian — a kind of Statist Utilitarianism, where *the criterion of morality is the interest of the State*.

Many national leaders have this Platonic notion about journalistic ethics and responsibility to the state. In fact, it may be said that all forms of political authoritarianism are built on the rationale set forth by Plato: citizens must submit to the dictates of the rulers of the state who know what is best for the state and who morally can (and must) impinge on the freedoms of citizens in the interest of the state.

Some manifestations of this can be seen in the increased emphasis on press councils, and other proscriptions and normative "help" given to the mass media. Media autonomy is being made to appear irresponsible, and the old concepts espoused by Plato so long ago are returning to infect us with their antidemocratic and elitist "wisdom" — concepts which do, admittedly, have a very strong appeal for the multitudes who recognize the comfort of being directed, and also to intellectuals who are titillated by the deterministic ideas of Freudians, Marxists, and Skinnerians.

Consistent with such a philosophy, the information media must be thought of as contributing to social harmony and stability. Certain things the populace should know; other things — harmful things to society — they should not know. The power elite will either directly operate the mass media or control them, leading to a monolithic journalism of conformity and harmony. The goal is political and social equilibrium. And this is true whether the nation is authoritarian of the right or of the left.

Power, as Lord Action states, does tend to corrupt. Power is also active and insistent; it must intervene — it must direct, supervise, set standards, define responsibility, eliminate nonconformists and eccentrics, and generally make the society march to its unified and regular drumbeat. Aleksandr Solzhenitsyn was talking about literature in his Nobel Prize lecture (1972), but he could just as well have been referring to journalism when he said:

> Woe to that nation whose literature is disturbed by the intervention of power. Because that is not just a violation against "freedom of print." It is the closing down of the heart of a nation, a slashing to pieces of its memory.

But this "freedom to print" that Solzhenitsyn sees as being at the "heart of a nation" is seen by authoritarians as potentially bad because it permits error to circulate in the society, damaging the social structure and impeding the achieving of social goals. The authoritarian maintains that people in general desire leadership; they like simple, straightforward, easy solutions and actions; they want decisions made for them.

Persons, of course, as well as regimes, are complex and multifaceted; but in spite of this and the danger of overgeneralizing, we believe that there is a general tendency in each political system — and in each individual — toward authoritarianism. Now, let us turn to libertarianism.

Libertarian Orientation

This philosophical stance is as old as, and maybe older than, authoritarianism. It has many roots, and Christians and Jews might even trace it back to the Garden of Eden. Undoubtedly freedom lovers have always existed, but it was not until the seventeenth and eighteenth centuries that the libertarian movement took on a philosophical significance and began to have an impact on the press and public expression. John Milton and his "self-righting process" and John Locke and his stress on "popular sovereignty" were seventeenth-century pioneers in England, followed by Thomas Jefferson in eighteenth-century America. It was Jefferson who clearly expressed the necessary relationship between a free (even if it seemed irresponsible to him) press and good, sound democratic government. John Stuart Mill in nineteenth-century England added further philosophical status to the concept of press libertarianism.

These, and innumerable others, propounded a philosophy which was considerably different from authoritarianism. Unlike disciples of Plato, and later Hegel, they basically trusted the common man and believed that all kinds of information and ideas should be made public. They despised secrecy; they rebelled against prior censorship and felt that free criticism was essential to personal, as well as national, happiness and growth. They were fundamentally democrats and not autocrats, aristocrats, or some other variety of elitists.

A national libertarian orientation is one in which the leadership relates closely with the followship. There is a trust in the citizens, a belief that the majority, even if not always right, should be taken seriously and that it generally comes closest to the truth and makes sound decisions. This trust of the people is related to the mass media in that it is the media that can best inform the people so they can know enough to elect their representatives intelligently, direct them, and change them when necessary.

Actually, there is a theoretical *assumption* in libertarian theory that a free and unhampered press will serve, at least to a large degree, this idealistic function of adequately informing a democratic people. But in libertarian theory there is no *obligation* on the press to do so. This would, of course, contradict the principle of press freedom. In spite of many criticisms which can be hurled at a free and autonomous press for avowed errors and excesses and the like, it is probably safe to say that in the United States, for example, the people are very well informed about the issues of the day, the activities of elected representatives, and the strengths and weaknesses of their political institutions.

It must be admitted that there is, in libertarian press theory, what must be considered a kind of built-in paradox. And it is this paradox which really is at the root of so much of the controversy going on today about press freedom and responsibility. The paradox arises from: (1) the basic philosophical assumption that a democratic people need information upon which to base their decisions, and (2) the basic free-press principle built into the First Amendment of the U.S. Constitution (and into constitutions of many other nations).

Quite naturally there are many citizens who look at the mass media, or certain of them, and see weaknesses in the way they are informing the public. Cases of journalistic falsification, where the public is fed outright lies such as in the *Washington Post* and the *New York Daily News* cases in 1981, do not help at all the case for press freedom, and they increase the insistence of many critics that journalism be made more responsible. So, the natural inclination is to evolve such a principle as this: If the press, or any unit of it, fails to provide the kind of service the citizenry is entitled to in a democracy it must forfeit its freedom. However worthy or unworthy such a rationale may be, it clearly points out the paradox mentioned above. For, quite simply, the press is free or it is not; and of course, if it is regulated, controlled, or directed from without (even in the name of democratic utilitarianism), it has ceased being free.

Often the paradox is expressed in other terms; for example, some libertarians refer to two types of freedom, *positive* and *negative* freedom. Positive freedom is the freedom to achieve some good, whereas negative freedom is the freedom from restraint. Many would say that positive freedom is responsible and negative freedom irresponsible. This positive/negative dualism is troublesome, for it would appear that if we were not free of restraint, we would not have the chance to achieve some good (of our own choice). Therefore, it would seem that the heart of the concept of freedom is really what is called negative freedom. If one is *free from restraint*, one is automatically free to achieve some good (if one elects to).

The libertarians of the positive-freedom school emphasize doing a *good*; they are really utilitarians and have restricted their concept of freedom to freedom to do something good. Theirs is a limited view of freedom and one which only elitist descendants of Plato would approve. The libertarians supporting negative freedom (regardless of its unfavorable connotation) are, in many ways, the valid libertarians, for they view freedom as freedom from coercion and know that this is basic to *any* concept of freedom. The truly free journalistic medium does not have to *do anything* to be free; it is only necessary that it be unrestrained so that it can *choose* whether it wants to do anything or not.

Much more could be said about the authoritarian and libertarian theories. It has been admitted that this dualistic typology is basic and useful, but not very discriminating. From it many ways of looking at theories of journalism can be formulated. Probably the best-known typology of press systems is the four-theories concept. Let us look briefly at this popular classification.

The Four-Theories Typology

In 1956, Fred Siebert, Theodore Peterson, and Wilbur Schramm brought out their *Four Theories of the Press* which more or less established a four-theories typology in the minds of journalism educators and students. The little volume has become standard reading in journalism courses and has done much to legitimize the fourth theory — *social responsibility*. Almost every article and book dealing with philosophical bases for journalism has alluded to this book, commented on it, or quoted from it. Its impact has unquestionably been great in spite of what we believe are significant weaknesses.

Siebert, Peterson, and Schramm discuss journalism philosophy by presenting four theories ("concepts" might have been a more realistic term): (1) the authoritarian theory, (2) the libertarian theory, (3) the communist or Marxist theory, and (4) the social-responsibility theory. Very briefly, here are the essentials of each:

Authoritarian

The state, as the highest expression of institutionalized structure, supersedes the individual and makes it possible for the individual to acquire and develop a stable and harmonious life. Mass communication, then, supports the state and the government in power so that the total society may advance and the state may be viable and attain its objectives. The state (the elite that runs the state) directs the citizenry, which is not considered competent and interested enough to make critical political decisions. One person or an elite group is placed in a leadership role. As the group or person controls society generally, it also controls the country's journalism, since it is considered as a vital instrument of social control.

The journalistic media, under authoritarianism, are educators and propagandists by which the power elite exercises social control. Generally the media are privately owned, although the leader or the elite group may own units in the journalistic system. A basic assumption is that a person engaged in journalism is so engaged as a special privilege granted by the national leadership. This press concept has formed, and now forms, the basis for many media systems of the world. The mass media, under authoritarianism, have only as much freedom as the national leadership at any particular time is willing to permit. Countries embracing this theory include Paraguay, the Philippines, Iran, and South Korea.

Libertarian

The libertarian press theory is generally traced back to England and the American colonies of the seventeenth century. Giving rise to the theory was the philosophy that looked upon man as a rational animal with inherent natural rights. One of these rights was the right to pursue truth, and potential interferers (kings, governors) would (or should) be restrained. Exponents of this press movement during the seventeenth century, and the 200 years which followed, included Milton, Locke, Erskine, Jefferson, and John Stuart Mill. Individual liberties were stressed by these philosophers, along with a basic trust in people to make intelligent decisions (generally) *if* a climate of free expression existed.

In theory, a libertarian press functions to present the truth, however splintered it may be in a pluralism of voices. It is impossible to do this if the press is controlled by some authority outside itself. Through the years many new ideas have been grafted onto early press libertarianism; many of them tend toward directing the press. One of these, for example, is the general acceptance of a kind of obligation to keep the public abreast of governmental activities, of being a kind of fourth branch of government supplementing the executive, legislative, and judicial branches. This is actually a rather recent concept, having been grafted onto the original libertarian theory. There is a basic faith, shown by libertarian advocates, that a free press, working in a laissez faire, unfettered situation, will naturally result in a pluralism of information and viewpoints necessary in a democratic society.

Communist

The communist theory of the press arose, along with the theory of communism itself, in the first quarter of the present century. Karl Marx was its father, drawing heavily on the ideas of his fellow German, Georg W.F. Hegel. The mass media in a communist society, said Marx, were to function basically to perpetuate and expand the socialist system. Transmission of social policy, not searching for truth, was to be the main rationale for the existence of the communist media system.

Mass media, under this theory, are instruments of government and integral parts of the State. They are owned and operated by the state and directed by the communist party or its agencies. Some criticism is permitted in the media — e.g., of failure to achieve goals — but criticism of basic ideology is forbidden. Communist theory, like that of authoritarianism, is based on the premise that the masses are too fickle and too ignorant and unconcerned with government to be entrusted with governmental responsibilities. Thus, the media have no real concern with giving them much information about governmental activities or leaders. Mass media are to do what is best for the state and party; and what is best is determined by the elite leadership of state and party. Whatever the media do to contribute to communism and the socialist state is moral; whatever is done to harm or hinder the growth of communism is immoral.

Social Responsibility

This concept, a product of mid-twentieth century America, is said by its proponents to have its roots in libertarian theory. But it goes beyond the libertarian theory in that it places more emphasis on the press's responsibility to society than on the press's freedom. It is seen as a higher level, theoretically, than libertarianism — a kind of moral and intellectual evolutionary trip from discredited old libertarianism to a new or perfected libertarianism where things are forced to work as they really *should* work under libertarian theory. The explainers and defenders of this theory maintain that they are libertarians, but socially responsible libertarians, contrasted presumably with other libertarians who are not socially responsible.

Emergence of the New Theory

Increasingly we hear about this social responsibility of the press, and it is emerging as a dominant concept, even though nobody seems to be in agreement as to what it really is. The book mentioned above, *Four Theories of the Press*, attempted to put in intelligible language this new theory of the press. Whether it did so is debatable. But the term at least has made its way, largely unchallenged, into books, articles, speeches, and academic dissertations. On the surface this new theory appears noble. Writers and speakers enthusiastically expound its virtues. It is difficult for anyone to take issue with any such concept which is wrapped in the glittering garments of "people's freedom" and "public good" and "social responsibility."

Although journalists, statesmen, and academicians have for years been thinking in terms of responsibility as well as freedom, there had really been no significant effort to place the concept as a serious theory, parallel in importance to libertarianism, until 1947 when the Commission on Freedom of the Press, headed by Robert Hutchins, discussed it in *A Free and Responsible Press*. Previously, it had been thought that responsibility was somehow a *personal* concept or somehow automatically built into a libertarian press, or that various of the media units would interpret "responsibility" in their own ways. Actually, it had generally been felt that the multiplicity of interpretations was what actually constituted not only a free press, but also a responsible press. At least it was felt generally in the Western world that a free press in a democratic sense was responsible *per se* to its social system.

But the Hutchins Commission thought differently. After seeing a very clear danger in growing restriction of communications outlets and general irresponsibility in many areas of American journalism (the criteria for responsibility, of course, set up by the Commission), it offered the ominous warning that, "If they [the agencies of mass communication] are irresponsible, not even the First Amendment will protect their freedom from governmental control."

Two basic assumptions (and conclusions) stand out in the Hutchins Commission Report: (1) that the press has a responsibility (defined by the Commission) to society; and (2) that the libertarian press of the United States is not meeting this responsibility.

At first, American publishers were quite disturbed by the Commission's report and the implications which they read in (or into) it; but by 1950 the issue had largely settled down, the journalists perhaps thinking that the best policy was to ignore it. Certain ideas inherent in the report, however, had taken root in journalistic soil which was already well fertilized with the philosophy of welfarism and egalitarianism and a readiness to accept ever greater governmental power. In academic circles, at least, the new social-responsibility theory was being discussed and interpreted (searching for a definition) widely by the 1960s. It had emerged as a seemingly viable, if somewhat fuzzy, concept that was spawning in the media such innovations as press councils, ombudsmen, professionalism, and codes of ethics.

Some Implications of the Theory

Just what does "social responsibility" mean as used by the Hutchins Commission and others who have become attached to this new theory? We cannot really answer this question. But one thing is certain: It does *not* mean libertarianism, for social responsibility is seen as a theory growing out of libertarianism. Proponents of social responsibility see their theory closely related to the libertarian press system, but see it as going beyond the free-press theory in that it places many ethical — and, conceivably, legal and other — restrictions on the press. It is restrictive although its devotees do not stress the point. Instead of emphasizing freedom, it stresses responsibility to society.

According to the Hutchins group, press freedom is limited by a social responsibility to report facts accurately and in a meaningful context. Since such thinking inevitably leads to the advocacy of a regulatory system to watch the actions of the press and to keep it functioning properly, the Hutchins Commission suggested that some type of government regulation might be needed to assure that the press accept its responsibility.

The social-responsibility theory implies a recognition by the media that they must perform a public service (of some specific responsible kind) to warrant their existence. The main parts of the Commission's report which seemed to have antagonized many American editors and publishers were those that intimated possible government involvement in the press system. Also implicit in this theory of social responsibility is the argument that some group (a judicial or governmental one, ultimately) can and must define or decide *what* is socially responsible. Also, the implication is clear that publishers and journalists acting freely cannot determine what is socially responsible nearly as well as can some outside or impartial group.

Assuming that a nation's sociopolitical philosophy determines its press system — and undoubtedly it does — then it follows that every nation's press system is in one sense socially responsible. For example, the Marxist or communist press system considers itself socially responsible, and certainly it is responsible to its own social system. A capitalistic press, operating in a pluralistic and competitive context, would be diametrically opposite to what the Soviets consider a socially responsible press. It would be to the Soviets the most irresponsible press system imaginable.

So all press systems conceive of themselves as socially responsible. This does not mean that every citizen (or journalist) in every country *approves* of everything the communications media do; many individuals may well wish for something else, but so long as a sociopolitical reality exists in a particular society, the press will support it, for the press of a nation is caught up in the governmental philosophy and fits into the structure of its society. If it does not, then the sociopolitical system of the country is in flux; either the government must change to fit the press (unrealistic), or the press must change to fit the government (realistic).

Those who call the press of the United States irresponsible are seeing in it some danger to the national society — or those aspects of the society which appear to them as most important. Those who might view the press of the Soviet Union or Iran as irresponsible would do so if in their view the press was exhibiting mannerisms which endangered the equilibrium and ongoing of their respective societies. Responsibility and irresponsibility are thus relative to the particular national society under consideration.

Perhaps we should make clear that we believe in the press (of any nation) being responsible. We simply (1) cannot understand exactly what is meant by a *theory* of social responsibility, and (2) cannot help feeling that a growing emphasis on such a theory will lead a nation's press system away from freedom and toward authoritarianism. In the eyes of individual persons in *any* society various media at times will perform what they see as irresponsible actions; for irresponsibility, like beauty, is in the eye of the beholder. But in order to talk of a nation's press *system* being responsible or irresponsible, we must turn away from looking at specific cases of irresponsibility and ask the basic question: Is this press system compatible with the basic ideology and sociopolitical structure of the country?

If the answer is yes, then we must conclude that in a sociopolitical sense at least, the press system is responsible. If the answer is no, then the press is irresponsible. Such pragmatic considerations as these may not please those who look on responsibility as meaning that *all* media units must, at all times, be responsible to the society in some kind of monolithic way. Such macroscopic pragmatism applied to the media is, in our opinion, unrealistic and meaningless when we are talking about a *theory* of social responsibility.

Symbiotic analysis alone will answer the question of press responsibility to society, and the basic question asked earlier — Is this press system compatible with the basic ideology and sociopolitical structure of the country? — is the starting point for this symbiotic analysis. So it is our belief that social responsibility is not viable as a theory separate from authoritarianism, libertarianism, or communism. It is a term which must be applied (or not applied) to each of these press concepts.

For example, the press in a libertarian country would be irresponsible to its society if it failed to be free of outside control, and if it failed to provide a pluralism of information and ideas for the populace. On the other hand, the press of a Marxist nation would be irresponsible if it conducted itself in the ways of a libertarian press, stirring up trouble, providing criticism of the institutions, and giving the people a wide diversity of views and information from which to choose.

So, in conclusion, it might be well to emphasize that a libertarian press system such as that in the United States is socially responsible for the very reasons that many critics call it irresponsible: it contains maverick elements and dissident points of view; it contains units that seem to rock the proverbial boat and cause social dissention; it has the freedom to take editorial actions not thought to be sound ones by various groups in the society. In short, a libertarian press is contentious, pluralistic, even mischievous. So it is frequently thought of as being irresponsible. Actually, however, these are the very reasons that it can be considered socially *responsible*. It mirrors, or is compatible with, its society — a society which itself is contentious, pluralistic, controversial, outspoken, and mischievous.

Suggested Reading

Barron, Jerome A. *Freedom of the Press for Whom?* Bloomington: Indiana University Press, 1971

Becker, Carl L. *Freedom and Responsibility in the American Way of Life.* New York: Random House, 1960.

Berns, Walter. *Freedom, Virtue, and the First Amendment.* Baton Rouge: Louisiana State University Press, 1957.

Commission on Freedom of the Press. *A Free and Responsible Press.* Chicago: University of Chicago Press, 1947.

Fisher, Glen. *American Communication in a Global Society.* Norwood, N.J.: Ablex, 1979.

Hayek, Friedrich A. *The Road to Serfdom.* Chicago: University of Chicago Press, 1944.

Hook, Sidney. *The Paradoxes of Freedom.* Berkeley: University of California Press, 1967.

Lowenstein, R.L. "Measuring World Press Freedom as a Political Indicator." Ph.D. dissertation, University of Missouri, Columbia, 1967.

MacBride, Sean, et al. *Many Voices, One World.* London: Kogan Page, 1980.

Merrill, John C. *The Imperative of Freedom: A Philosophy of Journalistic Autonomy.* New York: Hastings House, 1974.

Popper, Karl R. *The Open Society and Its Enemies.* Princeton: Princeton University Press, 1930. See Chapters 6, 7, and 8 on Plato.

Richstad, Jim, and Anderson, Michael, eds. *Crisis in International News: Policies and Prospects.* New York: Columbia University Press, 1981.

Righter, Rosemary. *Whose News? Politics, the Press, and the Third World.* London: Burnett, 1978.

Rivers, W.L., Schramm, Wilbur, and Christians, Clifford. *Responsibility in Mass Communication.* New York: Harper & Row, 1980.

Siebert, F.W., Peterson, Theodore, and Schramm, Wilbur. *Four Theories of the Press.* Urbana: University of Illinois Press, 1963.

Smith, Anthony. *The Geopolitics of Information.* London: Faber and Faber, 1980.

Tunstall, Jeremy. *The Media are American.* London: Constable, 1977.

Whalen, Charles. *Your Right to Know.* New York: Random House, 1973.

CHAPTER 8

Metaphysics: Journalism and Its *Raison d'Être*

Of all the philosophical dimensions of journalism, probably the most important is the metaphysical one. Actually it could have — and maybe should have — been taken up first in this book, for it deals with basic or first principles of journalistic activity. The metaphysical aspects of journalism are so basic, so fundamental, that seldom are they really considered at all; they are simply assumed, or implied, ignored, or hinted at occasionally when journalistic talk strays into regions of impracticality and esoteric philosophizing.

When we talk of journalistic metaphysics, we are trying to deal with the basic *why*? We are trying to delve into the ontological level — the fundamental one really — where not only the nature of being is assessed, but the reason for being.

Since this is such an important dimension of journalism, we have decided to leave it until last. Certainly of all the philosophical dimensions discussed earlier, this one is the most speculative, the most nebulous, and the most debatable. Here we must deal with the most elemental questions which, at the same time, are the most profound ones. The world of journalism, like the larger world around it, refuses to sit still for careful analysis. It is not only relative, but is dynamic; it constantly changes, adapts, rises, and falls. The genesis of one part marks the end of others. What seems to work with one part, fails with another.

As we have tried to show in earlier chapters, the "press" as a *concept* or *term* is far less pluralistic than the actual press. Unfortunately, labels tend to stultify or make static mental concepts, and such stereotyping is unrealistic. The press is no monolith; journalism is really beyond conceptualization, and thus beyond debate as to purpose. But, in the real world of nation-states, differing ideologies, and propagandistically inclined leaders, making such philosophical pronouncements is a meaningless exercise and indicates only an intellectual proclivity to evade difficult questions that must be faced in the pragmatic world.

Journalistic theorists, on the other hand, tend to view the pragmatists in government and the communications media in much the same way: unthinking and unrealistic functionaries who see only the trees and never view the forest as a whole, people who are forever arguing and fighting over terms which are so full of semantic noise as to be beyond argument, people who are really only interested in power politics and in using power to force *their* meanings for journalistic terms on others who would prefer to live with their own meanings.

The metaphysical level is surely a misty one, filled with uncertainty at every turn. But it is one which — whether one takes an absolutist or a relative perspective — individual journalists must contend with sooner or later. At least it is one which is so basic to journalistic discourse that every journalist and journalism student should welcome the opportunity to speculate upon it and, we would hope, to come to some satisfying solutions or answers to journalism's most difficult questions.

Let us look briefly at some of these questions.

Journalism's Nebulous Nature

What is journalism? Here is a question which is seldom if ever asked, but one which cries out for an answer. If we are in journalism, what are we in? If we are journalists, what are we? What is the core meaning of the term, and what are the limits? Are public-relations practitioners journalists? Are advertising people journalists? Are publishers or radio-station owners journalists?

We can play many little games here. We can stress etymology and force journalism to stay close to the *journal*. But even here we are in trouble: How close must we stay to the journal? What activities related to the journal must we consider? Is everyone a journalist who has anything to do with the production of a journal? The typesetters, the secretaries, the business-office personnel? Advertisers? Also, a related question: What *kind* of a journal? Is the production of a stamp collector's magazine journalism? Is a magazine of romantic fiction journalism? Or a science fiction journal? Other questions: Is a cartoonist a journalist? Is a photographer a journalist?

Meaningless questions, many will say. What difference does it make who is a journalist? Perhaps no difference, but it should make a difference to the precise mind, to the person who wants to understand the terms being used. One might as well ask the question: What difference does it make what we call *anything*? The temptation is to give into linguistic and logical anarchy or definitional nihilism and simply say: No problem; just call anything anything — it will still be what it is. Call a person who drives a newspaper delivery truck a journalist; that's all right. Call an editorial writer and a printing press operator journalists; that's all right. Whatever is, is, and it matters not what it is called.

We have heard such rationale, such argument.

What is really strange, and disturbing, is that we have heard such argument from supposedly thoughtful and intelligent people, many of them in journalism and in the academic world, who should know better.

Of course it makes a difference what something or somebody is called, and not only in psychological ways, but often in very mundane and pragmatic ways. With the term journalism, it can be crucial, for it can impinge on the First Amendment right of press freedom — the journalist getting the right and the nonjournalist without such a right. On a more practical level, the journalist may get a seat in a legislative press gallery or the press box at a football game, and the nonjournalist may have to stand outside or sit wherever there is a seat.

We cannot settle this question of basic meaning or substance here. But we can insist that distinctions are, indeed, important, and that journalists of all people *ought to care* about definitions; they ought at least to want to know who they are, and who other people are. Perhaps that is at the core of their identity: the capacity to make distinctions for the public, to impart information in as accurate a form as possible, and to deal with basic identification of the subjects of their stories *in precise terms*. If this concept is not found somewhere in the province of journalism, then perhaps there is, indeed, no necessity to differentiate journalism from law or medicine or anything else.

What many people would say, trying to give some substance to "journalism," is that it essentially has to do with the *news* function of communication. For these people it does not matter whether the journalism is delivered through a *journal* or through a broadcast medium; what matters is the nature of the content. The basic question is this: Does the activity deal with collecting and disseminating news and the analysis of this news, or does it deal with some other activities? Therefore a Dan Rather of CBS is a journalist; so is a James Reston of the *New York Times*. So is a John Doe who writes an internal newsletter for Exxon Corporation.

The main problem with this function concept of journalism is that it places primary emphasis on "news." Although news is perhaps journalism's traditional basic ingredient, it is a term which, in itself, is as semantically difficult as journalism itself. Just what is news? To the editor of a corn-grower's journal it may be one thing, to the *Wall Street Journal* something else, to the *New York Times* something else, to the *National Enquirer* something else, to the small weekly in the town of 7,000 people something else, to *Pravda* of the Soviet Union something else, to the editor of the Dartmouth alumni magazine something else.

"News" is as hard to define as "journalism."

In spite of this difficulty, it must be said that news-related endeavors or news processing and disseminating appears to be at the core of the concept of journalism around the world. Journalism without the aspect of news would be unthinkable. Therefore, we must submit that when we are talking about journalism or about a journalist we must assume that news is involved in some way. If not, perhaps there is a legitimate question as to an activity being journalism.

If, for example, in the United States the general concept of a public-relations person is one who collects and processes news, then we can safely say that the PR person is a journalist. If one is thought of as doing other things, or *primarily* doing other things, then one should not be called a journalist. Here is the rub: Is one doing *some* journalism and some other activities? If so, is one still a journalist under such a news-related definition? How much news orientation must be present for one to be called a journalist? This is an important question, which, perhaps, must remain unanswered. Because at this point the question gets even stickier.

There are many who say that to be a journalist one must not only deal mainly with news and news-related material, but that one must also be hired by a news medium (e.g., a newspaper). Therefore, if one (e.g., a PR person) is hired by a university, a corporation, or a public relations agency, even if one mainly prepares news releases and disseminates them, one is not a journalist. Therefore, under this concept, a journalist must work for a news medium *and* must participate in news-oriented activities. So what we have here is a *place of work* plus a *function* definition of a journalist. According to this perspective, a person could work for a newspaper and not be a journalist (e.g., a business office worker), and *nobody* working for a non-news medium could be a journalist. This concept simplifies the definition considerably for it insists that only those working for a news medium can be journalists — and these news-medium workers *must also* be in the business of collecting, processing, and disseminating news-related material.

If we accept this definition of a journalist, it would mean that reporters for a newspaper, an independent newsletter, a newsmagazine, a radio or TV station, a news agency, and the like would all be journalists. It would also grant journalistic status to editorial writers, feature writers, columnists, and the like for such news media *if* their activities were related to *news*.

But what about special columnists working for newspapers — those who might write humor columns or garden columns, book reviewers, etc.? They are media people who create material for the media, but are they journalists since their activities are not *news* related? The practical answer to this, of course, would be to say that they are journalists, since, undoubtedly, they do other things — things that are related to news — for their newspapers. Seldom does a writer write exclusively non-news-related material for a newspaper.

As you can see, all this becomes very tedious and confusing. Many will begin to feel that it is, indeed, better to forget the term journalist or the term news and seek other, more general, terms. But do we want to do this? Should we not, instead, try constantly to use terms more specifically, more precisely, more accurately, instead of seeking to find more general terms? At least it would seem that workers in the word world would want to be as precise as possible.

Purposes and Functions

Why journalism in the first place? Certainly such a question is related to the substance of journalism, to a kind of core definition of journalism. And we have seen in the foregoing section how difficult such a definition can be. But perhaps it is valuable to phrase the question a little differently so as to get at the metaphysical *why*: What are the purposes and functions of the news media, or of journalism?

Of course, we are presented with many more perplexing questions when we attempt such an ontological confrontation. By introducing another term, "news media," we pose additional perplexities: Just what is a news medium? Is a TV station one? Is a radio station one? Most of the broadcast time is obviously *not* concerned with news, although such stations do, indeed, see as one of their functions the presentation of news. Since we have posed such a question about broadcasting, it would be a logical follow-up for someone to point out that newspapers themselves do not use most of their space for news. This is certainly true, and this brings up the question of whether or not even a *news*paper is really a news medium. But let us assume that media which do provide regular news *can* be called news media — and this would include mainly newspapers, newsmagazines, radio, and television. And let us go back to the original question: Why — what are the purposes of — these news media?

One obvious answer, but one which does not provide much help, is that they provide news. They provide other things also, such as entertainment and advertising. But obviously most people would say that the main purpose of a *news* medium would be to provide news. If this were not the case, then, of course, we would not even refer to the medium as a news medium.

Why, then, is news considered so important?

Theoretically, news is important in a societal way as it provides information of a utilitarian nature. It gives the people of the society useful information so that (theoretically) they can make better decisions. They can know what is going on around them; they can know when and where these things are going on, and whether they feel them important enough to take part in. They can know the dangers — and the opportunities — around them. They can know who their leaders are and where responsibilities should be placed. They can learn about the norms of their society. They can learn through the news all sorts of information — much of it useful and much (probably most) of it not — about the world around them. And this information is usually considered important for some reason. Journalists, especially, think it is important. Other segments of society, such as politicians, educators, businessmen, also consider news — or many parts of it — very important. Here is some of what they say:

> We would know very little if it were not for the news media.
> We would have a hard time making our communities, our states, our countries, and our world work if it were not for the news media.
> News is the cement of society.
> News sets the agenda of our lives.
> News is the mechanism which makes democracy possible.

Of course, we often hear the flip side of the record: News distorts reality; news exacerbates social frictions; news creates and perpetuates stereotypes; news distracts people from serious matters; news fosters an emphasis on atypical behavior and antisocial activity; news creates a pseudoworld of basically negative and sensational dimensions.

But generally, at least among the intellectuals of the world, news is looked upon as a positive and necessary force in society, something which no reasonable and creative people can be without, something which is a mark of progress and civilization.

Most students of the press seem to think that news shapes society; but it would seem just as reasonable to consider various societies as shaping news. News, it would appear, is socially determined, being tied very closely to the values and interests of particular peoples at certain times. News, then, varies from place to place and from time to time. Who is to say absolutely what news is? Answer: Nobody! Each journalist — or for that matter, each audience member — determines what news is. News is, then, what *I* want it to be, and what *you* want it to be. But in all cases it is *something* and it has a *factual* base. We can say that news is personal, individual, and exclusive; it is social only to the degree that it is shared and to the degree that it has an impact on social action. Each bird that falls, we are told, is news to God — and, it might be added, to the bird lover of Boston who has housed them in a special tree apartment. But this Boston bird is not news to me, unless, perchance, I am in Boston and it falls on my head.

"This is the news," says the TV anchorman.

"What's news with you?" asks the neighbor upon greeting you as you are both leaving for work.

"No news is good news," says the cynic.

"What we need is more news about our accomplishments and progress," states the delegate from the Third World at the UNESCO meeting.

News, it seems, is many things. Like beauty, it is in the eye of the beholder. Even so-called good news and bad news. What *you* may think of as good news may cause *me* trauma; it may raise the level of my frustration; it may bring out in me thoughts and even actions which I should keep under control; it may cause me to think in ways not consistent with my best interests; it may serve only to cause me to conform when I should deviate or to deviate when I should conform.

In addition, news is something that I always take on faith. I am never sure of the validity of a news story, or of how much of the story is true. The case of the falsified Pulitzer-prize-winning story by a *Washington Post* reporter (revealed in April 1981) brought this point home to millions of readers in a well-publicized and forceful way. Even if I have several versions of a story, I am not sure which one is correct, or even best. If the truth wins out in a free news marketplace, I am always unaware of it. I believe what I want to believe; I make decisions subjectively from so-called objective news stories — knowing full well all the while that the stories are not really objective and that the reporters can do nothing other than report subjectively.

Many persons would state without hesitation that news to be news must be truthful. Others would even say that the report must also be objective. Overlooking the fact that truth is subsumed in objectivity, there is the general belief that news somehow must equal or closely approximate the reality it presumes to report. Of course, a little reflection will dispel such ideas; news — even the best written — never comes close to equaling or approximating reality. In an earlier chapter on epistemology we went into this matter, so there is no need to rehash it here; suffice it to say, in the words of Alfred Korzybski and the general semanticists: "The map is not the territory" — abstracted bits and pieces of an event presented in symbols do not equal the event.

No story is objective. Even those in which the reporter attempts to remain neutral and dispassionate (a subjective stance in itself) are filtered through the subjectivity of the reporter and are so biased by his or her value system and predispositions. Journalism, then, consists in essence of the dissemination of personal perspectives, biases, distortions, opinions, and judgments — all structured and selected according to conscious and subconscious value systems. Therefore, we might say that journalism — even that which revolves around the concept of news and news interpretation — is a kind of camouflaged fiction, where the world is, in effect, created by the journalist to suit his or her own whims and desires. Journalism is little more than subjective world-building by men and women obsessed with the mystique of objectivity and a love of power and influence.

Truth and Its Levels

The journalist — certainly in the best traditions of the term — is also obsessed with truth, or at least with the purported pursuit of truth. Truth must certainly be the key word in the journalist's lexicon, however it may be conceived. Most journalists, wherever they are found, would probably say with considerable sincerity: "I am dedicated to the truth." Perhaps a more honest and realistic treatment would be: "I am dedicated to *my* truth or to bits and pieces of the truth, interpreted from my perspective, which I feel are worth reporting." News is, in a very real sense, what the individual journalist wants to consider news — and truth is, in an equally real sense, the degree of verifiability which the journalist wants to build into a story.

"Truth" is, of course, used very carelessly. Seldom does a journalist, or anyone else for that matter, know exactly what he or she means when using the term. Journalists use it in a very general way, covering everything and covering nothing. There are five main levels of truth, and journalists should always know which of these levels they are talking about, or thinking about, when trying to write a story. Very briefly, let us look at these levels of truth:

1. *Transcendental Truth.* This is THE truth, Truth with a capital T. This is the Great-What-Is. And it is beyond human knowing. It is the complete truth with all of its ramifications and causations; it is beyond distortion, complete, accurate. It is What-Is prior to human abstraction and biasing. It is a nonverbal Truth — out there and in here, all-encompassing and all-inclusive, and is what really *is*, regardless of what human beings might *think* is the case. It is not a journalistic level of truth; no journalist can ever reach it, much less report it. Bits and pieces of it might be caught in the journalistic net from time to time, but these serve only to form a new or different type of truth, much lower and much inferior to the Transcendental Truth. Journalists might as well forget it, except, perhaps, to indulge in personal speculation about it; it cannot really be a part of their journalism.

2. *Potential truth.* Here is where the journalist comes in. There are some limited facets of Truth at this level, and the conscientious journalist can get at them. It is at this level that the journalist has the possibility

of grasping portions of the Truth with perceptive powers. This is Truth breaking into the real world, with a ray of light here and a ray of light there. This is the truth that is available to the human mind. It is a kind of skeleton truth, a partial truth which can be ascertained and reported. This does not mean that it will be. It is here that the sensitivity, effectiveness, skill, and perception of the journalist comes into play; some journalists can get more of this truth than others can. Some are simply more perceptive, more skilled, more determined than others, and therefore some journalists can abstract from this potential truth a much greater body of verifiable information than others can.

3. *Selected (abstracted) truth.* This is the heart of journalistic truth in that it is the raw material from which the reporter fashions an actual story. It is the reportorial-perception-level of truth. It is here that the concern is with the *what* the reporter chooses to abstract or select. The reporter never selects all the potential truth; he or she leaves much of it, or most of it, unselected and thus unreported, but does get some of it. And it is this "some" that we are referring to as this third level of truth — the selected truth. This is what forms the core of the journalistic news story. It is this selected portion of the truth that the reporter weaves into subjective patterns, calling the final product "news." At this level of truth the journalist selects from the potential truth certain things which *may* actually be used in the story. The journalist never really does use *all* of this selected truth in the story, but theoretically all of it *could* be used.

4. *Reported truth.* At this next (lower) level of truth the reporter presents parts of the selected truth. In other words, the reporter further abstracts. The reported truth is the journalistically pragmatic truth — the truth which is actually *used* in the story. It forms the basic substantive fabric of the story, and in a very real sense is what counts. It is what is submitted to the reader or the listener/viewer. It is the portion of the truth to which the audience member is *exposed*. All the preceding levels of truth are important, of course, but it is only at this level that the journalist's work shows up. If it is not here, it might as well not have been available and abstractable for the journalist. This is the most important level of truth for the journalist — and for the prospective audience member.

5. *Perceived truth.* Here we come to the last level of truth: the truth as perceived by the audience member, abstracted from the truth reported by the journalist. At this level, really, the journalist has faded from the picture; he (or she) has done his work; he has reported his version of the news. How it will be understood, perceived, or acted upon by the audience member is out of his hands now. This is the ultimate phase of truth-communicating, where certain portions of the reported truth are admitted to the perception of the audience. And it might be

stressed here that every audience member perceives the reported truth differently — which means, really, that the same news story is actually a *different* news story every time it is read by a different person. If news is originally in the eye of the beholder (the journalist), then news is ultimately also in the eye of the second beholder (the reader). Said another way: The news story which the reporter writes is not the news story which the audience member reads. The selective exposure, selective perception, and selective retention which afflicted the reporter earlier now afflict the reader.

Regardless of what the reporter may have felt to be the truth of a story, the real truth in the story is what each individual reader concludes or perceives to be the truth of the story. It is interesting to note that the reader's problems with truth are the same as the reporter's — except that they are working at different levels. The reporter tries to abstract (perceive) truth from a larger (and often firsthand) universe of facts, whereas the reader has only the reporter's abstractions from which to choose.

Objectivity: An Elusive Goal

Whatever the overriding *raison d'être* of journalism may be, certainly it has something to do with objective reporting. And, of course, as we have seen, this means different things to different people. It has to do with truth, but objectivity implies something more than truthful information; it implies *thoroughness* as well; it implies realistic organization and balance; it implies proper focus; it implies unbiased selection of facts and true-to-nature emphasis and deemphasis of these facts. Perhaps it implies much more, but this is enough to convince most journalists that objectivity in journalism is at best an elusive goal and probably even an unrealistic one.

Most journalists claim to have a high regard for objectivity in journalism and believe that they are trying to reach it; many, in fact, say that they *are* reaching it. One of the main problems with any discussion of objectivity is that there are so many ways of viewing it, so many definitions of it. William Stephenson, noted psychologist and long-time professor at the University of Missouri, was fond of saying that many journalists think of objective journalism either as being factual and accurate, composed of verifiable bits of information, or as being something far more complex and sophisticated, something that goes beyond the mere reporting of acts and statements and brings to the story another dimension which might be called reportorial discernment and sensitivity. The first concept, according to Stephenson, is far too narrow, and the second too fuzzy and esoteric. Probably a synthesis of the two would describe rather well the meaning which most journalists carry around in their heads. Objective journalism, then, would imply accurate and veri-fiable bits of information to be sure, but would also call on reportorial discernment and sensitivity necessary to putting flesh on the story's fac-tual bones. Just as a tree is something more than trunk, branches, and leaves, so also is objective reporting more than verifiable facts. There is something more: Just what this something is escapes precise description, but any thoughtful person recognizes its overriding and integrating character.

Stephenson refers to the two dominant views of objectivity as "fact" reporting and "factuality" reporting, the latter being the "something more" in the report that supplements the bare facts and gives a cohesion and meaning to the whole story. Undoubtedly there are many other views of objectivity in journalism than the fact and factuality ones just mentioned, but they are probably closely related to these two. The first view dominates today and insists on reportorial detachment and neutral-ism; it glorifies the separation of fact and reportorial opinion. This con-cept is well described by Barry Goldwater in his *Conscience of a Major-ity* in these words:

> I am a great believer in the device, practiced by most responsible American newspapers, of separating the news developments and the newspapers' editorial opinion. The first should be a flat, un-embroidered account of the facts surrounding the item of news. It should be, so far as is humanly possible, free from the writer's or the commentator's personal interpretation or views. [p. 157]*

Goldwater catches the essence of one main view (the fact concept) of objectivity and expresses it briefly and succinctly. Erich Fromm points out the opposing view (the factuality concept) just as cogently. As Fromm discusses objectivity in *Man for Himself*, it requires more than simply seeing an event or object dispassionately and neutrally, and it requires something more than mere accuracy; it requires the observer to become related in some way to that which is being reported. The na-ture of the object and nature of the observer (or subject) must be merged and considered equally important if we are to get at what constitutes objectivity. Fromm goes on to say:

> Objectivity is not, as it is often implied in a false idea of "scien-tific" objectivity, synonymous with detachment, with absence of interest and care. How can one penetrate the veiling surface of things to their causes and relationships if one does not have an in-

---

* Much literature and many speeches have dealt with journalistic objectivity in recent years; one of the best articles is Donald McDonald's "Is Objectivity Possible?" *The Cen-ter Magazine* (Santa Barbara, Calif.), Sept.–Oct. 1971, pp. 29–43.

terest that is vital and sufficiently impelling for so laborous a task.
[p. 111]

Fromm is stressing that objectivity does not mean detachment;
rather he says, it has more to do with "respect." And he points out that
the idea that lack of interest as a condition for recognizing the truth is
fallacious. All productive thinking, observing, and communicating are
stimulated by the interest of the observer, according to Fromm. And it
would seem that productive journalism, or journalism that reaches
furthest toward objectivity, would also be that which involves the interest of the reporter. It is impossible for journalists to detach themselves from their stories if they are to give an honest and full account.
And in this reluctance to detach themselves from the stories, journalists
dedicate themselves to subjectivity. But it could be said that this dedication to subjectivity is the pathway to greater objectivity, a seeming paradox. It is not paradoxical at all, however, if we admit that objectivity is
something more than mere factual reporting from a neutral perspective.
If we admit that one's own judgments and ordering of a story's substance are necessary for the most complete and meaningful story, then we
are simply saying that subjectivity is essential to what might be called
objective reporting.

Someone will object: "What about facts. Are not they undistorted
and objective reflections of reality?" We doubt it. Not only can facts be
meaningless, but they can be untrue by their very selection; they can
take attention away from what is relevant, or they can scatter and frag-
ment one's thinking so much that one is incapable of making meaningful
decisions. Why is this? Because the selection of facts implies evaluation
and choice. So even the presentation of facts, however they might be defined, is *subjective*. The fact of a fact, or the factual foundation under-
neath a fact, is in reality part of the fact, something that a journalist
often forgets. For example, if a journalist were to report objectively on
the activities of a certain individual, he or she must know the individual
thoroughly — even to the motives out of which the individual acts. The
journalist needs to provide the reader with such evaluation of motives
to deal properly with "the facts." Such evaluation of an act — the motive for doing it, etc. — is part of the objectivity of the act.

Facts in themselves have little correspondence to objectivity; they
can distort and mislead. It is well known by successful propagandists
that there is no more effective way of distortion than to offer nothing
but a series of facts — disjointed, isolated, unrelated, and taken out of
context.

Most citizens, concerned with getting the truth, and most journalists, concerned with providing the truth, have a certain respect for objectivity. They simply have various theories about how it is achieved.

The Goldwater perspective presented above seems to dominate journalism today, although the Fromm perspective appears to be on the rise.

The search for journalistic objectivity goes on; but there is no agreement on its nature or on when it has been achieved. This is especially true in libertarian societies, and it is perhaps a good thing that this is the case. It is certainly unrealistic to expect a common definition of objectivity to develop or a monolithic journalistic objectivity to emerge in a country like the United States as long as journalists are willing to fight against all manner of subtle and insidious authoritarian influences which would define for us the nature of objective journalism.

Two Faces of Objectivity

Although the discussion of objectivity goes on and seemingly will not be resolved (especially in open societies), there is something within us which keeps us trying to analyze and understand the concept. One interesting way to analyze objectivity in reporting is to consider two epistemological perspectives: *realism* and *idealism*. Although epistemology has been discussed in an earlier chapter, it might be well here to say a little more on the subject as it relates to objectivity.

The *realistic* view of objectivity would consider objective reporting — or the objective report — as a relational concept involving the event (object) and the report of the event (another object). It would put little or no stress on the audience members who perceive the report. On the other hand, the *idealistic* position on objective reporting is primarily a relational one involving the audience member and the report of the event. It has little or nothing to do with the actual event out there, for the only event of any real importance is the one in the mind of the audience member. In other words, the emphasis here is put on the fifth level of truth (the perceived truth) discussed in an earlier section of this chapter.

Let us look a little more closely at these two views. First, the realist would postulate that (1) a news event is a news event even though it is not reported; (2) a news story is an *object* in itself even though an audience member does not ever see or hear it; and (3) even if an audience member does see or hear the report, his or her perception of the report has nothing really to do with the objectivity of the report. A news story, for example, is a news story even though nobody reads it in the press, just as the original event existed in reality even though no reporter reported it. A story in a newsroom wastebasket is just as much a news story as one on the page of the newspaper. News, to the realist, is not a report of what happened; rather, it is *what happened*. And a news *story* is not what is *read* (perceived) by an audience member but what is *written* (or otherwise transmitted) by a reporter. The realist places the relational focus on the *event reported* and on the *report* itself. The question of importance so far as objectivity is concerned is this: How closely does the report approximate the actual event? The realist sees objectivity having to do mainly with events and reports of events, and reportorial objectivity as referring to the correspondence (relationship) between the actual event and the report of the actual event.

Next, let us consider the idealist. As applied to news, the idealist would postulate that (1) a news event is basically what happens in the mind of the audience member; (2) a news story is the device which triggers a perception (image) in the audience member's mind; and (3) there is no news except that which is perceived by the audience member. For the idealist, news is not news until it is reported — i.e., perceived — by an audience member via a report. Therefore, we cannot talk about objectivity in a news report without considering the audience. A report cannot be objective until (and unless) it is perceived by the audience member. Here the relational focus is on the report and the audience member — with major stress on the latter. The idealist says, in effect, that objectivity is a personal thing with the audience member. It is the individual perception of the report that really counts; therefore there may be as many *objectivities* as there are perceivers or audience members. The main question for the idealist is this: How do the audience members perceive the report?

Now, to draw a few inferences from what has just been said, the realist is more object-and-event-minded than the idealist. The realist is also more concerned with keeping out of the story than is the idealist; more concerned with reportorial neutrality. Therefore, the realist would embrace essentially the Goldwater perspective on objectivity discussed earlier. The realist is less concerned with audience perception than is the idealist, and more concerned with factual and tonal correspondence between the report and the event reported. How various audience members perceive the event via the report is of secondary interest to the reporter who is a realist; certainly the realist does not think these perceptions in any way affect the objectivity of the report. The report is either objective or not — independent of the perception of the audience.

The idealist, on the other hand, tends to be a subjectivist when it comes to objective reporting — believing that the reporter's own feelings, reactions, conclusions, judgments (as well as those of the audience members) are necessary for the production of objectivity. The idealist is concerned primarily with the perceptions in the minds of the subjects. The idealist is more likely to be a New Journalist or one dedicated to involvement and advocacy. The idealist is also more concerned with how an audience member *perceives* the event than with the actual event itself. The only event, in other words, that is important to the idealist is the perception in the mind of the audience member. Therefore, the idealist would be more interested in audience analysis than in content analysis, and would be considerably more psychologically oriented than the realistic journalist. Being interested in what is lodged in the mind of the audience member, of course, also forces a reporter to have a related concern for the perception in the reporter's mind. It would be meaningful and interesting to try to compare the audience perceptions with those of the journalist who did the reporting.

These are two important ways of considering journalistic objectivity, and they are related to other orientations mentioned earlier in this chapter. For example, the realist is akin to the neutralist, event-oriented journalist who believes in impersonalism and uninvolvement. The idealist, on the other hand, tends to be more closely related with subjectivism, personalism, people-orientation, and involvement.

More Questions than Answers

Metaphysical discourse tends to be rambling, esoteric, and often fuzzy. It is the kind of philosophical conjecture and rumination which provides more questions than answers. But, then, a basic philosophical principle is that the raising of serious questions is exceedingly important, even if no answers are forthcoming. Simply dealing with them, thinking about them, turning them over and over in the mind, discussing them, struggling with them — all of this cogitative activity is valuable to a person concerned about basic issues. Certainly a journalist or a person planning to become a journalist should welcome such metaphysical discourse, for it serves to open new doors of interest, challenge old concepts and ideas, stimulate concern with fundamental issues and problems in the field, and finally — and perhaps most importantly — to help form the habit of logical analysis and speculative thought.

Certainly many questions have been posed here. In fact, one of the main purposes of the entire book has been to raise questions for speculation by the serious reader. Obviously we have not answered all we have posed, and those answers which we have attempted to give will not find favor with all our readers. This is to be expected. What the reader brings to a book such as this is as important — if not more important — than what the authors bring to it. We have tried to deal with basic questions, with essential issues, with seeming paradoxes, with first principles of journalism, and have eschewed the more pragmatic or professional techniques approach. There are plenty of books around which can satisfy the trades-oriented practitioner in journalism.

In one sense this whole book has dealt with journalistic metaphysics. It has struggled with basics, with first principles, with fundamental issues and questions. We have tried to discuss such questions as the nature, grounds, and limits of knowledge as this subject impinges on the field of journalism; we have delved into the realm of axiology, discussing value and differences in journalistic quality. And we have discussed journalistic morality, considering basic questions of ethics which continue to confound journalists everywhere. We have dipped also into the area of logic, trying to highlight various kinds of logical fallacies endemic in modern journalism. We have also dealt with rhetoric in journalism, turning attention on persuasive techniques and irrational discourse. From there we have taken up an area often neglected in journalism literature: linguistics and semantics. Then, in conclusion, we have discussed political theory and journalism, and have rounded out the book with some thoughts on basic metaphysical or ontological questions.

So, all through the book, we have raised more questions than journalists or journalism students can ever resolve. Many of these questions should touch off argument (Is journalism a profession? Do the people have a right to know?), and other questions (What is news? What is journalism?) are more speculative and should cause the reader to think about possible answers in a calmer, more reflective manner.

The Future of Journalism

One last question: What lies in the future of journalism? Such a question is often asked these days, and authors plunge into the fray with little trepidation and great conviction and certainty. In the world of modern journalism, the temptation is for us to couch our answer — which will conclude this book — in science-fiction terminology, easily dredged up from the technological treatises which proliferate through the field and environs of journalism and mass communication.

Nothing should surprise us in journalism in the next two or three decades so far as technology is concerned. We can visualize all manner of computer terminals bringing a rich assortment of information right into the home. We can see conglomerates and multinational corporations involving themselves more and more in collecting, processing, and distributing information. We can see direct satellite hookups splashing international news and entertainment everywhere. We can visualize giant regional and national (maybe even international) computers storing all kinds of data for every purpose — all to be called up by specialized groups and persons in a flash. We can see the slow passing of the traditional newspaper and magazine as the electronic computerized technology presents the world's citizenry cheaper and cheaper and fancier and fancier toys. We can see ever more information flowing in a more equal fashion among nations and regions of the world. We can, indeed, visualize a New World Information and Communications Order, ushered in by UNESCO and other transnational organizations and groups, where gadgets and sophisticated technology dump worldwide communication — much of it garbage — on everyone's doorstep.

Technologically, the future world of journalism will be astounding, fabulous, fantastic, incredible. Quantitatively, journalism will improve. Messages will flow more quickly and in more profusion — everywhere. Information — general and extremely specialized — will be available at the push of a button. If a profusion of messages available for the world's people indicates progress and a more peaceful world, then we will have a future world of great progress and peace.

But while we are speculating and looking into the future, there is no reason for us to stop with this upbeat look at technology What we wonder is this: Will journalism be any better in the future — better in the sense of providing people with more insightful, sophisticated, meaningful, thoughtful, and helpful messages?

Will journalism be more ethical and logical? Will journalism present more viewpoints in more thoughtful ways? Will journalism draw more intelligent and serious practitioners? Will journalism, as it develops, permit more freedom for those who practice it?

Will journalism emphasize news more or will it turn increasingly to interpretative pieces, features, polemic, and propaganda? Will "news" significantly be redefined (at the insistence of the Third World and UNESCO) in the future?

Will journalism take on more and more of the characteristics of a profession, with the accompanying loss of individualism and pluralism?

Will journalism continue in the future to get most of its new practitioners from journalism education programs of the universities, or will journalists come increasingly from more traditional or more specialized academic departments?

Will the journalism of the future be more socially responsible? What will be the result of the present emphasis on responsible journalism and the cult of government-press partnerships?

Will larger and larger corporations and multinational concerns dominate world journalism? What will happen to the small publishers and the eccentric and individualistic journalists in the more collectivized and cooperative and "responsible" world of tomorrow?

What will happen to readers in the world of tomorrow where television and other electronic innovations will further simplify the process of message dissemination?

What will happen to literacy, and to linguistic sophistication — already dying out on the attitudinal level — among young people everywhere?

How long will it be before the courts or special governmental agencies (like the Federal Communications Commission) make the major editorial decisions for the mass media, and the editors and publishers turn completely into simple functionaries or businessmen?

Will the future news media be edited or directed by lawyers, who have already become extremely important in determining the news content of the media?

Will future journalists be licensed? And will there be an elite professional body which can kick out (de-press?) so-called irresponsible or eccentric journalists?

Will there be in countries like the United States a Federal Press Commission (to supervise and control print media) as well as a Federal Communications Commission (to supervise and control the broadcast media)?

Will governments increasingly have the power to direct the press systems of their countries so that journalism can more "responsibly" aid in the development and progress of these nations?

All of the above are significant and pertinent questions as journalism enters the two decades leading up to the year 2000. We can all speculate on their answers. Perhaps such speculation will actually affect the answers or solutions to these questions and problems. The discerning reader will recognize that the way many of the above questions were phrased indicates a certain pessimism on the part of the authors. But these are basically pessimistic times, and journalism, we believe, quite accurately reflects its times. For example, as ethical standards erode in society generally, they erode also in journalism.

Perhaps a golden sun of optimism will dawn over a future journalism that shows more courage, vitality, honesty, integrity, independence, and credibility than is generally shown in journalism today. Perhaps, then, much of the current malaise in journalism will be dispelled, and authors of the future writing on philosophy and journalism can frame more optimistic and heartening questions reflecting a new vitality and strengthened credibility of a truly New Journalism of a New Day.

Suggested Reading

Commission on Freedom of the Press. *A Free and Responsible Press*. Chicago: University of Chicago Press, 1947.

Fromm, Erich. *Man for Himself*. New York: Fawcett, 1966.

Goldwater, Barry. *The Conscience of a Majority*. New York: Simon & Schuster, 1971.

Hayakawa, S.I. *Language in Thought and Action*. New York: Harcourt, Brace, 1949.

Hedebro, Goran. *Communication and Social Change in Developing Nations: A Critical View*. Stockholm: Economic Research Institute, Univ. of Stockholm, 1979.

Korzybski, Alfred. *Science and Sanity: An Introduction to Non-Aristotelian Systems and General Semantics*. Lancaster, Pa.: Science Press, 1933.

Langer, Susanne K. *Philosophy in a New Key*. New York: Pelican, 1948.

M'Bow, A-M. *Building the Future: Unesco and the Solidarity of Nations*. Paris: Unesco, 1981.

Richstad, Jim, and Anderson, M.H., eds. *Crisis in International News: Policies and Prospects*. New York: Columbia University Press, 1981.

Schramm, Wilbur. *Mass Media and National Development*. Stanford: Stanford University Press, 1964.

Toffler, Alvin. *Future Shock*. New York: Bantam, 1971.

Index

EP31